The Atlantean Irish

IRELAND'S ORIENTAL AND
MARITIME HERITAGE

For Miriam

The Atlantean Irish

IRELAND'S ORIENTAL AND MARITIME HERITAGE

BOB QUINN

For my godson
Robin Shackleton
on this auspicious evening

THE LILLIPUT PRESS • DUBLIN

Antony Farrell, publisher
1 January 2005

First published 2005 by

THE LILLIPUT PRESS LTD

62-63 Sitric Road, Arbour Hill, Dublin 7, Ireland

www.lilliputpress.ie

A CIP record for this title is available from the British Library.

ISBN 1 84351 024 3

An
Chomhairle
Oidhreachta

The
Heritage
Council

Set in 11.5 on 14.5 point Centaur
Designed and typeset by Anú Design, Tara
Printed by βetaprint of Dublin

Contents

All photos by Bob Quinn unless otherwise noted.

Acknowledgments

I have relied much on the labours of those who are referred to in the text and list of sources. However, I should also acknowledge my debt to many who encouraged the work, but who are otherwise unmentioned: they include the staff of the Thomas Hardiman Library, NUIG, Helen Carey of the Centre Culturel Irlandais, Paris, Dr Ferdinand von Prondzynski of DCU, Hakim Bey of Autonomedia, Beatrice Kelly of the National Heritage Council, Miriam Allen and my extended family, as well as D.G. Bradley, Oisín Breathnach, Mary J. Byrne, Dr Richard Crampton, Michael Cregan, Clíodna Cussen, Jean le Du, Grattan Healy, Fred Johnston, Barry McDonnell, Gareth Murphy, Dr Harvey O'Brien, Padraig Ó Mathúna, Alex Ó Scanaill, Caomhán Ó Scolaí, Norbert Payne, T.C. Rice, Michael Rudd, Sture Ureland, Ethna Viney and Dr Alfred Winter. I also owe much to Aosdána, and above all to Antony Farrell and to his staff at The Lilliput Press, who felt that *The Atlantean Irish* was worth revising and publishing.

Foreword

One of the great joys of studying prehistory is that the subject is ever-changing. Every day, whether as the result of carefully directed research excavations or simply as chance finds made during construction work or farming, new evidence is pouring out of the ground. Some of it is spectacular and headline-grabbing but much is unsurprising and, let us be honest, superficially rather dull. Some years ago there was a revealing cartoon that showed an excavation with a pontificating archaeologist and a television team who were packing up in bored disgust. The archaeologist was saying, 'No, no treasure but a host of fascinating detail about the socio-economic structure of the Iron Age' – ourselves as others see us! But it is in these details and in the painstaking search for patterns in the data – and then for more data to help consolidate and expand the patterns – that the very basis of archaeological reconstruction lies. Upon these studies prehistory is written.

Those of us who are 'dirt-archaeologists' spend a disproportionate amount of our lives struggling to contain the detail and may perhaps be forgiven for sometimes allowing our vision to be restricted by the edge of the trench or the strict chronological limits of the period we profess to specialize in. There is still, I believe, far too much chronological or regional blinkering in the approach of the discipline. Eighty years ago the great French historian Lucien Febvre, one of the founders of the *Annales* School of History, wrote in characteristic style, 'historians be geographers, be jurists too and sociologists and psychologists'. He went on to encourage us to *abattre les cloissons* (smash down the compartments). As a student, my own rather pathetic response to the clarion call was to smuggle into the pages of the august *Proceedings of the Prehistoric Society* a description of some Roman potsherds – then an unthinkable intrusion.

The *Annales* School, and in particular the writing of its most famous proponent, Ferdinand Braudel, has had a profound effect on the work of archaeologists and prehistorians. Braudel has taught us to think in terms of different rhythms of time. Perhaps of most use to those who work in deep time is his concept of *la longue durée* (geographical time) – it is 'a history in which all change is slow, a history of constant repetition, of ever recurring cycles'. Such a way of looking at things is particularly helpful in the study of the intricately textured Atlantic façade of Europe – a landscape whose communities have forever been dominated by the constant rhythms of the ocean. It was the ocean that, for over 10,000 years, has bound these maritime communities together, encouraging them to turn their backs on the land. It has provided a corridor of communications along which commodities, people, ideas and beliefs have flowed with changing intensity over time.

The physical detritus of these contacts, and their echoes in written anecdotes and song and in the genetic make-up of the population, are the raw materials from which archaeologists, historians, linguists, ethnomusicologists and biomolecular scientists attempt to build models of the past. Each specialist will have a viewpoint – their own cognitive model of the past conditioned by the traditions of their discipline. These undoubtedly have a value but it is only when the compartments separating us have been swept away will new, and perhaps unfamiliar, pictures begin to emerge.

Bob Quinn, intuitively, has grasped the excitement of it all and has begun to explore many of the more crucial issues. In the story he tells there is much with which we can agree and things that we might feel less happy about – so, in bold reconstructions like this, it will always be. That said, his gentle, provocative style nudges us to confront our prejudices. If, at the end, we go away inspired by the author's love of his subject, seeing the familiar in different perspective, making new connections and eager to know more, he will more than have achieved his purpose.

Barry Cunliffe, Professor of European Archaeology, Oxford
Pont Roux

Introduction

The original Atlantean project took four years to fulfil – from 1980 to 1984 – reading, researching and filming as I went. It was the most exciting and intellectually stimulating time of my life, and it resulted in three films and a book.

My purpose was to show that Irish culture – and especially that of my neighbours in Conamara – was not just a vestigial remnant of Celticism, a European culture that had washed over the island 2500 years ago, retreated and left us high and dry, to make an exhibition of ourselves with 'the blind hysterics of the Celt'.

There were two starting-points: sean-nós singing, and the sea that surrounds Ireland and up to recently was the only approach to this island. The same sea touched many other shores and cultures. Was it a coincidence that the lateen sail used on the traditional Conamara púcán was an Arab invention still used on Egyptian dhows? Naïvely, then, I hypothesized that the Irish might owe as much to one of the great civilizations of the world, Islam, as they did to a focus on Eurocentric origins.

In pursuit of this hypothesis I wandered from Armagh to Árann, from a knitting shop in Oxford to the Coptic Museum in Cairo, from a sean-nós session in Carna to the monasteries of the Wadi Natrun Desert. I mostly travelled alone, was never mugged, never robbed (except by Moroccan security forces who appropriated a crucial part of my cine-camera), and I learned that the world was a far safer, friendlier and more interesting place than contemporary journalism would have had me believe.

The people I met during my quest were equally colourful. The expert

Arabist in the Chester Beatty Library in Dublin, who pointed out the similarity of style between the Book of Durrow and early Islamic manuscripts, was convicted of selling some of those same manuscripts to unscrupulous dealers some years later. The late John M. Allegro, author of books such as *The Mushroom and the Cross* and one of the first Westerners to decipher the Dead Sea Scrolls, enthusiastically supported my interpretation of the obscene *Síle na gCíocs* (Sheela-na-Gigs). When, in the Isle of Man, I introduced him to these images for the first time, his glee was palpable. Subsequently I found that mention of his name was the only way I could enrage a calm friend of mine, the late Dominican priest, Father Romuald Dodd.

When it came to writing a book about my adventures I was academically ill equipped. In cramming entire courses of archaeology, navigation, religion, politics, history, geography *et alia* into frequent, sharp intensive bursts of reading and studying in libraries and museums, I aimed to restore the neglected faculty of imagination to the disparate details being uncovered while trying to view them as a coherent whole united by the sea. It was like learning joined-up writing having been taught only block capitals. Encouraged by the geographer E. Estyn Evans' insight that in future all new discoveries would be made in the cracks between the disciplines, my approach was less scholarly than sociological, a discipline with which I had at least a passing familiarity.

From an academic viewpoint, my sin were twofold: not only did I confront the simplistic construction called Irish/Celtic/Catholic identity, I also recovered much of the Anglo-Irish, pre-Independence scholarly research that had proved inconvenient to the new state's image-builders and had been dismissed from official history books. But my greatest sin was to attribute to oral culture and to personal observation – that is to say, common sense – as much respect as I accorded written evidence and armchair scholarship. In short, I went beyond theologically acceptable versions of history and tried to interpret the 'good books' for myself. However, it was an upstart amateur archaeologist, Heinrich Schliemann, who followed his instincts and uncovered the city of Troy in 1871, and Alfred Wegener's suggestion in 1922 that the earth's continents had moved in the geological past was vigorously dismissed until surveys of the sea floor in the 1950s compelled acceptance of the tectonic-plate theory.

E. Estyn Evans' 'Personality of Ireland' lectures, first delivered in 1973, confirmed for me the limitations of exclusive reliance on written historical records. This Welshman, a Queen's University Belfast scholar for fifty years, was a passionate advocate of reading the land and listening to the people, differentiating 'dirt-archaeology' from 'desk-archaeology'. In some circles (as Paul Durcan wrote in a foreword to the current edition of the resulting book) Evans was referred to as 'a crypto-Unionist'. His parallel between introspective scholarship and the rise of nineteenth-century nationalism clearly raised many hackles. However, the late Liam de Paor had long shown that the trappings of all European nationalisms, not just the Irish, were products of nineteenth-century Romanticism, and the Irish were not the only sinners in this respect. Retired Professor P.L. Henry of Galway University (who, along with musicologist John Blacking of Queen's University, first suggested the Berbers to me as a relevant area of research) reconciled me to the professional silence that greeted my original research and findings; I had had to travel to Dublin and deliver copies of the original book to individual newspapers to encourage them to review it. He pointed out that I had touched on so many different disciplines that no single scholar could handle this vast canvas without betraying gaps in their own knowledge. It was more prudent for them to pass over my work.

One professional scholar, Dr Michael Ryan, now director of the Chester Beatty Library in Dublin, was courageous enough to review the first edition of this book in *Archaeology Ireland*. While disagreeing with me about almost everything, he paid tribute to my attempt to restore Islamic learning to its due place in the intellectual development of Europe. Dr Ryan had inadvertently encouraged me already by drawing attention (in his essay on the Derrynaflan Chalice) to 'the problem of eastern influence on all aspects of early Irish art', pronouncing that 'there is need now to reopen the question'. My book was not at all what he had in mind, but it was a start. Other reviews were more encouraging, but Professor Henry had already warned me that my findings would be ignored, as I was not an accredited scholar.

There have since been encouraging indications that an academic frost can thaw. In 1995 the then president of Dublin City University, Dr Danny O'Hare, reproduced my original (out of print) book and distributing fifty copies to colleagues in the United States. In *Ireland's Others* (2001), Elizabeth Butler Cullingford put me in the company of Brian Friel (*Translations*), Frank McGuinness (*Carthaginians*) and even Joyce: 'Quinn's idiosyncratic researcher may be seen as performing what Luke Gibbons has called "lateral journeys along the margins which short-circuit the colonial divide".'

Earlier, in the 1980s, Professor Hilary Richardson of University College Dublin showed me some of her comparative studies of Armenian cross-stones (*kachkars*) and Irish high crosses. 'Alone in the Christian world,' she wrote, 'the extreme east – Armenia/Georgia – and the extreme west – Ireland – preserved an established convention of erecting monuments in stone.' She emphasized Françoise Henry's mid-century support for the idea of oriental influences on insular Irish art, an idea that was disputed by some of the old-school Irish archaeologists.

The opportunity to write the original version of this book had come when Naim Atallah, the Palestinian owner of Quartet Books in London, saw the films and commissioned the book. When the manuscript was ready he entrusted it to a young Lebanese editor. She dismissed it as wild imaginings and passed it on to Jeremy Beale, a man of patience, who shepherded it from then on. I wondered whether her reaction had anything to do with the Beirut war, which was still at its cruellest. How else could a Lebanese react to a book that did not condemn the Muslim Palestinians? Sadly, Quartet published the book without its intended illustrations and left my literary baby to fend for itself, with no launch or any publicity. It went out of print in 1994.

It is as unprofitable to be twenty years before your time as a score too late.

In 1993 a scholar named Orin Gensler completed his PhD at the University of California, Berkeley, with a thesis on Afro-Asiatic languages and a study of eighty-five languages throughout the world. He is now attached to the Max Planck Institute in Frankfurt. In his thesis he described my book as 'the best overview of extralinguistic connections between the British Isles and North Africa that I have come across'. In fairness to Gensler, he stated that he was not equipped to substantiate my extralinguistic findings but he confirmed that his own conclusions supported Dr Heinrich Wagner's North African substratum ideas, on which I had relied extensively in my text. In the following pages I report for the first time on my subsequent field research and findings on the phenomenon of 'pre-Celtic' languages in Ireland.

In 1999 Simon James, an archaeologist on leave from the British Museum, produced *Atlantic Celts: Ancient People or Modern Invention?* In an acceptably scholarly manner he covered much the same ground and did an even greater demolition job on the Irish (and British) 'Celtic' invention than ever I could. His findings were greeted in an *Irish Times* article with disbelief as well as incomprehension by a friend of mine, Irish-language poet Gabriel Rosenstock. The most informed and devastating analysis of the whole 'Celtic' invention, however, was Hildegard L.C. Tristram's essay, 'Celtic in linguistic taxonomy in the nineteenth century'. In the same collection George Watson wrote: 'the "Celt" has been a construction of urban intellectuals imposed on the predominantly rural denizens of what has come to be called the "Celtic fringe"'. Very recently a team of geneticists from Trinity College Dublin and the universities of Leeds and Cambridge published the results of their study of mitochondrial DNA in Ireland. They concluded that 'the Irish are not Celts'. In this text I also refer to Oxford professor Bryan Sykes' equally supportive findings in the same specialized area of DNA.

Dr G. Frank Mitchell, late of Trinity College Dublin, wrote a review in the *Irish Times* in 1987 suggesting that a study of the North African Latin Church would be rewarding and was quite overdue: 'Art motifs could easily have reached Ireland from North Africa.' My own investigations in Tunis and Carthage into this forgotten dimension of Latin Christianity were also supported by the words of Dr Michael Richter (a medieval specialist who lectured in University College Dublin for twelve years), who wrote in 1988 in his book *Medieval Ireland: The Enduring Tradition*:

> The beginnings of systematic study of the Latin language in Ireland can be traced back to the end of the 6th century. As Latin was not dispensed with [i.e. could not be ignored] in the Irish Church, it was considered necessary to learn and teach the language thoroughly and for this the recognized *authorities* were used, particularly Donatus. [my italics]

Dr Richter went on: 'By 650 AD ... the Irish scholars had discovered Latin education for its own sake; in the following century they were to become famous and very quickly infamous for it. A Latinity developed which displays particularly eccentric features.'

In *Atlantean* I had featured a personality named Donatus, a fourth-century North African bishop excommunicated by Rome for leading a revolt. I suggested that the brutal persecution following his revolt might have driven many of the more ardent Tunisian Christians to a safe haven, far from Rome — even, possibly, as far as the Skelligs monastic outpost off southwest Ireland. Clearly this could not be proven, but at least it was possible to suggest that a heretical namesake of a North African dissident (if not the heretic Donatus himself!) had a direct intellectual influence on Irish monasticism and ultimately on the Great Western Church.

This 'eccentricity' or individuality of early medieval Irish monks was alluded to disapprovingly by Alcuin, the eighth-century Northumbrian adviser to Emperor Charlemagne. He said the Irish scholars were suspiciously more interested in philosophy than theology, i.e. they dared to enquire into the realities behind the approved ecclesiastical party line. Irish scholars had this in common with contemporary Islamic philosophers in Spain: they both tried to reconcile reason and religion and suffered much criticism for their efforts.

The most thrilling endorsement of my emphasis on the importance of a maritime interpretation of the Irish identity came quite recently. In *Facing the Ocean* (2001), archaeologist Barry Cunliffe's groundbreaking study, he revealed his development from a Celt-based interpretation of Britain and Ireland to a view focussed on the Atlantic seaways. He argued convincingly for what I had only speculated on many years ago: that the Irish language evolved not as a result of continental 'Celtic' influence but as a maritime language of the western coastal areas of Europe. Colin Renfrew suggested the same thing in 1987, when he wrote that the origins of 'Celtic' tongues were not to be found in the Iron Age but 6000 years ago with the first farmers on these islands. In 1958 Glyn Daniel wrote, 'it seems certain that the megalith-builders did not speak an Indo-European language. We should expect them to speak a Mediterranean language, some pre-Indo-European language which may have survived to the present day as Berber or Basque'.

The ideas in *Atlantean* were originally greeted with good humour. RTÉ television producer Larry Masterson gaily assailed me outside his prefab office: 'Listen here! St Patrick came here in 432! He drove out the snakes! He converted us with the shamrock! Get that straight, OK?'

'Are you the fellow that says we're all Arabs?' commented a judge in Kinvara, Co. Galway, before dismissing a minor charge against me. He added, glancing wearily around the miscreants in his court: 'I'm sure you have found plenty of confirmation for your theory today.'

I was reminded how many Europeans, fed by racist and stereotypical images culled from feature films and other media, are completely unaware of the actual world of Islam. There is not a single reference to Islam in the

1075-page *Oxford Dictionary of Quotations*. Centuries before Middle Eastern and North African peoples succumbed to colonialism and were carved up into manageable (and variously corrupt) client states, they had a world influence whose impact is rarely, if ever, mentioned. This convenient amnesia has resulted in a culpable ignorance of the Muslim world, one that has inexorably allowed a political exacerbation of the current artificial confrontation between 'Eastern' and 'Western' civilizations.

I hope this book may soften some of the crude strokes with which this confrontation is painted — by Henry Kissinger, among others. At a time when BBC commentator Robert Kilroy-Silk feels safe in describing two billion Muslims as 'suicide bombers, limb amputators, women repressors', Western society has a long way to go. Fortunately he is no longer employed by the BBC.

While professionals on whose disciplines I dared to tread in the first edition of this book maintained a dignified silence towards it as well as, in many cases, a privately expressed disapproval, others were less reticent. 'A compendium of nonsense' was a description reported back to me of a late-night tirade by a fine Irish-language poet; her beloved Ottoman Empire had not been given sufficient credit for Islamic influence on this island. My rejoinder is that all empires use the indigenous peoples they control to carry out their further depredations: witness the Gurkhas, the South Vietnamese, the Afghans and, especially, the Berbers. The Mediterranean may at one stage have been described as a 'Turkish lake', but few of the sailors themselves were Turkish.

On another tack, an American lecturer attached to the University of Coleraine publicly proclaimed in 1985 in Miltown Malbay, Co. Clare, that the musicological ideas of Seán Ó Riada — which had made a good deal of sense to my ear and on which I had relied greatly — were really quite far-fetched. That late and much-loved composer had said that Irish traditional music was non-European in that its original genesis was Indian and it had reached Ireland through North Africa and Spain. The American lady, on the other hand, followed the 'Celtic' trail and claimed an east European origin for sean-nós singing. She even played musical examples. What she appeared to be oblivious to was the 800-year Muslim control of the region from which she took her evidence. The same airy disregard was shown recently in *The Journal of Music in Ireland* by Dr Lillis O'Laoire, who attacked Ó Riada's and my ideas on this music as 'exoticization'. How many of us

— apart from the late Hubert Butler — realized, before the sickening war in the Balkans, the extraordinary proportion of Muslims who are native to and still reside in these European regions?

Traditional Irish musicians are not usually burdened with such theological agonizing about the origins of their discipline; they simply play the music as they hear and feel it. Thus the wandering troubadour Andy Irvine pioneered the rhythms and harmonies of Bulgaria and Hungary (in the nineteenth century the latter banned all Turkish trumpets) and paved the way for the bouzouki in Irish traditional music. It is perhaps twenty years since Irvine, in Slattery's of Capel Street, Dublin, exposed Irish audiences to the powerful sean-nós singing of the Hungarian, Márta Sebestyén. Not long after that P.J. Curtis introduced Irish radio listeners to the extraordinary *Le Mystère des Voix Bulgares*. All of these musical forms have been informed by the Muslim presence in Europe. In 1994 Bill Whelan, a collaborator of Irvine's, based his exciting *Riverdance* music on the same exotic rhythms.

In short, my findings were no surprise to the more adventurous of Irish musicians. Nothing I suggested about oriental influences had not already been intuited by them. But they did not go far enough east or south, to the original sources.

Visual artists in the main were also supportive, and indeed elected me to Aosdána principally on the strength of the *Atlantean* films. Painter Brian Bourke said: 'There is nothing so potent as an idea whose time has come.'

And what exactly was this time, this context, this idea?

The 1980s were a period of intense revision of conventional ideas about Irish identity. Renewed emigration, decimating a generation of the newly educated, suggested that the Republic was also a 'failed entity'. The barbarism of the war in Northern Ireland, and the fear of it spilling over into the South, produced a concerted political, journalistic and scholarly campaign to play down traditional ideas of identity such as Catholicism, the Irish language, a Gaelic culture, anything that could be depicted as underpinning or giving comfort to the Provisional IRA campaign. At the time it was as dangerous to be a free thinker as it was to be a fundamentalist; as intimidating, indeed, as it is now, post-9/11.

As I sailed unconcerned through that period, absorbed in my speculations, it surprised me how interested Irish people were in my alternative historical and cultural scenarios. It was as if, traditional bulwarks against life's uncertainties having been discredited or discarded, we needed another identity, however fanciful, that our national make-up was much broader, more complex and even, yes, more exotic than had been hitherto taught. More through luck than judgment, my revival of the Atlantean/Oriental idea fell neatly into this category.

In 1995 I set out to show in a documentary film that in the so-called European Dark Ages business was actually carried on much as usual – a theory originated by a Belgian, Henri Pirenne, and supplemented by the late Professor Sture Bolin of the University of Lund, as well as by Hodges and Whitehouse in their book *Mohammed, Charlemagne and the Origins of Europe* (1983). The latter quoted Pirenne's maxim: 'Without Mohammed, no Charlemagne.' The theory propounded was that civilization did not die after the Roman retreat across the Alps; it was happily carried on by, among others, the Vikings and the Muslims on the seas and waterways surrounding and penetrating the European continent. I called my project 'Navigatio: Completing the Circle'. It involved travelling widely in Scandinavia and even as far as Tatarstan, east of Russia, to search out and record musicians and singers.

In 1988, as a curious by-product of the original book, I was invited to write a biography of Colonel Muammar Qaddafi. Even the Libyans appeared to have heard of *Atlantean*. For a worrying week I was the leader's personal guest in his desert refuge and was promised access to a world of Arab scholarship. It was soon realized by his handpicked young lieutenants that I was not in the business of writing an unquestioning hagiography of their boss. The commission did not transpire. So far I have not written in detail about this Libyan experience (apart from an unpublished fictional account) for fear of putting some of Qaddafi's lieutenants in peril; it is enough to say that during that strange week in Libya I was brought to a remote beach in Cyrenaica, west of Benghazi, and urged to inform the USA that this was the ideal spot to invade the country! How time heals all wounds; now Qaddafi is the prodigal darling of the West, having renounced weapons of mass destruction and paid millions in compensation to the relatives of the 1988 Lockerbie disaster victims.

Apart from many new ideas and the illustrations that give the reader practical examples of the argument, this edition differs slightly from the original in the following respect. When I gave a draft of the 1986 edition to Bearnard Ó Riain, an ex-military friend, he said: 'Your readers are your company of soldiers. You are leading them on an assault, up the hill of imagination. You can't afford to hesitate. Take them over the top with confidence.' He was referring to an apparent diffidence in style I had adopted in order to seduce the reader and appease professional scholars. With more research and the reassurance of varied and nuanced reactions to the work, I can now develop and support my original ideas confident that they are as valid as anybody's, and perhaps nearer the truth than many. If the pendulum has indeed swung from diffidence to arrogance I can only plead a different kind of naïvety, perhaps one that accompanies advancing years.

My object of attack remains the extraordinary adherence by generations of scholars, propagandists and tourists to the 'Celtic' explanation for all things Irish. This Celtic delusion seems to me to be one of those incantations described by E.H. Carr in his George Macaulay Trevelyan Lectures of 1961 as 'designed to save historians from the tiresome obligation to think for themselves'.

Historical Origins: Vallancey and Ledwich

I

CHARLES VALLANCEY, chief engineer of Ireland from 1794, was angry when he saw what Edward Ledwich, the upstart vicar of Aghaboe, Co. Offaly, had written. Vallancey's work of a lifetime was dismissed as 'soporiferous' and 'the ravings of a bedlamite'. The chief engineer, who had spent years studying the customs and antiquities of Ireland through the prism of the Irish language, who had even founded the respected periodical *Collectanea de Rebus Hibernicis*, was accused of producing a 'fairy labyrinth of absurdity'.

Vallancey (1721–1812), an Englishman, had developed such an interest in the small island of Ireland and its people that it had inspired him to construct proof of their antiquity. He maintained that not only was their language inherited from Eastern civilizations, but that the people themselves were almost full-blooded Phoenicians. Had he not demonstrated beyond doubt that their famous Round Towers were the ruins of ceremonial monuments built by Persian fire-worshippers? Who better than an engineer to analyse such structures? But the presumptuous Ledwich was dismissing all of that as 'such a tissue of Hiberno-Oriental adventures as never before appeared on paper'.

Ledwich (1737–1823) even had the temerity to propose a system of his own: the Round Towers had been built by the Danes, who had also been

⊠ *Charles Vallancey (1721-1812) by George Chinnery (courtesy of The Royal Irish Academy, Dublin)*

responsible for megalithic Newgrange and constructed it in the ninth century. Ledwich declared that it was from these wild Northmen – whom he fatuously claimed had preceded the 'Celtes' – together with the Saxons, that anything worthwhile in Ireland was derived. With no command of Irish, the vicar presumed to ridicule the chief engineer's linguistic discoveries, and wrote that Vallancey could not prevent his interpretation of the traditional Irish fables from 'sinking under their own imbecility'. The famous mythologies of the Fianna were 'total inventions, to amuse an ignorant and barbarous people'; the Irish were as nothing until the Saxons redeemed them. This criticism must have appeared outrageous to Vallancey.

The bitter argument between Charles Vallancey and Edward Ledwich was paradoxical. An Englishman was proposing a substantial pedigree for the Irish; an Anglo-Irishman was declaring them to be barbarians. Each seemed to invoke the discipline of his opponent. Vallancey, whose training

⊠ THE ATLANTEAN IRISH

as a military engineer was practical, had used imagination and an Irish dictionary to construct an oriental and religion-centred past for the Irish. Ledwich purported to be a man of God, yet used the rationalist tools of the Enlightenment to demolish such a construct and erect a pagan Viking context in its stead.

If Vallancey was right, the Irish were civilized before the English took over; if Ledwich was correct, and the Danes had built Brú na Bóinne, then the Irish were doubly barbarian because everybody knew that the Northmen were uncivilized. To the modern reader, to whom such questions are academic and who reads these writings as literature rather than history, there is no doubt which is the more entertaining writer. The exuberance of Vallancey's speculations is infinitely more attractive than the intemperate sneers of Ledwich.

The dispute between Vallancey and Ledwich might now appear to be the insubstantial squabble of two educated hobbyists, but at the end of the eighteenth century it was one of the seminal themes of the day. Vallancey was an idealist, while Ledwich was an opportunist, seeing clearly the political dimension of a respected antiquarian's attempts to revive interest in a Gaelic past. In the growing pressure for an Act of Union with Britain, perhaps Ledwich also saw the possibilities of increasing his chances of advancement within the Established Church.

The Ledwich faction won. The Act of Union was passed in 1800, the possibility of Irish autonomy went underground and the vicar's thesis was republished four years later. Although even James Joyce quoted Vallancey's findings without demur, the engineer is still dismissed as an impractical romantic. Ledwich, who has earned no comparable odium, must have realized that Vallancey was more than politically incorrect, that it was essential to destroy his reputation; the antiquarian engineer was a figure of stature who showed too much sympathy for the native Irish and their language. Variations of the opposing perspectives of Vallancey and Ledwich are still the poles around which private and public debate inexorably revolve in the Irish cockpit. Even on that tiny eighteenth-century stage, the native Irish were rarely consulted. In a sense, Ireland may be approached as a figment of the imagination of visiting observers and their native agents.

Vallancey was treated kindly by many, such as the Earl of Rosse (Sir Lawrence Parsons), by the politician Henry Flood (stimulated by Vallancey's intention to earmark £50,000 for Trinity College Dublin for the study of the Irish language) and, in recent years, by the essayist Hubert Butler. However, the Ledwich tactic of simple abuse is still echoed by modern historians; Roy Foster recently described Vallancey's work on Irish philology as 'hokum'. In other words, that 200-year-old squabble is still alive among the learned classes. But what proportion of these learned classes has bothered to wrestle with Irish philology? In 1901 Douglas Hyde, first president of Ireland, could write:

> It is simply amazing that most Irish and many English writers, who have had to deal with Ireland from that day to this, have in their sketchy and generally unreliable accounts of the island, its people, and its social conditions, simply ignored the fact that any other language than English was spoken in it at all.

Vallancey was the principal exception. He over-elaborates, to put it mildly, and often reads surreally, rather like Lucky in *Waiting for Godot*, evacuating gobs of unintelligible erudition to the bewilderment of the reader. I have also encountered the sterile prose of Ledwich. Their arguments are irrelevant to subsequent assessments of them; Vallancey tried to understand the island's complex history and was enthusiastic about the place and its people, Ledwich despised both. They each ended up as pawns in the intellectual schizophrenia that has bedevilled discussion in and about Ireland for over 300 years.

Another visitor to Ireland, the French Chevalier de Latocnaye, in 1796 supported the theory that Ireland's origins lay to the west, that it represented the remaining fragment of a landmass submerged by the Atlantic in prehistoric times. A century later, this theory re-emerged in United States Senator Ignatius Donnelly's *Atlantis, the Antediluvian World*. However, these theories that the Irish came from the north, south or west were never as widely accepted as the theory that they came 'overland' from the east, that they were Celts.

It was (and still is) widely held that a people called the 'Celts' migrated westwards across Europe. By the mid-fifth century BC, it has been maintained, these northern Europeans had begun to colonize Britain and Ireland. Whatever about parts of Britain, the archaeological evidence does not support the idea of a Celtic colonization of Ireland, or that such a people re-placed or mixed with the indigenous population.

But it was a useful myth.

The modern myth's beginnings may be traced to a Welsh naturalist and polymath named Edward Lhuyd (1670–1709) who in 1700 was the keeper of the Ashmolean Museum in Oxford. Lhuyd was inspired by the writings of a Breton, Paul-Yves Pezron, whose patriotic aim was to distinguish between the French and the Bretons. In 1707, in the parallel context of antipathy between Wales and England, Lhuyd followed the Breton's example; in his *Archaeologia Britannica* he proposed that Irish, Breton, Welsh, Cornish, Manx and Scottish sprang from the same linguistic Celtic loins, and that they were all closely related to the ancient Gaulish and Iberian languages, thus making them 'Celtic'.

In this context at least, both Lhuyd and Pezron applied their considerable energies in a spirit less of scholarship than of politics and culture. Romantic nationalism was at the embryonic stage. In retrospect this was not in any sense ignoble; the pipe dream of value-free science has long run out of tobacco. Can any modern scholars – any human being – declare themselves uninfluenced by socially interiorized cultural predispositions?

A century after Vallancey and Ledwich, the Gaelic Revival in Ireland came into its own. It supplied Ireland's need for an identity other than that offered by the increasingly unpopular ascendancy. The foundation of such groups as the Gaelic Athletic Association, the Society for the Preservation of the Irish Language, the National Literary Society and the Gaelic League reinforced the 200-year-old theory that the Irish were radically different from the English, i.e. that they were uniquely Gaelic and Celtic. It helped to focus the national feeling that led eventually to a form of Irish independence.

The theories of Vallancey, Ledwich, de Latocnaye and others were dismissed as quaint; a new orthodoxy was established that has ultimately produced, among other things, a Celtic ragbag into which everything from new-age religion to saccharine pop music can be awkwardly crammed. The term 'Celtic' has become a kind of cultural smog that has demonstrably impoverished Irish culture. Even the Gaelic Revivalists assuredly must be turning in their graves.

The sixteenth-century Anglo-Irish poet Edmund Spenser wrote: 'It is certain that Ireland had the use of letters very anciently and long before England.' But for obvious political reasons, Spenser was impatient with claims that the Irish were related to the Spanish: 'Of all the nations under Heaven the Spaniard is the most mingled and most uncertain; whereof most foolishly do the Irish think to ennoble themselves by wresting their ancestry from the Spaniards.'

If Spenser had read that marvellous libel, *Topographica Hibernia*, by a Welsh cleric named Giraldus Cambrensis (1146–1223), he might have torn his beard out. Cambrensis purveyed his account of the Irish in the twelfth century. He was a churchman who accompanied the early Norman invaders, essentially a war correspondent with special privileges. He was given access to all available literary sources, but even if he had quoted accurately from these he would still have been in trouble. As Eoin MacNeill pointed out:

> The 10th and 11th centuries produced a school of Irish historians whose chief work was to reduce the old miscellaneous matter of tradition to unity and sequence. In dealing with the pre-Christian period they tampered with tradition in two ways; when they found definite elements of 'heathenism' they either cut these out or furbished them in a guise which they considered consonant with Christian belief. This can be shown to have been done consciously and deliberately.

Historical revisionism is no new phenomenon; MacNeill called its first practitioners 'the synthetic historians'.

Spenser might also have been incited to rage by Seathrún Céitinn/ Geoffrey Keating's *History of Ireland* (c. 1630). In this, using such Irish literary sources as *An Leabhar Gabhála* (The Book of Invasions), no fewer than five invaders are credited with an input to Irish identity. They are, variously, a granddaughter of Noah called Cesara; a grandson of same called Partholon; a Scythian named Nemedus, who held the country for 216 years 'and for 200 years afterwards the land was empty'; somebody named Dela who came from Greece; and, finally, two brothers named Hibemus and Hermanus who came from Spain. To this list Keating added tribes called the Dé Danann, the Fomorians and the Fir Bolg.

Vallancey tore Keating's ideas apart: 'The Translator [Geoffrey Keating], entirely ignorant of geography, has given this history an English dress so ridiculous, as to become the laughing-stock of every reader.' He also dismissed the classical authors: 'The Greeks, to whom we are much indebted, are still more *fabulous*; they knew little of the geography of the Globe; and the Romans even less ... Herodotus, the oldest Greek historian, knew nothing of Britain.'

Such exchanges tarnish the image of scholarly gentlemen discussing

 *Newgrange, Co. Meath, after its 'reconstruction'*

matters calmly. The groves of academe can sometimes resemble a jungle.

Neither did scholarly habits seem to improve in later centuries. According to Séamus Delargy (1899–1980), a leading folklorist, the scholars and literary men of Ireland, whether they were Irish or Anglo-Irish, wrote exclusively in English and were, in the main, 'completely ignorant of Irish and contemptuous of the language and the people who spoke it'. Oddly enough Vallancey, the most ridiculed of these scholars, seems to have been one of the rare exceptions, having at least gone to the trouble of familiarizing himself with Irish.

Delargy continues on a mournful note: 'The loss of the language over most of Ireland brought about the destruction of the oral literature enshrined in it, leaving a gap in our knowledge of Irish folklore which can never be filled.' This is a pity because the oral traditions of a people can valuably complement empirical evidence.

Throughout the twentieth century, scholarship in Ireland lost much of the exuberance of the Vallancey-Ledwich controversy and seemed to be governed by an orthodoxy imposed by the hidebound perspective of the area traditionally called the Pale, centred on Dublin. Interlopers were discouraged from offering opinions.

In the late 1970s a young American, Martin Brennan, dared to interpret the famous Boyne Valley passage tombs in terms of astronomy – positing that they were solar laboratories as much as burial places and therefore built by a highly sophisticated people. His book, *Boyne Valley Vision* (1980), suffered an unprecedentedly savage review from the widow of Michael O'Kelly – a fine archaeologist/excavator but tourist-oriented reconstructor of Newgrange; Liam de Paor described O'Kelly's reconstruction as 'kitsch'. The young American's reputation was further damaged when he left Ireland, allegedly deported for drug offences. In fact, Martin Brennan recently confirmed to me by letter that he had been harassed, but that it was a case of mistaken identity by the Special Branch – they had taken him for a well-known IRA member who was later deported.

In the light of this – the condition of Ireland that W.B. Yeats called 'Great hatred, little room' – nearly a quarter of a century ago I began to research the subject of Ireland's connections with, among other places, North Africa.

I sympathize with the prudence of scholars. Too often their findings, carefully qualified, have been plucked out of context and used for crude propaganda purposes. The pleading by Herder in the eighteenth century for the dignity of the German language and people was a reaction to the arrogance of the Frankish courts. Who could have foreseen there the seeds of an Aryan nightmare in the twentieth century? English chauvinists in 1912 tried to 'prove' that a certain skull belonged to one of the earliest examples of *Homo sapiens* in England. This became known as the Piltdown Man, and it was forty years before it was exposed as a hoax.

The history of such hoaxes and fakery has its serious side. Truth may always be relative, but provisional intellectual findings can often coincide with the prevailing political and national ethos. Such arbitrary conclusions can then become conventional wisdom. Thus, the British will say that the reason the Romans did not invade Ireland was because there was nothing there worth conquering. The Irish will retort that the Romans were nervous about taking on such a redoubtable foe. The British will contend that they sent the first people over the Scottish landbridge to Ireland in Palaeolithic times; the Irish will say it's just as likely they came directly from the Continent. The British will claim the Book of Kells for the north of England; the Irish grow indignant at such a suggestion, because they know their own scholarship was the basis of Northumbrian learning.

In the island of Ireland itself a parallel friction persists. Northern scholars traditionally pointed to a greater incidence of Mesolithic flints in their area as evidence of the earliest habitation of the country. Their southern

⊠ *Seán Ó Loideán with his find on the Seana Mhac bog, south Conamara*

counterparts might reasonably say that if as much attention had been paid by colonist antiquarians to the south, a similar density might be found.

Rarely are the footsoldiers, the people who actually live on the land, consulted. An elderly neighbour of mine in Conamara, the late Seán Ó Loideán, told me that he was cutting turf on the Seana Mhac bog in 1941 when, beneath the 4000-year-old blanket of peat (from the medieval Irish *puiteach* – boggy) and lodged in the granite below, he found a polished stone axe. It was identified by the National Museum as being identical in style to those manufactured in Tievebullagh, Co. Antrim, and Rathlin Island, 320 kilometres to the north. Fifty years later Seán could proudly show me the axe and was able to bring me to the precise spot where he had found it. Countrymen like Seán Ó Loideán often retain a deep interest in the origins of things; he was the kind of man Estyn Evans respected as a keeper of invaluable, if unwritten, records.

Irish archaeologist Peter Woodman, who had conducted an up-to-date investigation of the flints in the north, came to the conclusion that they were not necessarily made later than their equivalent in Scotland, from where it had been suggested the first settlers came. Subsequently, archaeologist Michael Ryan found material in Lough Boora showing that such early first settlers could have arrived in Ireland at almost any point on the east coast. Woodman moved on to work in the south-west of the island

and expressed confidence that he could find similar flints there. It was not long before he had found evidence in Ferriter's Cove, Co. Kerry, that pushed back by 2000 years the estimate of the earliest date at which people were arriving on the Dingle peninsula in Kerry. Since then other sites in the area have suggested that the earliest settlers could have arrived as early as 8000–7000 BC.

In other words, the 'truth' in these matters is simply a working hypothesis to be confirmed or denied by whatever new evidence is found. However, as Thomas Mann once wrote: 'In modern times man's destiny is stated in political terms.' Archaeology is not immune to this disease.

Scholars themselves are most conscious of these grey areas; hence their prudence, but also their wrath when mere laymen intrude. It is akin to the relationship between theologians and the faithful. Robert Graves has written trenchantly on this subject from the perspective of the poet:

> That so many scholars are barbarians does not much matter so long as a few of them are ready to help with their specialized knowledge the few independent thinkers, that is to say the poets, who try to keep civilization alive. The scholar is a quarryman, not a builder, and all that is required of him is that he should quarry cleanly. He is the poet's insurance against factual error … the poet's function is truth.

I have found individual scholars to be unreservedly generous with their knowledge and time. Graves was harsh on them; a scholar can be as imaginative as a poet: each desperately, single-mindedly, tries to forge an order out of chaos. It would be interesting, however, for a sociologist to plot a graph showing the correlation between scholarly consensus in a society and the dominant political ethos that prevails at any given time. The relationship between Europe and the Middle East is a case in point. It is clear that the colonial experience has complicated the history of ideas here and significantly coloured the accounts. How much does the West owe to the East? Did ideas and cultures, even civilizations, move from East to West or vice versa? At one stage Mesopotamia and Egypt were credited with the beginnings of everything. Alternatively Western Europe is proclaimed to have had a separate and quite autonomous development. The truth always lies in the fissures between the tectonic plates of ideologies.

A *cause célèbre* of recent decades has been *Black Athena* (1987), Martin Bernal's thesis that ancient Greek culture is at its base Egyptian and that classical historians since the late eighteenth century have conspired to deprive Africans of credit for it. His thesis, subtitled *The Afro-Asiatic Roots of Classical Civilization*, implied that several centuries of European scholarship were guilty of racism. Afro-Americans instantly saw the implications and gleefully championed his thesis; the book became obligatory reading for millions.

It took a few years for American classical scholars to organize their defence. In 1996 classical scholar Mary Lefkowitz edited a collection of essays entitled *Black Athena Revisited*, the work of twenty heavyweight scholars who tore into Bernal's ideas with scarcely concealed rage, consigning them to perdition in terms such as 'Afrocentric fantasies', 'tendentious', 'incredible' and 'selective'. It reminded me of Vallancey's treatment. Fortunately not all academics agreed. Paul Edwards of the University of Edinburgh elsewhere described Bernal's work as 'carefully considered and very well informed'.

It would be impertinent of me to even attempt to arbitrate in this dispute, but Bernal was at least fluent in Greek and could also read Egyptian hieroglyphics. His target was the gradual establishment in the nineteenth century of what he called the 'Aryan model' of ancient history. He was not the first to air such a thesis. Gerard Manley Hopkins, who taught Greek in Dublin in the late nineteenth century, also desperately sought evidence of such Egyptian foundations for ancient Greek. He suffered the same fate as Bernal. According to Lefkowitz, even Hopkins' own biographer dismissed the poet's enquiries as 'wild linguistic surmises' based on 'obscure etymological instances'. Hell hath no fury like a scholar roused. There is an echo of this dispute in the ironical writings of Sir Samuel Ferguson (1810–66), as quoted by Daniel Corkery, when he suggests the Greeks should consider themselves to be 'Northwest Egyptians'.

Linguistics and archaeology were once the preserve of amateurs – gentlemen who had the money and leisure to read and excavate at will, collect archaeological artefacts and speculate freely; they had not the scientific equipment to date their finds precisely. But the advent of professional archaeology also had its limitations. It was not until techniques such as dendrochronology (tree-ring examination) and carbon-14 dating were refined that there was any hope of precision. In the constant pursuit of certainty the archaeologists had had to become historians and geographers; they now found themselves having to consult botanists, chemists, geologists, linguists, anthropologists and other specialists. The new techniques altered some agreed dates by up to a thousand years, challenging the entire canon of archaeological and historical faith. As one archaeologist, Colin Renfrew, stated: 'Once it is accepted that no model of the past can claim to be uniquely correct – any man is free to claim his own – it follows that no theory relating to past events can ever be final.'

However, 'any man' is likely to be so intimidated by the vastness and complexity of available evidence that he will rarely try to construct his own model of the past. The honest seeker of the truth will find himself drowned in a sea of statistics, scientific jargon and opinions so qualified as to be useless. Even the solid common sense of the archaeologist in the field tends to be overwhelmed by the flood of information. The ill-equipped antiquarians, with their romantic, sweeping generalizations, seem attractive in the face of what Canadian poet F.R. Scott has described as 'the rain of facts that deepen the drought of the will'.

Scholarship and science are invoked to support cultural and political attitudes. One scholarly hypothesis can become the orthodoxy of the mob; historians must despair at the use to which their findings are put. In Northern Ireland, Protestants could point to the fact that Catholic Irishmen in the British forces put down the Irish nationalist rising of 1798 in the north, where the rebels were largely non-conformist Protestant. Catholics, for their part, could quote the Protestant leaders of the United Irishmen support of their nationalism. And everybody knows that the Protestant William of Orange had the backing of a Roman Catholic Pope, who said a Mass in Rome when the Catholic King James was defeated at the Battle of the Boyne in 1690.

The Bible itself is one of the most abused products of scholarship. In the Middle East, the government of Israel still uses the Good Book to justify its increasing takeover of Palestine. Arabs can plausibly argue that the Old Testament and its writers had their origin not in the Holy Land but in the Arabian peninsula. The Bible was used in the seventeenth century by Archbishop Ussher of Dublin to prove that the world was created in exactly 4004 BC. Even today there are thousands of sincere evangelists relying on the book's authority to prove everything ranging from Armageddon to the reality of eternal life. No wonder the Roman Catholic Church traditionally discouraged the faithful from reading the Bible for themselves.

⬚ *Chart from* Libro de Todo el Universo *by Lazaro Luis, 1563 (Academia das Ciências de Lisboa)*

In the secular arena, the Irish, Norwegians and Spanish claim that, respectively, St Brendan, Leif Ericsson and Christopher Columbus first discovered America. The claims of the 'Indians' who were there before them all do not count as they were pre-literate Stone Age people.

No wonder scholars so cloak their words in circumlocution that few can misquote them, never mind understand them. Specialization in the sciences and the humanities can approach the point of absurdity. In the focussed world of the specialist — however brilliant the individual — the human capacity for making imaginative leaps is in danger of atrophying. Robert Graves stated: 'To know only one thing too well is to have a barbaric mind: civilization implies the graceful relation of all varieties of experience to a central humane system of thought.'

For over thirty years I have lived, worked with and observed a living community in a 'remote' spot on the edge of Europe: Conamara in the west of Ireland. From this perspective, Europe looks different. So, for that matter, does the island called Ireland. Instead of being a distant and unimportant planet on the edge of a European galaxy whose axis runs east/west, Ireland can be seen as the centre of a cultural area oriented north/south, based on the Atlantic seaways that reach from Scandinavia to North Africa. The squabbles of Vallancey and Ledwich may eventually be superseded by a more satisfying perspective: one based on common sense.

Such a view will, alas, still be provisional. Although the perspective the Irish imagination still cultivates is that imposed by traditional European history and geography, it also happens to retain an essential tool of survival: peripheral vision.

Sean-nós Singing and Conamara's Boats

2

On the periphery of Europe, midway up the west coast of Ireland, lies a region called Conamara. It occupies the area to the west of Galway city and forms the northern shore of Galway Bay. A much-visited part of a small island on the edge of Europe, it protects England and Wales from the full force of the Atlantic while at the same time deflecting the warm waters of the Gulf Stream northwards to Scotland. Conamara takes the brunt of the attack from the Atlantic. In the arc of its ever-changing skies the onset of whatever weather is in store for the two islands can be detected daily. In 1970 I exiled myself to this unpromising region and have made it my home ever since.

When visitors to Conamara extol the desolate beauty of mountain, bog and lonely lake, it is clear to me that they have not experienced the place at all. They have been shepherded by some tourist brochure northward through a countryside that looks well from a bus — particularly because there are no people to clutter the view. They have been consciously steered away from the coastal region, South Conamara, still the most densely populated region in rural Ireland although much less than its peak of 500 persons per square mile in 1841, before the Great Famine. North Conamara is more

⊠ *View of Cuan na Loinge, and the 'interdigitized' coastline of Conamara*

dramatically beautiful but relatively unpopulated; South Conamara is crowded and relatively untidy. In addition, the inhabitants speak Irish, show a disconcerting indifference to modern tourism, and sing songs that fall uneasily on Western ears.

South Conamara is about as far west as you can go in Europe. The people here are more familiar with Boston than Dublin. In the 1840s a local man is reputed to have packed his entire family into a small traditional sailing boat and, with a plentiful supply of salted pork, escaped from the Famine to North America – 4800 kilometres away. The exploit was repeated by the intrepid Paddy Barry in a Galway Bay *hucaer* only a few years ago. These adventures serve to highlight the most significant yet most ignored aspect of Conamara and its people: their obsession with boats and the sea. They seem to be the only large and identifiable community in Ireland that realizes we inhabit an island. For certain reasons, rooted in the colonial experience, the Irish of recent generations have all but ignored the sea. They even abandoned their small merchant fleet to creditors in distant ports some years ago. Consequently, most reporters on Conamara tend to overlook its predominantly maritime personality. In contrast to the rest of Ireland, where boating is essentially a suburban hobby, a rich man's sport or part of the neglected fishing industry, the average Conamara person has a feel for the sea. On every Sunday afternoon in summer, crowds still gather in the various bays and harbours to celebrate the survival of their own traditional craft: the hucaer, gleoiteog, púcán and currach.

On such festive occasions the sense of history is palpable, but sublimated to present enjoyment. The main attraction, apart from hotly contested rowing races in currachs, is the sailing competition. The most spectacular of these features the *hucaer* or *bád mór*, literally 'big boat'. It has a massive oak construction, a dramatic tumblehome or belly, dark heavy sails of canvas and can be up to fifteen metres in length. The sight of seven or eight of these boats scudding along in a brisk wind generates ripples of knowing comments among the onlookers ashore.

On the boats themselves the atmosphere is tense. Some skippers may have had their ships in dry dock for a few days in order to grease the hulls – I certainly witnessed one, the late Johnny Jimmy Mac Donncha, laboriously applying margarine for minimum water resistance to his *Maighdean Mhara* (the mermaid). His sons still proudly race the boat.

The races have been suspended in the past because of the dangerous rivalry and doubtful tactics occasionally employed. One outlawed technique was to send a sharp piece of flint whizzing across to rip into a rival's taut sail. This was considered fair when a rival had cut inside and 'stolen your wind'. It is part of the mythology that many years ago, when a crew member fell overboard and was clinging to a trailing rope, the skipper was so desperate to win the race that he cut through the lifeline, leaving the man to be picked up by the next boat, which the skipper knew was commanded by the unfortunate victim's cousin.

In these races the satisfaction lay not simply in taking part. Winning was everything and it was based on a sound economic tradition. These big boats were used for carrying turf from bog-rich Conamara to places that had none, the limestone islands of Aran as well as south Galway and Clare. Whichever boat first reached the small harbours made sure of the inside berth beside the quay wall. This made the unloading easier, saved hours of waiting and ensured the best price for the turf. The tradition of this trade is commemorated every August when a fleet of turf-boats, with billowing

■ *Conamara hucaerí and púcáin*

brown, black and red sails, sets sail from a pier in Carraroe and races across Galway Bay to Kinvara, in Co. Clare.

It is hard to reconcile the massive beams and generous scale of the *hucaerí* with the intimate lifestyle and organic architecture that, up to recent years, the people themselves cultivated. It is as if all sense of grandeur was siphoned off from domestic life and channelled exclusively into these boats. Perhaps this was how the people showed their pride in themselves when in all other areas they were modest, even reticent. The small thatched cottages and tiny plots of land were undemonstrative. The fact that this lifestyle has been largely replaced by modern bungalows and cars, while economic dependence on the sea has diminished, underlines the interrelationship between these two aspects of Conamara life.

The presence and impact of the sea expresses itself first in the physical environment: a series of islands and peninsulas hewn out by the Atlantic, the topsoil stripped off by the gales that begin in September and sometimes do not ease until March. This indented coastline means that virtual neighbours, a half-mile apart, might have to travel thirty kilometres by road to visit each other. As against this, the presence of shops, post offices, pubs and travel agents on the remotest tips of these islands and peninsulas suggests that it was not always thus. The location of these services makes no economic sense until one stops looking through the windscreen of a car and realizes that the logical connection between these places is the boat.

Within living memory practically all commuting and transporting was seaborne. Water was not a barrier but a lifeline. Even social life depended on the currach. On summer evenings young people would pile into these canvas boats, row to the next island or peninsula, dance all night and row home at dawn. There is sad evidence for this custom in the memory of occasional drownings; these were more likely if the indigenous brew — *poitín* — was indulged in. Even in the context of this illegal drink, and the efforts to suppress its manufacture, there is evidence of the native regard for boats. Poitín was — and still occasionally is — made on the islands and rocky shores of freshwater lakes. When the still is raided, the natural escape route is over water. The local forces of law and order would constantly bewail the fact that the powers that be would not supply them with a fast boat to engage in hot pursuit. Officialdom took a long time to realize that we are all surrounded by water and as a result captures were rare. The Conamara person's respect for boats has a practical as well as a sentimental basis.

This took on importance when I began to wonder about the strange music of the area: sean-nós singing. It is a pity the term is so imprecise; *sean-nós* simply means 'old style'. Nevertheless, the performers and their dedicated audiences know, with ferocious precision, what is meant by the term: an ascetic, unaccompanied form of solo singing that at its best has not succumbed to the emotional sogginess of pop music. It may not be too much to claim that whoever can be moved by the writing of Samuel Beckett has the capacity to enjoy sean-nós singing. In it, passion is pared away to reveal the extraordinary courage at the heart of the human being. Describing the most heart-rending events in song, an intelligent performer's face will betray not one wisp of emotion. This singing, at least in Conamara, defies comparison with the drawing-room tradition and its sentimental off-spring. There are no dramatic high notes, no hushed tones, and no build-up to a pyrotechnical climax; instead the good singer will concentrate on minuscule decoration.

In this there is an analogy to be made with the art of manuscript illumination. At their best, singers like Darach Ó Catháin and Seán Jack Mac Donncha could sing with a subtlety compared to a page from the Book of Kells. Under a microscope some of the lines on those pages are miraculously fine. The art in them seems to be to conceal art; the satisfaction seems to be in the achievement rather than the acclaim. Similarly with the good sean-nós singer: in performance the singer seems to escape into total intro-spection, as if communing with him or herself rather than with the audience. In this way the audience is drawn into the singer's semi-trance. As if to make sure he does not forget their presence, and also to reassure him of their

 *Sean-nós singer Sarah Grealish with Seán John Mac Donncha*

support, one of the audience will grasp his hand and move it rhythmically in a winding action.

Inevitably, this extraordinary art form is withering. Many of the songs relate to the sea, be they accounts of lovers lost or terrifying storms. As the maritime dependence of the people has lessened, so the musical form degenerates. This seems a more fundamental cause than that customarily offered: the decline in the use of spoken Irish. However, the singing is still the most popular event at the annual gathering of Irish speakers, the Oireachtas.

I encountered this music on the radio as a child in Dublin. It was quite alien to my urban ears, which were accustomed to Italian opera, the lighter classics and the pleasant treacle of Bing Crosby. Indeed, sean-nós singing was an occasional object of ridicule on stage and radio, being used as a symbol for an allegedly backward rural tradition that sophisticated urbanites should deride. In my father's house, sean-nós was switched off.

Twenty years later in Conamara I found it was the most popular form of musical expression and, as I learned, the basis of all traditional Irish music. It was still difficult to enjoy. It defied all of the conditions I had been led to believe were essential to enjoy music: it did not easily lend itself to harmony; it had none of the simple rhythms of European classical form, nor the dance rhythms of folk music. Also, it seemed to go on and on, endlessly. No matter how musical a person was – and I prided myself on my musical ear – it was impossible to pick up the style quickly and perform even remotely well. Although Conamara people stated that it could be learned, they added that it could not be taught. In other words, one would have to apprentice oneself to a singer and simply listen for years before acquiring the words, melodies, or styles of ornamentation. Even then, much would depend on the performer's inventiveness, because no two singers embellish a song in the same way. Its closest relation is modern jazz.

It became clear that this form of singing was an artistic response by a highly integrated community to a particular – and precarious – lifestyle in a long-settled environment. But this description does not match the conventional explanation of the origins of the people of Conamara. They are usually thought to be recent arrivals, descendants of the seventeenth-century victims of Oliver Cromwell and the famous dictum: 'To hell or to Connacht.' The explanation matches neither the Conamara sense of identity, the people's ancient singing style, nor their highly developed tradition of boat handling and design.

When I read descriptions of the place as 'lonely', 'remote', or 'out in the wilds', I looked out of my window and saw fifty houses across the lake. On Sundays I saw traffic jams outside the church. Social life was consistently more intense and gregarious than in the average city suburb. Whatever the depressing results of American sociologists' sallies into rural Ireland, their findings simply did not fit Conamara. Neither could those people who wrote the travel brochures about the place have spent much time here.

The social structure was so intimate, the channels of communication so efficient, that it was unwise to criticize persons behind their backs: your audience might very well be their cousins. The traditional naming system was biblical: surnames were shared by so many that it was wise to know, as well as the person's first name, those of his father and grandfather. This must have caused people in official agencies to tear their hair out; it was a sure way of confusing the computer. I found myself living in what felt like a slightly foreign country. Luckily, I had no private means and was forced to work with the people. This meant learning the language – quite different from the 'book-Irish' I had been taught in school – and this helped when I began studying sean-nós singing.

On examination, the music did not at first appear to be simply a survivor

Egyptian musicians (G. Angelidis, Cairo)

of a long-forgotten European tradition. The late and highly respected composer, Seán Ó Riada, in the course of three radio lectures, contended that sean-nós was not European, nor could it be understood in that context; it was much closer to oriental forms. Irish art had never adopted the forms 'spawned', as he put it, by the Graeco-Roman renaissance. The best way to understand the music, he said, was 'to listen to it with a child's fresh mind'. In other words, dismiss all preconceptions. Failing that, he suggested, one might try to hear it in terms of Indian music.

Sure enough, there happen to be faint resonances in sean-nós that would remind one of Indian music. And, of course, this would fit with the conventional Indo-European explanation of the origins of the Irish. However, when pressed as to how such music could have arrived in Ireland, Ó Riada suggested it might have come through North Africa and Spain.

Seán Ó Riada was a classically trained musician, had composed film scores, wrote some of the most important symphonic music in Ireland, formed a folk orchestra whose influence was seminal in the popularization of traditional Irish music, and the famous Chieftains folk group owes its origin to his inspiration. Not only was Ó Riada also an admired jazz pianist, his sophisticated company was much sought after. His analysis of sean-nós should not be dismissed; his tragic death at the age of forty halted a fascinating line of enquiry.

Generally speaking, when Irish people listen to the music of the Middle East and North Africa they experience an odd, aural equivalent of *déjà vu*. Charles Acton, late music critic of *The Irish Times*, once wrote an extensive article on the subject:

> If one has listened for hours in the desert of an evening to Bedouin Arabs singing narrative epics with as many stanzas as a long *aisling* [vision poem, in Irish] and then returned to Ireland and heard a fine sean-nós singer using the same melismata and rhythm, one finds the resemblance between the two almost uncanny. So too, if one listens to *canto jondo* [of Spain].

Mr Acton went on to say that he put this idea to Joan Rimmer, an ethnomusicologist of authority. Her crisp reply was: 'Of course!' He concluded: 'The connections between the Arab lands and southern Europe, Spain and Ireland are, apparently, commonplace to scholars of her eminence.'

The famed collector Alan Lomax shared this perspective:

> [I] have long considered Ireland to be part of the Old Southern Mediterranean–Middle Eastern family of style that I call bardic – highly ornamented, free rhythmed, solo, or solo and string accompanied singing that support sophisticated and elaborate forms.

One of the greatest exponents of sean-nós singing, the late Joe Heaney (Seosamh Ó hÉanaí), was described by the writer Máirtín Ó Cadhain as singing such songs

> effortlessly, one after another, in a manner which strongly reminds one of Gitano singing in the caves of Granada. In fact his splendid figure and face is the southern Spanish type. There is a strong tradition that survivors of the Armada remained along the Conamara coast.

The Spanish connection made sense; Irishmen always looked to Catholic Spain as a possible saviour. Salamanca had educated thousands of Irish priests. Spanish Arch in Galway commemorates the busy trade between the two countries. Even the typical Conamara dance called 'the battering' is the nearest thing possible to Spanish flamenco. But contact with 'the Arab lands'? Such an outlandish suggestion had never been made in my presence. It was completely at variance with conventional history, which took all of the divergent characteristics of the Irish, both negative and positive, and dumped them into the romantic category: 'Celtic'. The suggestion that sean-nós had a respectably authenticated connection with the Arabs was startling. Not world-shaking, of course, as the music has a relatively small, loyal audience of aficionados and these are principally located within the Irish-speaking areas of Ireland.

An acquaintance of mine spent three years in University College Dublin acquiring a degree in music without once hearing sean-nós singing. Little attention is paid by musicians of the classical or even 'contemporary' school to this folk-idiom, despite the fact that it is more subtle than a Scarlatti sonatina. I am aware of few serious Irish composers who have considered the form with insight; they include Frank Corcoran and Roger Doyle. Dr Seoirse Bodley has also perceptively written:

> The real oral tradition of sean-nós is often obscured for many listeners by several factors. There is often confusion in the public mind between: (a) the genuine sean-nós or oral tradition and (b) songs that are sung in Irish but without the style and without the traditional ornaments or tone quality. This does not mean that one objects to the songs of the Irish Language Revival, but that a clear distinction must be made between them and sean-nós proper.

In the tightly-knitted garment of Irish 'Celtic' culture, there now appeared to me to be loose threads. If sean-nós was (a) not European, according to Ó Riada, (b) to be distinguished from the mainstream of 'Celtic' culture and (c) was alien to the majority of Irish ears, then where on earth did it fit? I have spent many years tugging at these loose threads: the garment when unravelled is less a seamless jersey of pure 'Celtic' weave than a more interesting coat of many colours.

The first question to be asked was: how could there be any contact between two such apparently remote places – between Ireland and the Middle East, between two such different peoples – the Irish and the Arabs? They inhabited different continents, had profoundly different religious beliefs and, judged by the perilous barometer of ethnicity, looked different. Besides, one group lived in the sun, the other on a misty island 1600 kilometres away.

Yet listening at night with more attention to those obscure radio stations that sometimes trespass on our wavelengths with strange music from North Africa, the possibility grew. For instance, the folk orchestra that Seán Ó Riada developed so many years ago, consisting of fiddles, flutes, tin whistles, melodeons and a quite primitive drum called the 'bodhrán', did not, in retrospect, seem quite so remote from the distant strains of North Africa. Indeed, when I visited Iran in 1968 I recall being struck by the similarity between their 'classical' music and the Ó Riada invention. At the time I attached little significance to it.

However, the goatskin drum or *bodhrán*, which Ó Riada rescued from obscurity in Kerry to become the basic rhythm section of most traditional Irish music groups, has its exact counterpoint in the *bindir*, the drum of Morocco. It was interesting that Ó Riada had, in creating a 'classical' folk music, unconsciously followed the example of the 'Persians'. Like them, he had respect for indigenous modes and techniques evolved over the centuries that only required the sophisticated humility of genius to recognize and adapt. Admittedly, Ó Riada introduced a baroque note by using the harpsichord, but he excused this as the nearest sound he could find to the great Irish harp.

A musicologist would get down to a detailed examination of the modes employed, the different scales, the instruments, the chronology of these disparate manifestations of the same phenomenon. He or she would certainly soon realize the debt European music owes to Islamic culture: the violin's origin in the Middle East; the guitar's antecedent in the *ud* of North Africa; the influence of the Moors on the seminal Troubadour repertoire of France; the possibility that Europe may have got its first idea for a definite pitch notation from Arabic scholars (in particular an Iraqi named Ziryab, who spent an influential period in Moorish Spain). There have been efforts to confine sean-nós to a respectable European context through comparison with Romanian and Hungarian musical idioms. Scholars who do this are invariably ignorant of the Islamic world, and of the impact the Turkish Ottoman culture has had on those areas.

However, these details are overshadowed by the practical objection of the distance between Ireland and North Africa, and the dangerous stretches of water between the two areas. Returning to Conamara, the objection does not seem insurmountable. Geographically, it is similar to the rest of

The map contains the following labels:

HIBERNIA

purgatoriñ
Saint patriñ

laronel

Olibam

ragrnn

C·ligra
Abram
Cormadella

Iokam fl·
o fosso

O

don fobry
monesta
veiforbo o
chenostin
Effanforda o
Careforda o
daithe

Relm
O

Orozdao

·C· flct
losto
ordes
irlanda
donvelim
Bie
arbroim
vitello
arrello
renas

laratis
Confrendam
otorim
oram

Robs
O

Regia
O

Lamerich
O

C·altrombre

Braschei

Santbranbam
ledeng

O

fredir

Brezil

Ganaforda

orforda o
rifalt
elebam

dondal

ertamer
ninam
lrones

Conba
Gaclosbna
andelmoba
camela·
olarus
dombos
granari
·C· mulem

⊠ *A sea chart of Ireland by Martin Waldseemüller, Strasburg 1513 (National Library of Ireland)*

the western seaboard of Europe: there is the same threatening Atlantic in common, the same cruelly indented coasts, the same peninsular layout. If the people of Conamara could develop an unparalleled tradition of seamanship to overcome the apparent social disadvantage of their physical environment, could the same principle not apply on a larger scale to the entire Atlantic coast of Europe? If Conamara regarded intervening stretches of water not as insurmountable barriers to social intercourse but the very common means of achieving this intercourse, could not the same principle apply on a larger scale? Just as the Irish-speaking minorities in Ireland constitute a cultural archipelago in a sea of English speakers (and are now united through the airwaves of Raidió na Gaeltachta), could not the 'isolated' regions of Atlantic Europe constitute a similar archipelago, writ large? This would then include the Welsh, Bretons, Cornish, even the Galicians, in a unity much more solid than that normally suggested for them. I hope it is not too soon in my argument to point out that Morocco is also one such part of the Atlantic areas.

To most Europeans – but particularly to most Irish people – the idea of significant contact by sea, in the presence of trains and cars and planes, is a little quaint, despite the fact that every single influence that reached Ireland in the past came by sea – as do 90 per cent of its imports and exports still. The Irish mind is so paralysed in matters maritime that the boats between Rosslare and Fishguard or Pembroke, between Dun Laoghaire and Holyhead, between Larne and Stranraer – that is to say the shortest possible sea passages between Ireland and Britain – are about as far as the imagination can stretch.

Only recently have the *nouveaux riche* of Ireland discovered how relatively simple it is to sail their cruisers to the sunny climes of Marbella and the south of Spain. But there have also emerged some true sailors. Paddy Barry honed his skills by sailing to Santander, until he finally made the big leap and sailed his hucaer to Boston and later to the Arctic Circle. In 1989 the Kerry-based Roger Foxall sailed the first Irish yacht into Leningrad since the Russian revolution. His return voyage lasted 111 days and took in thirteen countries. The pioneer of them all was Conor O'Brien, who in 1923–5 circumnavigated the world in the boat *Saoirse*.

To revive such daring was appropriate because, as sociologist Michael D. Higgins has pointed out: 'The migrant is the norm in coastal parishes. The deviant is the person who does not move.' Sociologist Kevin Whelan agrees: 'Looking at Cois Fhairraige, for example, the variety of surnames indicates considerable mobility, especially from County Clare.' It is also borne out by finds on the remotest tip of the island of Leitir Mealláin in Conamara. Here the late Pádraig Mulkerns, an amateur archaeologist, found three groats from the reign of Henry VII (1490); coins identified as George II and George III; a Napoleon III piece; and many Victorian pennies, as well as a brass tap from a sixteenth-century wine butt.

Dr John de Courcy Ireland has laboured for years to restore to the Irish mind a consciousness of its sea-girt position. In a lecture in 1983 he passionately declared:

An té a mbíonn long aige, geibheann sé cóir uair éigin. (He who has a boat eventually gets a breeze.) A proverbial statement like that does not emanate from a people that is a landlubberly people. Long before the Irish language, or a Celtic language of any description, came into this country of ours, we were a maritime people, and the blood that flows in every one of us here, every one of us in the country, is blood that came across the sea. I do not accept that because we have a reputation for holiness in this country, our ancestors were dropped from heaven. And you can go back to the very earliest moment in history and you find that the first people who came into our country came here by sea, and they laid the foundations of a maritime tradition that this country has, richer and older than almost any country in Europe.

At this point it would be helpful if the notion of Ireland as a remote and isolated place receded. Ideally, it might be replaced by the image of a traffic island or even a trading post, centre of a vast traffic in ships up and down the Atlantic coasts from the Baltic Sea to the Straits of Gibraltar. Such, up to recent times, was the position of Ireland and there are many testimonies to this fact. Instead of a nervous hedge-hopping to and fro between Britain and Ireland – spending the least possible time on the ocean waves – a picture emerges of the sea not as a barrier but as an essential part of the multifaceted culture of this island. It is appropriate that in Conamara, whence I derived this untypical perspective, there exists a more solid image of the idea.

The *púcán* has an unusual and distinctive sailing rig called the dipping lug, or lateen sail. This sailing rig revolutionized the art of sailing in the thirteenth century by making it possible to approach the wind from almost any direction. Hitherto the square sail had enforced long delays in port waiting for 'a fair wind', i.e. from astern. With the lateen a boat could be sailed almost directly into the wind and, by using the technique called tacking, could travel at the master's, rather than the wind's, convenience. Its incorporation by the Portuguese into their renowned *caravelle* design contributed greatly to that nation's pioneering exploration of the world.

Having sailed in a púcán all the way down the west coast of Ireland, I was familiar with this strange rig. But it came as a surprise to me to learn that it was an invention of the Arabs and was still in use in North Africa. From Egyptian travelogues one can see the equivalent of the púcán in the dhows and feluccas of the Nile. Even in Tunisia, fishermen still use it. At one stage the púcán was the most popular fishing boat in Galway. Apart from those in Conamara itself, a considerable fleet of such fishing boats worked out from the Claddagh, in Galway city. They were built, like the hucaer and gleoteoig, in skeletal/carvel style – that is to say, with butt-joined planks over a framework, as distinct from clinker design where the planks overlap. An expert on vernacular boat-building, Michael McCaughan, has detailed the stark contrast between the proliferation of the clinker design on the north and east coasts of Ireland and the skeletal/carvel design on the west (Conamara) and south coasts of Ireland, which, he suggests, may be far more ancient, perhaps going back to pre-Roman times.

I shall conclude with an observation made in 1984 by a maritime observer, Arthur Reynolds, about a fine maker of miniature traditional craft in Conamara, Pádraic Ó hEidhin:

> When I called to his home I noticed that he also makes wooden fish traps for taking rockfish or ballan, popular with the Aran islanders and local people. Surely the use of traps for fin fish in Conamara must be unique in Ireland, *even though many Middle East and Far Eastern fishermen work with nothing else.* [my italics]

🔲 *Egyptian felucca sailboat on the Nile*

3 Gaels and Arabs: The Common Ground

THE CONFLICTING ELEMENTS on the island of Ireland are no less confusing to visitors than they are to the natives themselves.

Dublin is a microcosm of this confusion: a city developed by Vikings, overrun by Normans, taken over by the Tudors and now having the high-street ambience of a provincial English city. The first official language of Ireland is still Irish, but this is rarely heard in the capital – only a tiny minority of the nation's political, business and cultural class can muster more than a badly pronounced phrase in the language. The average literate Dubliner is more likely to get his or her opinions from English tabloids than from Irish broadsheets, and as much from SKY News as from the national broadcaster, RTÉ. Liam de Paor wrote in 1971: 'The symbols which once had meaning – harps, shamrocks, sunbursts – are now comical, embarrassing, or merely conventional ...'

The audience in Ireland for American films was once, *pro rata*, the largest in Europe. Now British and American soap operas dominate the citizens' tastes. There is little continental European influence in the media. The only regional accents proudly retained on the national broadcasting service come from Northern Ireland, which is still part of the United Kingdom.

Dublin, finally, still entertains a civil service more geared to running an empire than a small island.

Imagine being reared in this melting-pot and educated to believe you are something unique called a 'Celt'. This has been the experience of at least two generations of Dubliners, including my own. Such a paradox is not unique. Generations of Londoners have absorbed the fiction that they are something called Britons who 'never ever shall be slaves'; this despite the fact that the only people vaguely entitled to the label 'Briton' are the Welsh. Similarly, to describe the residents of Glasgow as 'Scots' is really to say they are Irish; 'Scotti' was the original name for the Irish. It is all very confusing but it is, and has been, a functional confusion. The myth of 'Briton' built an empire; the myth of 'Celt' built a tourist industry — and provided a good living for scholars, musicians and New Age travellers.

Names are always arbitrary, but customary usage over a long period tends to confer authenticity, render them as if carved in stone. They become reality; the word becomes flesh and people will eventually go to great lengths to prove that they are, incarnate, what was originally a scholarly, political or even propaganda category. Once the Irish adopted 'Celt' as a description and a working concept of who they were, they carried it to its logical conclusion. Not only was an insurrection in 1916 based on extrapolations of the concept, an independent state was founded as a result. To maintain consistency they were obliged to interpret the name racially and, as a result, decided that any other strain that contributed to the personality of the island was alien, or at least a superficial intrusion.

A group identity serves any social purpose and it is essential for a people intent on throwing off an intolerable colonial yoke. Socrates referred to it as the 'noble lie'. But, at a certain stage, a new nation must develop the confidence to dismantle its unitary foundation myth and replace it with the diverse richness that lies beneath. In this context, and that of my preoccupations, the suggestion that Ireland might owe something to the exotic world of the Middle East was very attractive.

After the trigger of sean-nós music, other clues followed. Early indications were superficial but exhilarating: even small things like the fact that the Arabic for Jesus is *Issa*, pronounced identically to the Irish *Íosa*; in Egypt, a knife is *sekina*, etymologically inseparable from the Irish *scian*; rosary beads, once the badge of devout Irish Catholics, are a Middle Eastern invention still used by Muslims and others; and not only is the recently

Arab astronomy, Pegasus; illustration from A Treatise on the Fixed Stars *by as-Sufi, 1009 AD, Arabic Ms. Marsh 144, Bodleian Library, Oxford*

discarded costume of the traditional Irish nun Middle Eastern in origin, the word 'nun' itself is Egyptian.

When two strangers with a halting knowledge of each other's language meet, the first thing they do is compare vocabulary. A culturally egocentric anglophone might be humbled by knowledge of the number of words he owes to Arabic: tartar, talc, almanac, alkali, borax, elixir. If interested in astronomy he will find many of the principal stars have Arabic names: Aldebaran, Betelgeuse, Rigel, Vega, Altair. His mathematics would not proceed far without zero, sine, root or algebra. A chef might know that the Arabs brought lemon, coffee, saffron, sesame, tarragon; and that the French croissant derives from the Islamic symbol, the crescent. Many an uneasy crowned head of Europe was soothed by the Arab *ud*, or lute, and where would Spanish music be without the Arabic *naq-quara*, or guitar?

Without the Arabs, the Europeans would not have had a Renaissance and might never have learned about classical thought. Christianity, represented by Julian the Apostate, had proscribed the teaching of pagan Greek writers. It was left to the Arab conquerors of Alexandria two centuries later to incorporate that learning into their own studies and to preserve it until Europe was receptive again in the thirteenth century. The above points are readily accessible to the most casual enquirer, and educated Europeans are, however dimly, conscious of them but, especially nowadays, find them convenient to ignore. Culturally, Europe owes much to the Islamic world. Ireland, being loosely attached to Europe, is similarly indebted.

But is there anything unique in the case of Ireland? Whenever this question was raised, the image of Conamara and its people hove into view.

In the late 1970s a party of Irish musicians and dancers visited Libya. Among them was Seosamh Mac Donncha, who after this experience I should probably call Josie ibn Seán ibn Jack ibn Donncha. Josie, as his friends call him, is a sean-nós singer from Ard Thiar, Carna, a village in Conamara famous for its unique singing style. He told me of his surprise at the reception his singing received in Libya. Without the faintest understanding of the words of the songs, the Libyans gave him the attention he would normally expect only in Conamara. All became clear when Josie heard Libyan singing; to his surprise he found that if he closed his eyes he could easily imagine himself listening to a neighbour at home. It was hard to pin down the similarity, he said, but there were phrases here and there, perhaps a half-line now and again, and an overall likeness in the style of ornamentation that made it all sound very familiar. His impression was confirmed by other members of his party.

When a Lebanese visitor to the Royal Irish Academy in the 1850s was asked to read from an ancient copy of the Qur'an owned by the academy, he proceeded to chant it in the style of a muezzin. Coming up the stairs at the same time was Eugene O'Curry, a well-known antiquarian and native Irish speaker. As soon as the visitor stopped, O'Curry took up the refrain but he continued in the strain of a Keener, or sean-nós singer of the West of Ireland. The people present said they could not distinguish between the two forms of chant or the words used. They concluded that the two musical forms were related.

Such speculation has a long pedigree and was quite prevalent in the nineteenth century. Even then some aspects of the island's culture did not fit into the classical European perspective. What was remarkable was the apparent haste with which this speculative line was dropped in the early years of the twentieth century. Its abandonment coincided with the adoption of Gael and 'Celt' as badges of national identity.

Oriental speculation such as this did not happen in a vacuum. Since Napoleon's 1799 invasion of Egypt, orientalism had become an obsession for educated and wealthy Europeans. In Dublin, second city of the British empire, it was an interesting distraction. The Grand Tour to the 'Near East' was highly desirable. One man-about-town, Buck Whaley, wagered that he could visit Jerusalem and be back in his club – à la Phileas Fogg – within a specific time; in 1789 he succeeded and pocketed £7000. In 1750 Sir John Browne, 1st Earl of Kilmaine, was so impressed by his tour to Egypt that he built a miniature pyramid on his estate in Cong, Co. Mayo, to commemorate his brother. It is still visible and was renovated by the Office of Public Works in 1990. Coincidentally, in the same western region of Ireland are found the famous Turoe and Castlestrange stones. These stelae are intricately carved in what is described as La Tène, i.e. 'Celtic' style, and illustrations of them are regularly invoked to support this exotic past for Ireland. The designs might just as easily be described as 'arabesque', and such a suggestion would not have been greeted as fanciful in the nineteenth century. Besides, the base of the Turoe Stone has a geometric pattern that is unmistakably Greek.

The pyramid at Cong, Co. Mayo

⊠ *Inscription on the Cong pyramid*

On 24 May 1866 the old dispute between Vallancey and Ledwich was revived at an open-air lecture in Clondalkin, Co. Dublin. Two valiant orientalists, Messrs Caleb Palmer and John Darling, challenged the members of the Royal Irish Academy, together with the 'antiquarians of Ireland generally', to come and hear their proofs that the famous Irish Round Towers had an Eastern, even Phoenician origin. They stated:

> Traditions existing in this country which derived from Eastern fable, manners and customs substantiate the analogous evidence between the habits and predilections of the Irish and Eastern peoples: the Patterns and Pilgrimages, Particular Holy Wells and Fountains, the celebration of Lá Bealtaine, the Irish Ullagone, the lighting of fires on St John's Eve, the Baal-ist names of bridges, towns, mountains, brooks, rivers & co.

Predictably, Charles Vallancey wrote a long poem in praise of those 'men of true genius and sterling worth'.

Navigating carefully between these dusty disputes and the phenomenon of modern sean-nós singing, I visited the Chester Beatty Library in Dublin. Located at the time in Shrewsbury Road, Dublin, this library contains the greatest private collection of oriental manuscripts in the world, bequeathed to the Irish nation by the Canadian millionaire after whom it was named.

Ninth-century cross found in Co. Cork inscribed, 'Bism'llah' (British Museum)

The collection illustrates the history of civilization from about 2500 BC to the present time and therefore attracts more foreign scholars than Irish.

The curator at the time, David James, a fluent Arabist, was intrigued by my interest in finding musical connections. Sadly, he could not help much in this area. However, he had just published an article in which he compared Islamic illuminated art to its Irish equivalent. He detailed surprising affinities between an illuminated Qur'an produced in Baghdad in the ninth century and those products of the golden age of Irish art, the Book of Kells and the Book of Durrow.

The Abbasid Qur'an, James said, is the only surviving manuscript produced by a famous Arab calligrapher. Using this Qur'an and a facsimile of the Book of Durrow, he demonstrated the points of coincidence. The prominence of the design known as interlace was the most obvious; the central 'tree of life' symbol was also traceable in this and the Book of Kells; even to me, the similar geometric composition of certain pages was striking. He emphasized that there were no exact likenesses, but he considered it intriguing that the two areas, Ireland and the Middle East — at opposite ends of Christian Europe — should have, as he put it, 'expressed spiritual and metaphysical ideas by means of an art that was either wholly non-representational, abstract, or in which the human element was subordinated to anti-naturalistic concepts'.

Abbasid Qur'an, ninth century (Chester Beatty Library)

THE ATLANTEAN IRISH

In short, the Christians of Ireland and the Muslims of the Middle East, at approximately the same period, were expressing their opposing beliefs in similar ways.

I entertained, for a moment, the wild hope that the Arabs might have directly influenced the Irish in this art, but this was dispelled by the fact that the books of Kells and Durrow were produced in Ireland two centuries before this particular Qur'an was written in Baghdad. Still, it seems indisputable that both schools of illumination were influenced by the visual repertoire of Egypt, Syria, Iran and Central Asia. Further, it appeared likely that the emergence of a Christian art form – of which these Irish books were the most distinctive – and an Islamic form that resembled it could not be accidental. There must be a connection. The only tentative suggestion that David James had for me was something called 'Coptic Egypt'.

This was the point at which my simplistic categories began, fortunately, to crumble.

Were not all the peoples of North Africa and the Middle East called Arab? Yes, but only because they spoke the Arabic language; in fact, the happily surviving indigenous population of North Africa also speak Berber, which has a Hamitic base (as distinct from Semitic, which is Arabic). There are Arabic-speaking Jews and Christians, too: the Copts in Egypt, for instance, are Christian. The latter at one time spoke Egyptian – the original language of the Pharaohs – but since the ninth century had adopted Arabic. All that remains of their original language is their liturgy.

To a neophyte this was very confusing. In the midst of investigating the origins of the Irish, a doubt was emerging as to who and what the Arabs were. At about this time, a piece of physical evidence surfaced to illustrate the problem precisely: a strange brooch that had been found in a bog in Ballycotton, Co. Cork, many years previously. Although it was made in the shape of the Christian symbol – the cross – the inscription on it was Arabic: 'Bism'llah' (In the Name of God). How did such a brooch get to Ireland? The British Museum, which now looks after it, told me the following:

> The brooch dates from the reign of Charlemagne (768–814) and was manufactured somewhere in his Empire, but under the influence of Anglo-Saxon metalwork ornamentation. One can only guess at how this piece came to Ireland, perhaps in the luggage of an Irish ecclesiastic visiting one of the great monasteries such as

Corbie, which flourished under Charlemagne's patronage, or more prosaically, brought in by a Norse trader or raider.

I found this explanation inadequate. First, was it likely anywhere in the Christian empire of Charlemagne – at war with the Muslims who controlled Spain – that a craftsman would risk inscribing one of the commonest expressions of the 'infidel' on the holiest symbol in Christendom? Second, it overlooked the existence of the Christian Mozarabes of Spain, who at the period of this object's manufacture lived comfortably with their Islamic masters; they even fought beside the Arabs when Charlemagne and the Franks entered Spain in the eighth century. These Christians might happily have tolerated the Christian symbol with the Islamic invocation. Further, there had always been direct maritime contact between Spain and Ireland. As to how the cross got to Ireland, Norse raiders seemed a likely conduit.

In the eighth and ninth centuries the Norse moved comfortably throughout the Atlantic reaches of Europe. They were familiar with the riches of the Islamic world. In 859 two Vikings called Hastings and Bjorn journeyed from western France down the coasts of Spain and Portugal, through the Straits of Gibraltar, where they encountered Muslim ships intent on blocking their passage. The raiders passed through to attack Italy, call on Egypt and return by the same route. They fought the Muslim ships again at Medina-Sidonia in Spain, and reached home safely in 862. In the course of their adventures they attacked Asturias, Seville, Catalonia and the Balearic Islands – all Muslim strongholds, with the exception of Asturias. These daring marauders even wintered on the Camargue in the south of France. With such activity going on down the Atlantic coasts of Europe and into the heart of Islamic civilization, it seemed feeble to credit Anglo-Saxon craftsmen with the design of the cross in question, or Irish ecclesiastics with the provenance of this Muslim artefact.

Idries Shah, a prominent writer on Sufi thought, referred to this cross in the context of Sufism. He has also claimed that 'Sufi ideas, and even literal texts, were borrowed by or lay behind (European) theories and teachings ... as diverse as Chivalry, of St John of the Cross, St Teresa of Avila, Roger Bacon, Geber, the father of Western alchemy ...'

Meanwhile, I gradually became aware of more connections between North Africa and Ireland. Evidence of a Barbary ape had been found during an excavation in Eamhain Macha, or Navan Fort, not far from Armagh

Barbary ape *(British Museum)*

City. But Barbary apes are associated with Gibraltar and have been there only a few centuries, their natural home being North Africa. The excavations put the remains of the Navan Fort ape at around 390–320 BC.

The ape, whose sad skeletal remains I inspected in the British Museum, may have been somebody's pet. But how could it have travelled to Ireland from such a distant place? Had it come in the luggage of a 'Celt' from central Europe, via Britain – the route attributed to practically every unusual feature of Ireland?

The puzzle was compounded by a literary reference in *Deirdre* by William Butler Yeats, a tragedy set in a mythological Ireland two thousand years ago. The action takes place in the court of King Conchubhair, located at Navan Fort where the Barbary ape was found. In the play were references to Libyan dragon skins and Libyan mercenaries. These dark-skinned fighters had apparently been hired by the frustrated old king to guard his interests, especially the beautiful Deirdre. What were Libyan mercenaries doing in the north of Ireland over two thousand years ago? Did some hard-bitten soldier, to remind him of his Mediterranean home, keep an ape as a pet? And how had he and his companions found employment for their deadly profession on an island at the edge of the known world?

Yeats explained none of these puzzles; he had not, of course, invented the basic theme. The saga of Deirdre and the Sons of Uisneach is part of the ancient heroic literature of Ireland. Archaeological evidence shows an impressive centre of activity existed at Navan Fort. As in all so-called 'myths', there was a central core of truth.

Some scholars have suggested that accounts of heroic ages contained in the oral tradition of a people are the result of invasions by people of a 'higher civilization'. To accommodate an incursion on a large scale, the victims weave stories in which eventually their own ancestors become the heroes. Scholars spend their lives extricating the facts of invasions from the imaginative web in which they are embalmed. The historically documented invasions of Ireland are straightforward: the Vikings in the ninth and tenth centuries, the Normans in the twelfth century, the Tudors in the sixteenth. Beyond those dates – and in the gaps between – there have been many permanent callers to the island. The farthest south to which anyone reliably attributes any kind of invasion is Spain, but historical incongruities, such as the Barbary ape, suggest wider influences.

In the epic literature of Ireland there are many exotic references to places beyond Europe. The *Táin Bó Cuailgne* (The Cattle Raid of Cooley) describes one of the heroes as sporting a helmet 'do chumtach ingantach tiri Arabiae i crichi na Sorcha', that is of the wonderful workmanship of Arabia, i.e. the land of Syria. (Sorcha is a common name among my neighbours in Conamara.) The hero's charioteer is described as wearing a cloak that Simon Magus had made for Darius, King of the Romans, who had in turn given it to the King of Ulster. This king, Conchubhair, was the same king credited with hiring the Libyan mercenaries and whose court included a Barbary ape. These allusions are explained by scholars as later interpolations in the text, originally written down in the eighth or ninth centuries, with the scribes of the eleventh and twelfth centuries introducing new references learned, presumably, from crusading contacts with the Near East.

It seemed one should attribute all connection with the Middle East to a series of literary and cultural accidents combined with a vivid imagination. The unusual wealth of Irish epic tradition was simply a local re-working of universal myth; the Irish were great storytellers, not averse to bending the truth a little; they had simply adapted travellers' tales to their own needs; the mound of dirt at Navan Fort they transformed into a palace; a hillock in Co. Meath became 'Tara of the Kings'. These items were testimony to the marvellous Irish imagination, but they were really based on Greek mythology and, where that did not fit, on a 'Celtic' source. Even in their imaginative life, the Irish were locked into Europe – Barbary ape or no Barbary ape, Libyan mercenaries or not. Was there any escape from this historical straitjacket, any way of showing that Ireland was influenced by anything other than the Caucasian and Graeco-Roman worlds? The only escape route apparent was the sea.

Seafarers, Smugglers and Pirates 4

GRÁINNE MHAOIL, or Grace O'Malley, was a pirate queen of the sixteenth century. She controlled much of the west coast of Ireland from her castle fortress, Clare Island in Clew Bay, Co. Mayo.

The castle still stands, a grim presence overlooking the little harbour. Gráinne's coat of arms is visible and now beautifully restored on the wall of the island abbey away towards the west of the island. When, in 1593, Gráinne decided to make her peace with England's Queen Elizabeth I, she did it in style. Dismissing the idea of travelling overland to London, she sailed down and around the west and south coasts of Ireland, across the English Channel, through the Straits of Dover and up the Thames to Greenwich. It was probably her way of showing the Queen that she was no ordinary petitioner, that the supposed perils of the deep – fogs, storms, other pirates – held no fears for her. The same seas enabled her to preserve her defiant autonomy for forty years.

Gráinne Mhaoil saw which way the political wind was blowing and cleverly anticipated its possible vicissitudes. While the English queen graciously afforded the pirate queen a respite fourteen years after her visit, the last of the Irish aristocracy in Ulster were given no such option. Realizing that

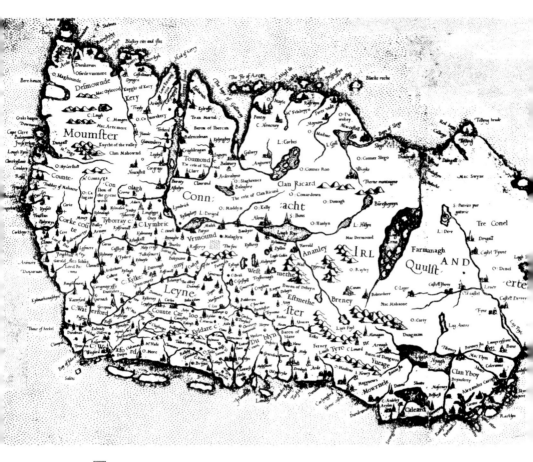

🗺 *Map of Ireland, Gerard Mercator, Duisburg, 1564 (National Library of Ireland)*

they could no longer maintain their stand against the English, they decided on exile. The O'Neills and the O'Donnells did not take the short route to Scotland but piled their families and goods into ships in Lough Swilly and sailed the long way round to the Continent. Similarly, the Wild Geese — remnants of the broken Irish armies in the late seventeenth century — sailed out from Limerick to places as far away as Cadiz (the original Phoenician settlement of Gades).

These examples suggest that historically the sea was seen by the Irish not as a disadvantage but as a medium of power, a protective barrier and a means of escape. It was also an economic advantage, as the merchants of Galway proved. When amassing their considerable fortunes and in the process turning that port into the second largest trading city on the island, they did not rely on dealings with Dublin or London. They sent their wool and hides to Spain and received wines and silks in return. So strong and long-established were their commercial links with the far south that the burghers had a system of mutual fosterage with their counterparts in Spain. The crime for which the infamous Judge Lynch (as in 'Lynch law') hanged his son was the unforgivable one of murdering a Spanish youth who was in the judge's own care.

The defeat and wreck of the Spanish Armada in 1588 does not appear to have interfered too much with this trade. Four years later, the Lord Deputy was still naming Spain as the chief cause of disorder in Ireland. He attributed this to the immense trade between the two countries. In 1625 Sir James Perrot, governor of Galway, described the town as 'next to Spain and trading with it'. This odd perspective – the west coast of Ireland being nearer to Spain than to England – is confirmed by an Islamic map in the Chester Beatty Library. On it, Ireland is clearly shown as lying to the south of England. This is not simply bad cartography. It illustrates how Ireland was perceived by sailors and is in the tradition of 'portolans', the earlier

⊠ *Islamic map showing Ireland to the south of Britain (Chester Beatty Library)*

written instructions by which mariners had traditionally navigated. For most of its history, Galway looked to the sea and to Spain.

In 1834 a traveller named H.D. Inglis wrote the following:

> Galway, the capital of the wild west, is a large and on many accounts an extremely interesting town. I had heard that I should find some traces of its Spanish origin; but I was not prepared to find so much to remind me of that land of romance. At every second step I saw something to recall Spain to my recollection. I found the wide entries and broad stairs of Cadiz and Malaga; the arched gateways with the inner and outer railings and the court within needing only the fountains and flower vases to emulate Seville. I found the sculptural gateways and grotesque architecture which carried the imagination to the Moorish cities of Granada and Valencia. I even found the sliding wicket, for observation, in one or two doors, reminding one of the secrecy, mystery and caution observed where gallantry and superstition divide life between them. Besides these Spanish resemblances, Galway has a more Popish aspect than any other Irish town.

However, to limit Irish maritime contacts to Spain alone would be a mistake. The seas around Ireland have always teemed with strangers. Pirates in the sixteenth and seventeenth centuries frequently assumed command of the waters between Ireland and England. In 1608 a Venetian visited the coast of Cork and reported that it was one of the chief nests of 'pirates'. In the south-west, off the coast of Kerry, on 7 August 1626, a French merchantman was ignominiously chased into Berehaven by a 'Turkish' pirate. In 1627 a French pirate named Campane is reported as taking shore leave in Killybegs, Donegal, where he was 'always drunk and with loose women'.

The image of Ireland as a traffic island was never more apt than at this period. But the maritime orientation went back a long time. As James Kenney put it: 'From the years when the great forests succeeded the Post-glacial steppes down to comparatively recent times, the easiest and most frequented means of travel was the sea, or rather the sea coast, and Ireland's position is most favourable.'

As long ago as the second century AD a Greek geographer based in Alexandria, Claudius Ptolemaeus, was able to list the latitude and longitude

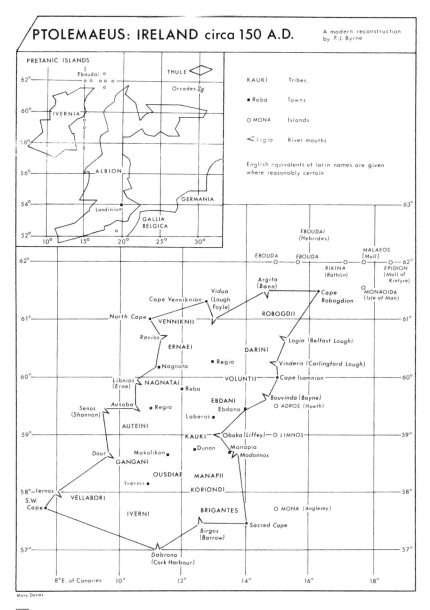

PTOLEMAEUS: IRELAND circa 150 A.D.   A modern reconstruction by F. J. Byrne

PRETANIC ISLANDS

KAUKI	Tribes
■ Reba	Towns
O MONA	Islands
< logia	River mouths

English equivalents of latin names are given where reasonably certain

Mary Davies

⊠ *Ptolemaeus: Ireland circa 150 AD*

of sixty features of the island, including the names of tribes and forts, all of them on the coast. From whom did he get his information if not from Mediterranean sailors who had ventured into these cold northern waters and, on arrival in Alexandria, were obliged to lodge a copy of their portolans

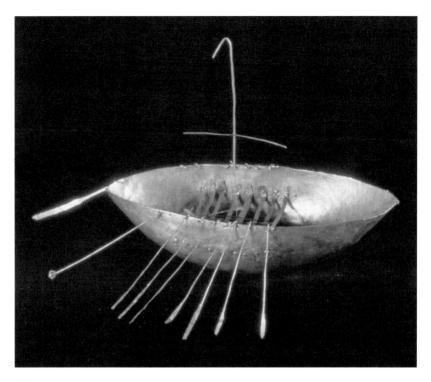

Broighter boat, Derry (National Museum of Ireland)

in the Great Library there? This library, tragically destroyed by fire in 642, no doubt contained numerous accounts of voyages in and beyond the Mediterranean.

Other potential sources for early contacts with these islands had also been destroyed centuries before: Carthage and its colonies in Spain – Gades, Tartessus and Carthago Nova. The Romans wiped out almost all trace of the Carthaginians' first recorded voyage to our northern islands. These North Africans, known as the Phoenicians, came from the Lebanon and built up a trading network second to none in the Mediterranean. Their second home, Carthage, beside present-day Tunis, was founded in 813 BC as a colony of Tyre and Sidon. Carthage outgrew its founding cities and became the third largest city in the ancient world. I sauntered through its ruins, besieged by guides who wanted to sell me 'authentic' Phoenician coins and lamps. They showed me plenty of evidence, beneath the subsequently built Roman villas, of the Phoenician custom of infant sacrifice. Hundreds of tiny coffins made of stone were stacked in the basements. It was as if

the Romans had purposely left this evidence of an ugly custom so that future generations would think them right to have razed the city.

According to the historian Pliny and the poet Avienus, a man from Carthage voyaged through the Straits of Gibraltar and explored the Atlantic coasts to the north. From the Phoenician/Carthaginians' Tartessus base on the Atlantic coast of Spain, it must have seemed logical to see what lay farther north. The Phoenician Himilco is credited with reaching Armorica — now Brittany — and describing the skin-covered currachs, versions of which are still in use in Wales and Ireland. A people named 'gens Hiernorum' (the Irish) and a place called 'insula Albionum' (England) are mentioned in references to his voyage, suggesting that he reached these areas, too, and paved the way for the exploitation of Cornish tin.

As this man was sailing northwards, his fellow North African Hanno sailed south, around the coast of Africa. He was hoping to emulate the feat of a Phoenician ancestor who in 600 BC had circumnavigated Africa on the commission of the Egyptian king, Necho. That ancestor appears to have succeeded, according to Herodotus, because he reported that, as they sailed westwards (logically, round the Cape of Good Hope) the sun was on their right. This could not have happened in the northern hemisphere. Though Hanno, sailing west from Carthage and then south, only succeeded in getting as far as Sierra Leone, it still indicates that these Phoenician North Africans, as early as 425 BC, were familiar with extensive stretches of the Atlantic coasts. For almost 500 years they controlled that half of Spain south of the river Tagus.

There can be little doubt that to these courageous men the Atlantic ocean was a vast and unknown quantity. They saw it as a kind of huge river flowing around the known world of the Mediterranean. In a sense this was, as we say in Conamara, 'true for them', as I discovered later in Tatarstan. In the meantime, if the world was as disc-shaped as everybody believed at the time, there was a serious danger of ships being blown over the edge, a belief that persevered in many minds until the end of the fifteenth century.

When navigation was in its infancy, direct observation of the sun and the stars was the only guide. If on emerging from the Straits of Gibraltar you head north towards Cape St Vincent you are, in effect, in the open Atlantic. The easiest star to locate in the sky is the North Star, indicated by the pointers of the Great Bear, Ursa Major. From Cape St Vincent, if you follow that star, you will be led safely and directly to the southern and western coasts of Ireland. It was the Phoenicians who taught the Greeks to find this North Star.

There was good reason why North Africans such as the Phoenicians/Carthaginians would want to venture on the Atlantic seaways. They had blocked the Straits of Gibraltar in 600 BC to protect their valuable silver deposits at Tartessus as well as to monopolize whatever rich mineral resources lay farther north, especially in the Cassiterides, the Tin Islands. The Mediterranean was, for centuries, divided between the two peoples: the Greeks controlled the eastern and northern shores, while the western and southern shores were dominated by the Carthaginians. A thousand years later this division would be replicated approximately by Islam and Byzantium.

But the Greeks had founded and controlled Massalia – now Marseilles – thus giving them an overland route to the Loire and thence to the tin deposits of the British Isles. The Carthaginians were, therefore, forced to seek a different route to this raw material which, mixed with copper, was essential to the manufacture of bronze weapons and implements. The uncolonized waters of the Atlantic seaways were theirs for the taking or, at least, the traversing, and they made sure the Greeks had no access to this route. It would be centuries before a Greek from Massalia named Pytheas dared to pass through the Straits, enter the Atlantic and explore the sea-route to the British Isles. This voyage is better recorded than that of the Carthaginian Himilco, probably because Pytheas had more prolific historians on his side, both Greek and Roman.

Ironically, although the ancient Phoenicians developed the alphabet,

 *Algiers Inn, Baltimore, Co. Cork*

their exploits are the least recorded. This may be because they were traders rather than conquerors, less interested in writing glorious histories than recording prosaic transactions. It is also suggested that their curving script was less amenable to being carved on stone than the straight lines of Roman numerals. But the overall reason is more acceptable: their records must have perished when Carthage, their nerve-centre, was wiped out in 146 BC by Scipio Aemilianus, whose grandfather Scipio Africanus had stormed the colonies of Carthago Nova and Gades forty years before.

Carthage perished, North Africa and its indigenous people stayed; Romans and Vandals came and went, empires rose and fell in the following 1500 years. But this seagoing contact between North Africa and the British Isles persisted, however sporadically, throughout all those centuries. The most dramatic evidence of this occurred one balmy summer's night in 1631 when the town of Baltimore in West Cork was rudely awakened by pirates from Algiers.

> *All, all asleep within each roof along that rocky street,*
> *And these must be the lovers with gently gliding feet.*
> *A stifled gasp! A dreamy noise! The roof is in a flame.*
> *From out their beds and through their doors rush maid and sire and dame,*
> *And meet upon the threshold stone the gleaming sabre's fall*
> *And o'er each black and bearded face the white or crimson shawl,*
> *The yell of 'Allah!' breaks above the prayer and shriek and roar —*
> *Oh, Blessed God, the Algerine is Lord of Baltimore.*

This ballad, 'The Sack of Baltimore', was written 200 years after the event by Thomas Davis, an Irish Protestant nationalist. His object was to show how heroically the Irish had resisted these 'savages' from North Africa. Davis got most of the details wrong. The term 'Algerine' – from Algiers –

was interchangeable with 'Turk'. It was indiscriminately applied to the many privateers who dominated the Atlantic coasts from Iceland to the Mediterranean. The Spanish Main, the Barbary Coast, the Salley (Salé) Rovers, are all terms that date from this period. Algiers was under Turkish rule and, along with Tunis, Tripoli, Salé and other ports of the North African coast, was an organized entrepot for what respectable people called piracy, but which was simply the ordinary cut and thrust of commercial maritime activity in that period. The picture depicted by romantic histories, novels and Hollywood epics completely overlooks the highly structured nature of this trade.

On the night of 17 June 1631 two ships from Algiers anchored at Baltimore, a quiet seaside town. They ransacked it and took the entire population – 163 souls – back to North Africa.

> Oh, some must tug the galley's oar and some must tend the steed,
> This boy will bear a Sheik's jibouk and that a Bey's jereed.
> Oh, some are for the arsenals by beauteous Dardanelles,
> And some are for the caravans to Mecca's sandy dells.

Although captives from raids like this sometimes ended up as slaves, they had other uses too. Their captors placed them in four categories: as labourers (men); as companions or concubines (women); as a source of income, i.e.

⊠ *Ransoming slaves (from* Barbary Corsairs, *National Library of Ireland; photo: Bob Hobby)*

☒ *Murrough O'Brien, Lord Inchiquin, captured off the coast of Portugal in 1659 (National Library of Ireland; photo: Bob Hobby)*

tradesmen for hire; and – as a step towards paradise according to Muslim belief – small boys who could be 'converted' and thus add to the new master's store of grace. But all these were secondary to the prime aim, ransom. This was the most lucrative aspect of the trade and is probably the main reason why captives, despite contrary reports, were treated so well. As early as 1618 an Irishwoman had a royal licence granted so that she could beg for funds to retrieve her husband from North Africa. These were the bread-and-butter captives, ordinary people. Occasionally there was a bonus, as when Lord Inchiquin was captured off Portugal in 1659. It took six months of delicate negotiations for him to be released in exchange for the handsome sum of 7500 crowns.

It has been elsewhere remarked that a number of the inhabitants of North Africa have red hair and blue eyes. Nineteenth-century historians claimed they were the descendants of captives from Ireland. But with the possible exception of five people, all the hostages from Baltimore were in fact English. Baltimore was what is known as a 'planted' town, occupied by settlers; the Irish lived outside.

The man charged with piloting the pirate boats into Baltimore was named as Hackett, a 'papist' from nearby Dungarvan, Co. Waterford. Guilty or not, the man was hanged for the crime. It could be pleaded that his 'treason' was justified, that Baltimore was considered a fair target because it was not inhabited by the native Irish. Like many places on the south and west coasts of England and Ireland, Baltimore was regarded as a watering place for what were termed 'pirates'. It was certainly a centre of smuggling, a normal, respectable means of building a fortune in such remote areas. The family of Daniel O'Connell – known as the Liberator because he was the architect of Catholic Emancipation – achieved prosperity by 'importing' luxuries, despite being locked away in the fastnesses of Kerry. Smuggling in those days was a reasonable way of avoiding the oppressive English tax laws.

Corsair attack (from Barbary Corsairs, *National Library of Ireland; photo: Bob Hobby)*

In this light, to a considerable proportion of the population – at least on the coasts – privateering was a normal activity. Only the minority who agreed with, and had a stake in, the ruling class's arrangements for distributing the wealth of the world could have frowned on this entrepreneurial spirit. While the Barbary corsairs were plaguing Europe, English and French pirates were doing precisely the same in the Caribbean. Francis Drake and Walter Raleigh, whom British schoolboys were taught to admire, were experienced and successful pirates.

To North Africans, the rich vessels of European merchants were treated as fair game. A fine service industry was built up on the Atlantic coasts to employ the many not yet absorbed in the tentacles of centralized power. There had to be what in criminal parlance is termed a 'fence' – a disposer of stolen goods – and a market-place for the captives. North Africa, being Muslim and therefore antipathetic to any rules of the sea that Christian Europe might proclaim, was the obvious centre. The ports of that part of the world became the regulators of a large and healthy commerce. Some of the most successful captains of these North African-based pirate ships were themselves Europeans. The leader of the Baltimore expedition was a Dutchman. Jan Jensen from Haarlem became such an outstanding success at the game that the Pasha of Algiers bestowed on him the title 'rais' – the equivalent of admiral.

Whatever about the morals, these privateers were magnificent seamen. Three Algerian ships sailed as far as Iceland in 1627, raided the capital and still had the energy and skill to navigate home with 300 captives. They must also have been masters of the art of naval warfare: between the years 1613 and 1621 they took 447 Dutch, 193 French, 120 Spanish, 60 English and 56 German ships, and brought them to Algiers as prizes.

There was a strict apportionment of the booty. In 1633 the rates were as follows: in Algiers, 12 per cent went to the Pasha – it being at least nominally controlled by Turkey; 1 per cent went to maintain the mole or sea barrier that protected the city's harbour from surprise attack; 1 per cent went to the holy men attached to the city's mosques; 43 per cent was divided between the ship's captain and its owners; and the remainder was allocated to the crew in order of rank. For most of those details I am indebted to John de Courcy Ireland, that indefatigable advocate of a maritime perspective on Ireland, who did exhaustive research in Algerian archives and found many examples to show how this trade affected Ireland.

In February 1641 the Rev. Devereux Spratt of Tralee, Co. Kerry, was sailing for England from Youghal in the ship of John Filmer of that town, but Algerian corsairs took their vessel while still in sight of land and carried them off to Algiers. Spratt was quite well treated and stayed to preach to the captives in Algiers even after his ransom came. But Dr de Courcy Ireland adds that in exactly the same year the Irish Viceroy, Wentworth, was credited with wiping out piracy off the coast of Ireland: 'evidently,' the researcher says, 'the Viceroy's intentions have been mistaken for facts'.

In reality, it took until 1843 for the combined British and American navies to put an end to this economic activity now called piracy. They described their action as 'imposing European trading practice', which simply meant establishing their own monopoly. The involvement of America indicates how widespread the influence of the corsairs was. The Salley Rovers, from Salé in Morocco, were often active as far away as the banks of Newfoundland and the coast of Nova Scotia.

On my visit to Baltimore, a local resident invited me to see a newly acquired treasure, a large ivory tusk, found locally by a diver a few days beforehand. It was an appropriate trophy for a town that has a significant link with North Africa and this significance was realized by its possessor

– a Breton. It shows what a reticent archivist the sea is, holding its secrets for years and then releasing a tiny detail of evidence to jog our memories.

As a footnote it should be mentioned that the Irish were not always passive in this impressive traffic. A scholar of the period told me that among the 'Algerines' who operated off Howth in the Irish Sea, there was a pirate named O'Driscoll. He was certainly no Turk.

> *The maid that Bandon gallant sought is chosen for the Bey.*
> *She's safe – he's dead – she stabbed him in the midst of his Serail;*
> *And when to die a death by fire that noble maid was doomed,*
> *She only smiled – O'Driscoll's child – she thought of Baltimore!*

Damsel in distress (from Barbary Corsairs, *National Library of Ireland; photo: Bob Hobby)*

St Brendan, Sindbad
and the Viking Connection

5

I HAVE DWELT UPON the North African corsairs because the regular traffic between 'isolated' coastal areas of these islands and North Africa has been practically ignored in history books.

Freebooting ships sailing up and down the Atlantic reaches of Europe carrying goods and people year after year – no matter how illegitimately – reflected badly not only on the official agencies charged with controlling such traffic but on their superiors, the European powers who supposedly divided the world between them. Subordinates tend to tell their superiors what they wish to hear.

From the sixteenth to the nineteenth centuries there was unofficial, possibly sporadic, but significant contact between these islands and North Africa. Gráinne Mhaoil, as a pirate queen, had more in common with the 'Algerines' than with the Queen's navy. When she married her second husband, Richard Bourke, the contract stipulated that either party could, after one year, end it simply by saying, 'I dismiss you.' This form of divorce had more in common with the Muslim faith than with the rigid tenets of Christianity.

Naturally, evidence of contact in preceding centuries is piecemeal. There is the belief that Columbus called into Galway to collect stores and crew for his trip to America – an inscribed stone has been recently erected in Galway city near Spanish Arch to commemorate the idea which, though plausible, is mainly intended for tourist consumption. The Portuguese certainly collected seamen from the western coastal towns of Britain and Ireland. An obscure legend of the seventh century is contained in the story of St John the Almsgiver, patriarch of Constantinople. In this there is a reference to a large Alexandrian grainship voyaging to Britain and exchanging the wheat for gold and tin. Hagia Sophia in Constantinople is also referred to as having been built partly with Irish marble – ideal ballast for a returning ship.

But a maritime legend that has endured and can be taken seriously is that of St Brendan the Navigator. The Irish claim he went to America before Leif Ericsson. This is based on the medieval story called 'Navigatio Sancti Brendani Abbatis', which existed in over a hundred different versions. St Brendan is reputed to have lived at the end of the fifth century, and the story appears to be a compendium of all the tales of wandering Irish missionaries of the following centuries. The earliest date to which the actual writing of the story is attributed is 800 AD. The legend of St Brendan's 'Fortunatae Insulae' was printed thirteen times in German between 1476 and 1523, but as late as 1721 a Spanish expedition was mounted from Santa Cruz in Tenerife to find the 'Ila da San Borondon'.

When the Vikings reached the Hebrides, the Faroes and even Iceland, they found the Irish had been there before them. These places are logical stepping-stones on the route to North America – as Tim Severin reported in 1976 in the account of his re-enactment of the saint's voyage, *The Brendan Voyage*. Mr Severin, a specialist in testing the physical possibility of historically attested voyages, showed, among other things, that references to strange natural phenomena in the 'Navigatio' could have their equivalent in existing geographical features. The Faroes were perhaps the 'island of sheep' referred to in the text, the volcanoes of Iceland the 'Fiery Mountains', huge icebergs might be what were referred to poetically as 'Columns of Crystal'.

Several places in the text were too vaguely described to be capable of identification but as the 'Navigatio' might include references to many voyages, in many directions, this was not unreasonable. For instance the term 'Eastern Beach', which in context means 'Eastwards', is a strange direction to follow if one is looking, as Brendan was, for the promised land in the west.

The adventures recorded in the 'Navigatio' paralleled those of another sailor, Sindbad. The equally legendary voyages of Sindbad constitute a

 *Sindbad and the Roc (from* 1001 Nights, *National Library of Ireland; photo: Bob Hobby)*

separate block of stories in the 'Tales of the Arabian Nights'. The first coincidence concerns Sindbad's crew landing on an island that turns out to be a sea monster. Exactly the same thing happens to Brendan and his companions: when they light a picnic fire on a small islet, it turns out to be the great whale, Jasconius. Sindbad encounters the great bird, the Roc. In Brendan's account this becomes a flying gryphon. A blinded giant throws great boulders at Sindbad as he and his companions escape on a raft. This becomes, for Brendan, the natives of an island who throw fiery lumps of slag at them as they try to get away on their frail craft. The reality underlying this last adventure may well have been a volcanic eruption, a feature of Iceland.

Both Sindbad and Brendan discover island paradises, see monstrous fish, find underground palaces and meet strange people. The similarity between the two voyages is particularly noteworthy because they are attributed to the same period and happen to representatives of cultures apparently separated by geography and religion – Ireland and the Middle East. The relationship between the two works is as curious as that already noted between Irish and Islamic manuscripts. This coincidence tends to be underplayed by scholars of the classical school, who attribute practically everything first to Greeks and Romans and, when that does not fit, to the Indians and Persians. The Rev. Geo. Fyler Townsend, MA, in a nineteenth-century edition of the

Sindbad stories, does not even credit the Arabs as the originators of the tales. He attributes them to Plutarch, Aelian, Diodorus Siculus and Pliny. However, as A.A. Aleem, the Egyptian scholar and oceanographer, demonstrated at a St Brendan Conference in Trinity College Dublin in 1985, many of the wonders detailed in Sindbad could be related to existing biological phenomena in the Indian Ocean. These, when experienced by early Arab mariners, were interpreted in fantastic forms.

What is also not easily explained away is how a writer in the ninth century – long before the Crusades – on an island in the North Atlantic could have had access to the literary wealth of the Middle East, and be so familiar with it as to plagiarize it and issue it in a Christian and Irish disguise. Surely everything could not be explained away by reference to twelfth-century copyists with a penchant for Middle Eastern embellishment? Certain light might be thrown on this matter by considering the Islamic domination of Spain, which began in 711 AD and continued for 800 years – longer than England controlled Ireland and, coincidentally, about the same length of time as the Carthaginians were there, a thousand years earlier.

■ *Sindbad (from* 1001 Nights, *National Library of Ireland; photo: Bob Hobby)*

If there was any substantial influence from North Africa and the Middle East on these North Atlantic areas, it had to come a long way by sea. If one could establish a continuity of voyaging between the two areas, from prehistoric times to the present, one could reasonably attribute otherwise inexplicable features of Ireland to a more exotic origin than, say, Britain or continental Europe. A practical instance is the ancient and continuing tradition of courageous Iberian fishermen braving the northern seas to poach fish in Irish waters. They did not always need refrigerated factory ships; the time-honoured preservative of salt was all around them.

Mark Kurlansky has established that salted cod was the staple diet a thousand years ago for the Vikings on their Atlantic voyages. It was the impetus for the Basques' long-distance voyaging (the Atlantic Cod, *Gadus morhua*, is not found in Iberian waters) and facilitated the European exploration of the New World: cod lasts longer than any other salted fish, tastes nicer and when dried constitutes 80 per cent concentrated protein. In the search for Faroean, Icelandic and Newfoundland cod, the island of Ireland was a natural stepping-stone for sailors from the Atlantic façade.

North African pirates came here, and before them, the Carthaginians. The Vikings, having braved the northern seas to establish colonies in Ireland, were certainly not intimidated by the milder southern waters; they sailed to Egypt and back. There was even a suggestion by R.D. Barnet, a reputable maritime historian, that a Phoenician design used by the Egyptians was the basis of the Viking galley with its high prow and stern. There is a carving of such a boat, found during excavations in Dublin, reminiscent of Pharaonic artwork, and a rock carving at Newgrange echoes these designs of 3000 years ago!

The Irish monks were well-known seafarers, albeit not quite so aggressive as the Vikings. They tended to let the wind blow them where it would, like religious pollen, hoping to blossom on whatever bleak coast they landed. That, at least, was the impression they gave King Alfred when three of them landed in Cornwall. They declared that they merely 'wished to go into exile for the love of God; they cared not whither'. P.W. Joyce posits three monks in Carthage in the seventh century who were Irish. Two of them were called Baetan and Mainchine, and they wrote 'in elegant Latin, wonderful things of the Sacred Scriptures'. According to John McNeill, the Irish geographer Dicuil based his *Liber de Mensura Orbis Terrae* on 'information furnished by one Brother Fidelis, probably an Irish monk, who had visited Egypt and

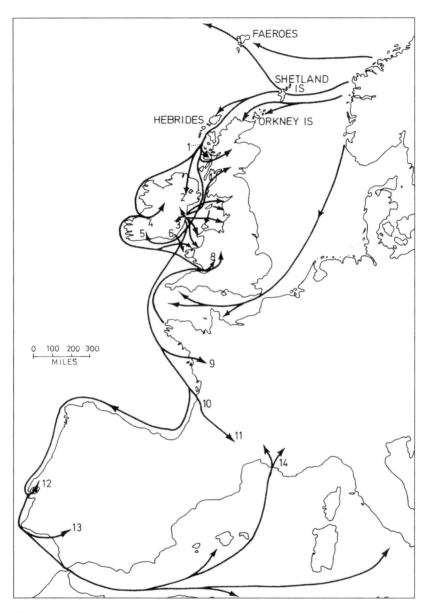

🔳 *Viking voyages (drawing after E.G. Bowen from his* Britain and the Western Seaways, *1972)*

Palestine'. These details are often regarded as exceptions: conventional history tends to ignore events that do not 'fit'.

The Vikings are a classic example of contrasting versions of history.

🔳 THE ATLANTEAN IRISH

Traditionally, they were considered to be only a temporary, if painful, intrusion on the quiet land of Erin. In Irish history these intrepid adventurers were described only through the eyes of their victims, the monks. Naturally only their depredations were mentioned: they were fierce pagans who arrived in their longboats, descended on the monasteries, pillaged the sacred vessels and books and disappeared back to Norway. However, the wealth of the monasteries made them an obvious target for any marauder; warring Irish kings had long established the monasteries as fair game. The *Ulster Cycle* records Irish attacks on monasteries in 757, 789 and 793 – before the first Viking attack in 795. By 823 the Vikings had circumnavigated Ireland, attacking points all round the coast. They built shelters at Annagassan, Co. Louth, and Dublin, thereafter establishing settlements. The *Ulster Cycle* mentions the loss of thirty boats on Lough Ree in 756 and other incidents showing that the Irish had substantial fleets. At first the Irish were unable to retaliate against the marauding Vikings but later defeated them at sea, in 856 and 926, and mounted raids on Viking settlements in England and the Orkneys in 913 and 941.

The 'settlements' of the Vikings became the first secular cities of Ireland. Dublin was the centre of the earliest Viking state recorded in Western Europe. The Vikings named Wicklow, Wexford, Waterford, Arklow, Dalkey, Lambay, Howth, Leixlip, Skerries and many other places. They gave Ireland its first minted coin. They influenced its famous metalwork. They gave the north and the east of the island the clinker, or overlapping-plank, tradition of boat-building.

It was taught, traditionally, that when Brian Boru defeated the 'Vikings' in 1014 they piled into their boats and fled back to Scandinavia. Some of their warlords may have done so; but these people had been in and out of Ireland for two centuries. Many had become Christian, raised families and fought beside, as much as against, the various factions in the country, becoming as integrated as any 'native'. It is only through the quite recent and artificial construct of a homogenous people or nation that the Vikings of Ireland could be viewed as alien. The 'Celts', by the same logic, must at one stage have been alien. Christianity at one stage was a novelty.

The political urge to forge a unified national image arbitrarily excludes certain categories of people in forming a coherent culture. The settlers called Vikings patently contributed much to the multifaceted personality of this small island located in the centre of a busy north/south sea route.

6 *Wales and Europe*

A MOUNTAIN IN WALES, frequented by hillwalkers and pony-trekkers, boasts the strange name 'Cader Idris'. The word *Cader*, like the Irish *cathaoir*, simply means 'chair'; 'Idris' is a fairly common personal name in Wales, but for centuries the kings and saints of the Muslim world of North Africa have also been called Idris. I visited the shrine of one such saint in Morocco, in a town called Moulay Idris, perched on a hill within sight of the old Roman town of Volubilis. The shrine itself was considered so sacred that even lapsed Christians like myself were not allowed to enter, so when I say visited, I really mean I stood outside while my Muslim film crew filmed inside.

This particular Moroccan Idris had founded a dynasty in Morocco in the seventh century – about the same time as Idris the Giant, a magician and astrologer, was reputed to have lived in Wales. However, topographical names attached to rivers, mountains and features of the physical environment such as Cader Idris tend to be much older than recorded history. If there was any connection between Cader Idris and Moulay Idris, it must have been long before Idris the Giant or the Muslim saint.

Generations of Irish people have passed through Wales without giving it much thought. They have been emigrants from Ireland bound for London.

As the Shamrock Express usually passes through Holyhead and Bangor in the dead of night, they did not see much of this delightful country. A cup of British Rail tea on a windy platform at midnight is no introduction to Wales. As that had been my only experience of the country, I decided to visit it formally, this time going by the southern route from Rosslare to Fishguard, the same route by which the Anglo-Normans came to 'civilize' the Irish in the twelfth century. Thus the Irish and Welsh are long-standing friends and rivals sharing a common linguistic root. The Lleyn peninsula, for instance, bears the same name as its neighbour just across the Irish Sea, the province of Leinster.

The topography of the Welsh coast, to me, looked quite similar to Conamara. Farther north the scenery was less dramatic, but the Welsh mountains made up for it. In Aberystwyth University I sought out the late E.G. Bowen, who I knew had recorded the same North African connections as myself and had applied them to Wales. He had been studying and writing about the Atlantic seaways for years. He brought scholarship to support the historical incongruity that I, in my ignorance, had intuited: that formal history was based almost exclusively on literary evidence from urban-based classical writers who were not concerned with what they deemed 'peripheral regions'.

Loss of peripheral vision is called 'tunnel vision'. It is fatal for a football player but a necessary form of myopia for empire builders. The Roman Empire was built on a network of roads (as was the expansion of Hitler's Third Reich). It was inevitable that both ancient and more recent authors should have concentrated on the land (tunnel vision) and rarely described the movements of coastal peoples (peripheral vision). What had happened to dent the fixed idea that 'the sea divided and the land united'? New archaeology was the key.

E.G. Bowen was primarily a geographer but thought as a historian and archaeologist. This seemed paradoxical to me until I realized that the physical context of an event is almost as important as the event itself. Man does not do his deeds in an ecological vacuum, does not build his shelter or manufacture his tools without direct reference to his environment. We should be able to trace the movements of people by the artifacts they leave behind. If they leave a trail of broken pottery as they migrate, this is much more reliable evidence of the migration than written accounts based on orally transmitted tales, although this too has its respected function.

Similarly, if artefacts are found in very different places, but are clearly

◪ *St David's Cathedral, Dyfed, Wales*

of identical manufacture, cultural contact can be assumed between these places, no matter how remote from each other. If a chart is plotted showing the relationship between these various finds, you can make a good guess at the extent of a culture's influence, the routes travelled and the mode of travel. Such a plotting of finds is tentative and entirely subject to whatever evidence might emerge in the future. E.G. Bowen, as well as Cyril Fox, Gordon Childe, O.G.S. Crawford and other eminent archaeologists, had applied this cartographical principle to the Atlantic seaways, concluding that in distant times the seas around Ireland were 'as bright with Neolithic argonauts as the Western Pacific is today'.

I had a number of enthusiastic sessions with Professor Bowen – a short, lively old man. He warned me that his ideas, for instance, about the progress of early 'Celtic' Christianity were unpopular in Dublin. His approach was defiantly sea-based. He had little time for the classical perspective of ideas moving slowly and ponderously overland to reach the peripheral areas of Europe and the British Isles. His vision included a host of seafaring monks moving from peninsula to peninsula by sea, carrying their light boats over the established paths to the next stretch of water. The jewel in his argument was the Cathedral of Dewi Sant, or St David, patron saint of Wales. This massive building is located at the tip of the Dyfed peninsula, rising impressively and surprisingly from a marshy valley, the Vallis Rosina. It is the last thing one expects to find in such a 'remote' spot.

Such a foundation had to be located, even 1400 years ago, in what was considered to be the centre of the area occupied by its religious adherents. If this were so, then half of Dewi Sant's parish consisted of seafarers. Most of the parish calls must have been conducted by boat. It was similar to what I had noticed about Conamara – the peninsular setting of shops and post offices. The position of this, the premier shrine of Wales, on such a peninsula implied that the original founders were seafarers. How they arrived at this place in Wales was debatable and whence they came even more so. It seemed ludicrous to suggest that they had got their inspiration from London and travelled through the dangerous land of southern England. They must have come by sea.

A photo acquired from the cathedral gives a clue to their origins. It shows a gathering of bearded dignitaries surrounded by their acolytes taken in the grounds of the cathedral in 1920, the occasion of celebrations to mark the disestablishment of the Church in Wales. They came from the East, from Nubia in Egypt, Alexandria and Jerusalem. The Russian and

◼ *Meeting of Eastern Orthodox patriarchs at St David's, 1920 (photo courtesy of the late E.G. Bowen)*

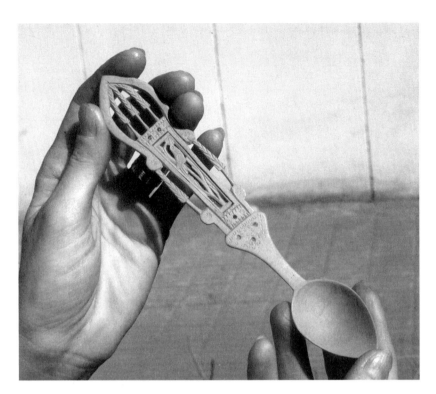

 *Egyptian love spoon (top); Welsh love spoons (above)*

the Byzantine churches were also represented. It stated clearly that the Welsh saw their traditional religious ideas extending farther than Westminster or Canterbury, and suggested that the Welsh were more aware of, and more willing, than the Irish to acknowledge their connection with and debt to the East. Was it their way of saying that the first carriers of this religion to Wales had also bypassed continental Europe?

I moved on. In the church of St Mary's in Haverfordwest I was directed to a sculpture that represented a pilgrim. This female figure was lying down and by her side was a scallop shell, indicating she had completed the journey to Santiago de Campostela, then the second shrine of Christendom. In addition to those who went overland, devout people of the British Isles travelled by sea, from places like Plymouth, directly down the Atlantic coasts to visit this shrine in Galicia, Spain.

The love spoons found in Wales are finely carved specimens of folk art. Little attention has been paid to their origins, though it is suggested that the custom of offering a carved spoon as a marriage proposal comes from Scandinavia or Germany. But in a town called Azrou in central Morocco, where exquisite wood-carving is a feature, I came across a man carving love spoons. He used the same clever motif of chain-links fashioned from a single piece of wood. Farther east, in Cairo, I was shown wooden spoons and forks carved with as much care as the Welsh versions. I wondered why the origins of the love spoon should be automatically attributed to northern Europe. The frequency of rope and cable and anchor designs on them indicated that sailors passed the tedium of long voyages by carving these spoons. I could suggest that Welsh sailors had picked up this custom from their long voyages to the warm south but, as one expert has said: 'Since in its simplest form there occurs a basic similarity among most expressions of peasant art, these influences may be more imaginary than real.' However, the collection of love spoons in St Fagan's folk museum in Cardiff showed that this activity achieved a standard far beyond the definition 'simple'.

In this folk museum there was also an account of a traditional game called *bando*. It was played with a stick and a ball and featured two teams with an indeterminate number of players on each side. Bando died out in Wales before the nineteenth century but was clearly related to the Irish game of hurling — the fastest grass surface game in the world — which has become the national game of Ireland. I have also seen photos of a similar game called *takourt*, played in Morocco until outlawed by the French authorities

☒ *Megalithic mound, Bryn Celli Du, Anglesey, Wales*

on the grounds that it was 'très brutal'. The Irish game similarly affects the squeamish. Fortunately, it has survived its critics.

In the National Museum in Cardiff I found a strange little model boat with what looked like eyes painted on the prow. It was called the Caergwrle Bowl, and the authorities attributed Phoenician stylistic resonances to it. It was dated to the Early Bronze Age, possibly even to 1100 BC, and was more evidence of a maritime predisposition in those distant days. The Roman historian Tacitus once described the people of south Wales – the Silurians – as 'a dark-skinned race with twisted curly hair'.

In Anglesey, north Wales – occupied by Roman armies in the second century AD – there was plenty of archaeological evidence for contrast with Ireland. One passage tomb, Barclodiad y Gowres, had designs described by archaeologists T.G.E. Powell and Glyn Daniel as 'mostly the disintegrated remains of a human figure, derived from those in Iberia'. Other parallels, they said, were to be found in Morocco and on the Niger, while the resemblance between the multiple arcs on stones from Pola de Allande, Asturias, and menhirs at Tondidaro on the Niger, was also to be found on Iberian bone idols. Such an openness to possible African connections was very refreshing to me, particularly as these designs were acknowledged to be related to their equivalent in Ireland. Up to a thousand years ago, it is maintained, Welsh and Irish were mutually intelligible languages. There has always been friction between scholars as to who is indebted to whom as far as names and language is concerned. Did the Irish colonize Wales or vice versa? Is Irish a late derivation of Welsh?

Other place-names in Wales are distinctly Irish. Cilgerran on the river Cardigan is such a name, commemorating the Irish saint, Ciarán. The village retains the use of what archaeologists call a 'palaeotechnic artefact'. This is simply a canvas-covered coracle, a diminutive boat in which big men still hunt salmon on the river Cardigan. These are descendants of the boats that Himilco the Carthaginian described so many centuries ago. The fisherman kneels in front of the boat, facing forward and, with one small oar, literally drags himself through the water. I tried one; after a very short while my knees ached. On the other side of the Irish Sea, on the Boyne near Drogheda, mussel fishermen used very similar boats before heavy industry destroyed the mussel beds. On the coast of Conamara a longer version, the currach, is used; this has a sharply upturned prow to breast the waves. In Kerry the same boat, called the *naomhóg*, also survives.

The Welsh have a much better-recorded tradition of seafaring than the Irish. It is surprising, though, how closely their maritime legends parallel those of their neighbours. They sailed the waters round Iceland before the Vikings; they were credited with discovering magical islands; they even had their American discovery myth. This held that twelfth-century Prince Madoc had been there three hundred years before Columbus. It was a particularly powerful myth, and led to the belief that somewhere in America was a lost tribe of white Indians who were Welsh-speaking descendants of Prince Madoc and his crew. It was revived in the fifteenth century by the English to counter Spanish claims to exclusive ownership of the Americas. If Britons (i.e. the Welsh) had been there in the twelfth century, how could such a claim be exclusive? From then on, Madoc was a recurrent phenomenon in the exploitation of America. In 1796 two Welshmen, John Evans and Morgan John Rhys, charted a large section of the Missouri basin in the search for their long-lost brothers. When they finally came upon the 'Mandans', as these Indians were known, they had to admit that there was not one phrase of Welsh among them. Still, the myth stimulated a flood of emigrants across the Atlantic and gave the Welsh pride in their seafaring abilities.

The strangest thing I experienced in Wales was neither myth nor museum artefact. It was a custom called *Cymanfaoedd Pwync* that consisted of musical chanting, the likes of which I had not heard before. It took place in a small

Dolmen at Pentre Ifan, Dyfed, Wales

chapel in a village called Maenchlochog Dhu, meaning the Black Monk's Bell. The entire congregation assembled in the body of the chapel, divided itself into four sections, two male and two female and, without benefit of a conductor, launched into a fierce and startling recital. The music was as far from any European form as sean-nós singing. Not that it resembled sean-nós; it was the exact opposite, like a war chant, loud and staccato. Each musical phrase was the same, simply two notes repeated for as long as the words required. I was intrigued to discover that they were reciting, in Welsh, from the Bible.

These people, worshipping in a perfectly normal way, appeared to have retained the uninhibited fundamentalism that must have imbued early Christianity. Explanations as to the origin of the chant were, as usual, vague. There was the prosaic explanation that this was a technique used by old missionaries to instil by rote the words of the gospel into the heads of children. The parents, as so often happens, learned from the children. Just as mathematical tables were once learned off by heart, without much comprehension, so the object was to imprint the words indelibly on people's minds.

It is just as likely that the chant was pre-missionary, part of the secular culture of the people; could it have been, like so many other things, absorbed into the Christian form of worship? I have heard of preachers in south Wales who could work themselves up into such a frenzy of oratory that it became almost a musical recital. The BBC once recorded them, intercut the sound with that of a muezzin, and dared anyone to tell them apart. It was reminiscent of that occasion, a century before in the Royal Irish Academy, when the man from Lebanon and the Irish antiquarian also, literally, exchanged notes.

The day after this recital I inspected a large megalithic structure called Pentre Ifan, similar to those I had seen all over Ireland, as well as in Brittany and much farther down the Atlantic coasts to Galicia. Following the cartographical lessons of E.G. Bowen, I made a mental note that all of the chapels and Sunday schools in which Cymanfa Pwync is sung are on the same Welsh peninsula that contains St David's Cathedral as well as the Cilgerran coracle. This is the peninsula that reaches farthest out towards the Atlantic.

At this stage, I discovered a study suggesting the sought-after links might be more than cultural. A 1952 survey by A.E. Mourant and I. Morgan Watkin of the blood groups, anthropology and language of Wales and western countries found that the peoples of the peripheral north-western regions

◩ *Dolmen de Dombate, Galicia, Spain*

of Europe – Iceland, Scotland, Ireland and parts of Wales – showed A, B and C blood groups with a frequency almost identical to those of the Sardinians, the Cretans and certain Berber tribes of North Africa. In 1987 Dr Morgan Watkins, a former Deputy Director of the Blood Transfusion Service for Wales and Medical Officer for Carmarthenshire, produced a survey that substantiated the idea that people in north Wales were closely related to the Berbers of North Africa.

This relative frequency of blood-types by no means proves that these people are the same, or are even descended from the same ancestor: the similarity could be due to the coincidental effects of environment and isolation. The theory that beyond cultural links there might be a racial link, the remnants of a migration in prehistory, is, I recognize, sailing in perilous waters. I therefore consider it prudent at this stage to quote David T. Croke of the Royal College of Surgeons who, in an essay on genetics and archaeology, wrote: 'In short, the findings of modern human genetics conclusively demonstrate that there is absolutely no biological basis for ideas of "ethnicity" or "race".' I subscribe to this, believing that people are indivisible as a species and that the concept of race is a dangerous extrapolation of the harmless and enriching activity of cultural comparison.

More solid evidence for my cultural speculations was to be found in Western Megalithic culture. Down the Atlantic coasts of Europe the megaliths (literally, 'big stones') reach like gigantic stepping-stones. They link places as far apart as Denmark, Scotland, Galicia and southern Spain (and, as I shall demonstrate, Morocco). They are the dolmens, menhirs, passage tombs, some of them immense in construction, that stand as permanent testimony to the imagination and organization of a people or peoples who were essentially seafarers. The Boyne Valley passage tombs of Newgrange, Knowth and Dowth, with their massive scale, strange carvings and astronomical precision, are exactly counterpointed by those in Morbihan on the coast of Brittany. The similar designs, the identical layouts, the location near water – a river in one case, the sea in another – all point to an undeniable relationship. There can be little doubt that the people who built them were in direct maritime contact. Even the esteemed Professor Frank Mitchell said that the kerbstone designs originated in Iberia.

These megaliths are the most solid evidence that at least as far back as 3000 BC, before the pyramids of Egypt were built, man carried his culture up and down the Atlantic coasts. Despite many local variations, the passage

⊠ *Dolmens at Poulnabrone, Co. Clare (top); and Proleek, Co. Louth (above)*

tombs in Maes Howe, Orkney, share the same tradition as those in Alcala, Portugal, or Huelva, Spain. They profoundly correct the delusion of cultural spread happening primarily overland.

Evidence has been produced to suggest that the megaliths of the northern areas, in fact, predate their counterparts in the south. The relationship to Minos and Mycenae is here invoked. Undoubtedly there is a clear similarity

Stone circle at Drombeg, Co. Cork

between the layout and designs of those eastern Mediterranean structures and those of the Atlantic areas. The entrances to the Palace of Minos on Crete and the Newgrange passage tomb are remarkably alike. But the dispute over chronology tends to obscure the main point: the Mediterranean and the Atlantic expressions of this culture are related directly. Gordon Childe made a direct analogy, in reverse, when he suggested that we should notice that the areas on which the Vikings made an impression are the same as those in which the megalithic forms appear. If the Vikings could have such wide-ranging contacts, why not accept the possibility of an earlier people doing the same thing? People have been sailing these waters for at least 9000 years!

There seems to be a lack of confidence in the idea that Neolithic man was technologically equipped to sail long distances, despite the fact that all scholars now agree that the sea was an easier and safer form of travel when the land was forested and filled with wild animals. Thor Heyerdahl insisted that man hoisted a sail before he saddled a horse. The evidence shows that even when early man penetrated inland, he clung very closely to the waterways.

The navigational abilities of our Stone Age forebears are greatly under-estimated despite clear evidence, from the alignments of their stone structures, that their astronomical observations were highly sophisticated. The repeated convention is that monumental constructions such as Newgrange, Knowth and Dowth, are nothing more than memorials to the dead. The

Swedish ship circle at Kaseberg, Sweden (photo: Susanne Johnson)

obvious fact that their construction required extraordinary knowledge of astronomy, of the movements of the sun, the moon, the stars and the planets, has been carefully obscured or at least sidelined by generations of archaeologists. There is hardly an architectural construction in the history of mankind that does not at least take account of the position of the morning and evening light. If a building had religious connotations, the designers invariably constructed it with an astronomical dimension in mind, be it as obvious as the rising and setting sun. Such constructions, from Maltese temples to American Indian mounds, all pay homage to the source of all energy and life and light, the sun. An agnostic attitude towards archaeo-astronomy seems to have plagued Irish archaeology, resulting in a summary dismissal of that perfectly reasonable approach.

In the summer of 2001 I listened to a young Newgrange guide dismissing a visitor's suggestion that the extraordinary rock designs (most obviously the snake-like coils that represent the nineteen-year Metonic cycle) have astronomical implications; he suggested they were hallucinogenic doodles! I have been shown, by workmen in Knowth, the entrance to the longest such passage in Europe, ignorantly stopped by a lump of concrete that precludes cognizance of the original orientation towards the equinoctial sun. I have witnessed the depredations that a tourist-oriented reconstruction is wreaking on Knowth's fabulous kerbstone designs – the simple matter of rainwater being allowed to drip relentlessly on those ancient configurations. I spoke to the workman who, in the early 1980s, actually found the famous Knowth flint macehead. So polished was the execution of this carving, he said it had initially been dismissed as a piece of plastic discarded by a tourist.

Perhaps basic astronomy should be included in archaeological courses. It might override the fear of attributing rationality to ancient pagans and thereby undermining established religious ideas of progress towards perfection. Such an idea would subvert all optimistic concepts of humanity's eschatological 'progress' towards the Pleroma.

All knowledge, including theories about the origins of peoples, cultures, nations, civilizations, is provisional and hypothetical, i.e. valid until better evidence arrives. There is no beginning and no end to knowledge; but the first requirement of truth is to preserve an open mind to every perspective. Modern light pollution renders Western man practically blind to the wonders of the night sky, which in turn suggests a blindness towards the sheer improvisational brilliance of our so-called primitive ancestors. They did, after all, survive a harsh northern environment without oil, electricity or the automobile.

In 1969 on Clare Island, Co. Mayo, I saw an islander conducting brain surgery on a sheep! The operation, called 'trepanning', is an ancient and well-attested procedure for relieving painful pressure on the brain, or 'water on the brain', colloquially, 'the head-staggers'. It requires keen powers of observation and a steady hand. The elderly farmer, Michael Joe O'Malley, had lived his entire life on the island. From this experience I learned never to think in terms of 'the primitive'.

Marine archaeology is still in its infancy. Water covers seven-eighths of the planet and is still encroaching, in some areas, at the rate of an inch a year. If this rate has been constant over the past 9000 years, the remnants of coastal dwellings of millennia ago must all be covered by water. To get a truer picture of the movements of people in the past, future archaeologists would benefit from a course in snorkelling.

The builders of the megaliths used wood and hides for their boats. These perishable materials do not survive on sea or riverbeds, awaiting discovery. Like music and language, they are the invisible archaeology. The oldest remains that have so far been found in northern areas are dug-out canoes made from single trees and preserved in bogs or lake floors, but Thor Heyerdahl has demonstrated that these are not necessarily the earliest form of marine craft. The ancient Assyrians – admittedly later than the megalith builders – were able to carry a complete chariot together with a crew of possibly twenty people in their 'quffas', the large equivalent of the coracle. If they could do this with skin-covered vessels, what could others have fashioned from wood?

The mysteries of the megaliths will never be solved until archaeology becomes as efficient on the sea as on the land. It does not seem too much to maintain that, independently of central Europe, the peoples of these Atlantic coasts were in direct maritime contact as far back as 5000 years ago, and that this contact extended from Scandinavia to the Mediterranean. We overlook the fact that the Mediterranean has two shores; the southern one being the coast of Africa, and the nearest landfall to Ireland on that continent Morocco.

7 Ireland and North Africa

I visited all the oceans, I saw the misty West,
There, where clouds are born, and beauty.
I saw Medina and also Mecca, and Egypt and Jerusalem.
In Sudan I watched the great rivers.
From the top of the plateau I saw the world.
Take my advice, friend, dismount here;
No place is lovelier than Amur.

'Amur' is an old Berber name for Morocco. I came across this poem in a magazine called *Amazigh*, published in Rabat and devoted to reviving the Berber language and culture. This magazine fascinated me because its arguments seemed to reproduce all the sentiments of the Irish-language revival of the early twentieth century. There was a difference, however slight, in that it appeared to me to be unlikely that the Berber culture and language could ever be indissolubly bound to the religion of Islam. The fortunes of the Irish language became linked to Roman Catholicism, a development that has, however well intentioned, ultimately worked against the survival of the language.

THE ATLANTEAN IRISH

Berber market, Meknes, Morocco

However, Berber revivalism is not quite the proper way to describe the philosophy of the *Amazigh* magazine; its object was to achieve formal acknowledgment that the Berber languages and cultures were central to the identities of Morocco, Algeria and the other countries of North Africa. The official language is Arabic, and French is universal in the cities, so Berber may end up, like Irish, as mainly a rural phenomenon. Morocco was a French colony for a century, but it is the only North African country that was not also dominated by the Turks, which means one less cultural layer to peel away.

My first exploration of Morocco over twenty years ago was also my first experience of the African continent. The initial glimpse of its brown earth from a plane produced an excitement in me I can still vividly recall. It felt like a homecoming. After all of my readings and speculations about the country, the emotion was strangely similar to those experienced on my many trips home to my native Ireland.

In a quiet street near the Grand Mosque in Rabat I came across the Louis Chatelain Archaeological Museum. The museum was mainly devoted to the glories of Greece and Rome, but there was also a fine collection of Phoenician coins to whet my interest. What I was looking for would not be prominent: it could be a coin, a map, a design, anything with a 'Celtic' echo – the only yardstick against which I could so far measure my disparate observations.

There were plenty of old stones in the museum, some with delicate carvings of animals, a reminder that the Sahara was once a green and fertile

 *Stele de Maaziz (Louis Chatelain Archaeological Museum, Rabat, Morocco)*

place supporting a large population of people – as well as antelope, giraffe, rhinoceros and the many other animals depicted in the rock art of southern Algeria. Some of the stones had inscriptions in Libyan/Berber, indicating that these people had been literate for at least as long as the residents of the British Isles.

A display of Roman metalwork showed designs to which I could easily attribute an Irish likeness. One in particular – a piece of harness – was fashioned as a triskele, a favourite detail of Irish art. However, this was explained by the possibility of the Roman armies including 'Celtic' trades-men. In fact, the triskele is as fundamental a design element as the spiral;

the running legs motif of the Isle of Man is the example nearest home. There were certainly Britons and Gauls in the Roman army; they were soldiers or tradesmen, or perhaps victims of the press gangs of the time. In Volubilis a figure of a man is shown wearing plaid trousers and the inscription identifies him as a 'Briton'. I had also read that in the Fayoum area of the Egyptian desert a sword was found dated to the third century and described as 'Celtic'.

A single stone called the Stele de Maaziz, tucked away in the corner of the museum, caught my eye. It was approximately one metre high and featured a carved figure of indeterminate sex surrounded by a snaky, wavy line and, outside that, a series of overlapping concentric half-circles. The arrangement of these circles reminded me of the entrance stone to Newgrange. I had also seen the snake-like line on stones in Ireland; in Rabat I learned that the design could be traced back to Egypt and that it symbolized a serpent protecting the sun god in his tomb. This seems to me a vivid way of describing the winter solstice, the recognition of which is the principal feature of the tumulus at Newgrange. There, on 21 December, the rising sun penetrates a passage twenty metres long and illuminates a central inner chamber.

The wavy and concentric designs on the Rabat collection were common on other stones collected from places with strange names such as Oukaimeden, Aougdal and n'Ouagouns – all Berber strongholds. The French scholar George Souville wrote that those could not be accurately dated; however, he pronounced the following:

> These different sorts of decorations are well-known on numerous monuments, stelae or engravings on the Atlantic coast from Ireland to Portugal, from Brittany to Galicia. The serpent-like motif appears on the menhirs from Minio in Brittany and reappears in Portugal and Spain. Concentric circles and semi-circles are motifs very widespread in Ireland, on Breton megaliths, notably at Gavr'-inis, also in Galicia and Portugal.

George Souville linked these stones with the Bronze Age and, more particularly, with what he referred to as the 'Civilization of the Bronze-Atlantic'.

Before I left the Louis Chatelain Museum, a French curator told me of a stone-circled tumulus in a place called M'Zora halfway between Rabat and Tangier. She even produced a faded photograph of the place. It was sufficiently intriguing for me to resolve to visit it. At the coastal town of Larache (El Araiche, originally Lixus, a Phoenician settlement), I was directed ten kilometres inland to a small town called Sidi Yemani. Its main street consisted of brown mud, churned up by the rain and looking like something out of an Alaskan gold rush. A young passer-by was amused by my pidgin French as I tried to describe a tumulus and a circle of standing stones. 'Ah,' he said in perfect English, 'you mean the cromlech. Come, I shall take you there.'

I drove the hired car for five kilometres on a track carved out by a stream. Due to the rain, the stream had now reasserted its authority. It was the busy pathway between Sidi Yemani and the village where, I was informed, the cromlech stood. Eventually, we had to abandon the car and start hiking. It took another five kilometres of squelching through the mud to reach the site. It was set in the middle of a cluster of houses and gardens and was dominated by a tall, phallus-shaped stone, referred to locally as El Uted. I had seen an identical erection at Punchestown, in Naas, Co. Kildare. Coming nearer, we could see the circle of stones, some of them trespassing on gardens. It was true; it was the remains of a tumulus. Most of its centre had been gouged out, probably for the stones and gravel, just as similar tombs had been pillaged in Ireland. Many of the adjoining cottages were probably built from the material. According to our count there were 167 stones in the circle. The pillar dominated the landscape. Newgrange once boasted such a pillar – Edward Lhuyd first reported it in 1699.

The guide told me there was a reconstruction of the original tumulus in a museum in Tetuan, seventy kilometres away. There, the following morning, after much bureaucratic difficulty – I had, after all, no academic credentials and no written permissions, so necessary in Morocco – I bribed a guide and managed to take two pictures of what was, to me, unmistakably a first cousin of Newgrange and Gavr'inis. I learned that a Roman historian, Sertorius, had mentioned the site. It was also described as being the grave of a native god, Antee, cognate with the tradition of Newgrange being the grave of an Irish pagan god, Aonghus.

What was disturbing was to have to go to so much trouble to learn about a prominent landmark with which many archaeologists must be familiar. Among British and Irish archaeologists, the only reference to North African Neolithic constructions I could find was from Glyn Daniel in his *Megalith*

⬛ *M'Zora burial mound, Larache, Morocco (top); M'Zora reconstruction, Tetuan Museum, Morocco (bottom)*

Builders of Western Europe. There was a reference to menhirs in Algeria, simple standing stones that were defined as being much later constructions than those on the Atlantic coasts. There was no reference that I could find to the tumulus of M'Zora, the strongest evidence of connections. I brought my findings to the attention of the late Michael O'Kelly, the Newgrange expert, and he admitted that 'at first glance one would see resemblances to Irish engraved art', but he added, the subject was 'quite outside my field of study and it would be presumptuous of me even to comment …' He recommended I write to Dr Emmanuel Anati, an Italian archaeologist in Brescia.

Certainly, French and Spanish archaeologists knew about it – the French and Spanish being, of course, the colonizers of Morocco. On my return to Ireland I was lucky enough to meet a visiting American, James W. Mavor, of the Woods Hole Oceanographic Institute, who had studied, measured and written in detail about 'The Riddle of M'Zorah'. He also made the connection with the Atlantic and pointed out that long ago the silted stream leading to the site would have been a navigable river – like the Boyne's access to Newgrange.

The most acceptable explanation I got for the startling similarity between Newgrange and M'Zora was contained in one word: polygenesis. This suggests that people with absolutely no cultural contact can easily develop habits of life, forms of worship and burial that are similar. They might discover fire or invent the wheel at the same time and without the slightest idea of each other's existence. It was not beyond the bounds of possibility that Neolithic man in Morocco developed the forms of the passage tomb, the tumulus crowned with a phallic-shaped stone and surrounded by standing stones, quite independently of the Neolithic farmers on the Boyne. Even the designs on the Stele de Maaziz could be explained away by polygenesis; the spiral and circle are universal symbols used in places as far apart as China and America. The spiral, for instance, is always 'at hand', as you can see by studying your fingerprints. Even the Japanese built what could be called 'megaliths'.

Not for one moment did I believe M'Zora could be thus explained away.

I was urged to consider the modern phenomenon of two physicists: working at opposite sides of the globe, they can quite 'independently' come up with the solution to an intricate problem. However, two modern physicists, no matter how geographically separated, are by virtue of their discipline working in precisely the same intellectual environment, have

⊠ *Berber woman (from* Tribus Berbéres du Haut Atlas *by André Bertrand, 1977)*

access to the same references and precedents; they belong, in fact, to a very specific scientific community. As Arthur Koestler pointed out, Leibnitz and Newton developed the infinitesimal calculus apparently independently, but they shared a long line of precursors. If the Neolithic peoples of North Africa hit upon the same method of burying their dead, or erecting monuments, and used the same designs as other peoples on the Atlantic coasts, what long line of precursors, what community of interest, did they share with the Irish?

Polygenesis or isolationism and its opposite – diffusion, meaning cultural spread – are theories that are used selectively. Similarities detected between the British Isles and North Africa are labelled polygenesis or coincidence. However, the cultures of Hallstatt or La Tène in Central Europe, as compared to that of British Isles, are classified under diffusion or direct cultural contact. It is quite respectable to see a solid Neolithic connection between the Aryan – or even pre-Aryan – 'races' of Scandinavia and the British Isles; one can even see connections with Crete – comfortably part of Mediterranean Europe. But it is going a little far to include what may be seen as lesser, dark-skinned people of North Africa.

The Berbers, however, are not remotely what one could call dark-skinned. Many Berber communities, who keep to themselves and maintain a traditional lifestyle, have a complexion lighter than some of my neighbours. They live mainly in the smaller towns of Morocco and on market day are easily distinguishable. The older women have tattoo marks on their faces; some have a simple, inconspicuous mark on their foreheads, others have faces and hands entirely covered with a complex tracery of designs.

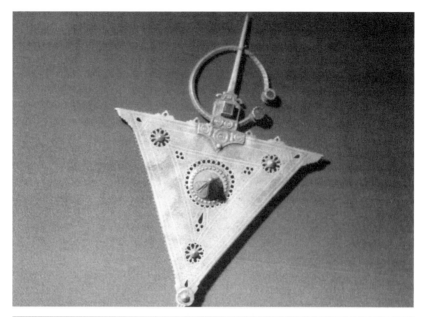

Berber jewellery

These patterns were consistent with the decoration on pottery and carpets for which the Berbers are famous and which, for subtlety of composition, are hard to match.

The Berber people are fascinating. The males were traditionally the shock troops of the various conquerors, having the same problem as the Irish; inability to pool their various tribal resources and collectively repel invaders. Their horsemanship is renowned and annually celebrated in summer festivals. In Meknes, a line of horsemen gallops furiously across an open space and suddenly, without any evident signal, they loose their rifles at the same moment as they halt their gallop. Then they turn and repeat the exercise time and again. This is called the *Fantasie*, but its origins are far from fantasy. Whenever the Berbers could combine forces, they formed impressive dynasties such as the Almoravids and the Almohads, which swept across Morocco and spread throughout Algeria, Tunisia and Libya. In the eleventh century they came to the rescue of the Muslim rulers of Spain whom Christian forces were threatening.

The French colonists in the nineteenth century were able to manipulate successfully the distinction between Berber and Arab on the principle of divide and conquer. The tension is still echoed today. Those who are aware of this period will say: we are neither Arab nor Berber; we are Moroccans. As successive historians have pointed out, the invasions of North Africa by Phoenicians, Greeks, Romans, Byzantines, Vandals, Arabs and Turks probably constituted small ruling élites, technologically superior but, in the main, transient. Thus, the cultural characteristics of the indigenous population, the Berbers, have remained substantially the same.

The Moroccan Berbers produced a succession of leaders – Massinissa, Jugurtha, Juba. These variously opposed and collaborated with the invaders according to the political expedients of the time. Their descendants across North Africa demonstrated this independence of mind in religious affairs; when Rome was pagan, the Berbers adopted Christianity and Judaism, when Rome became Christian they adopted the 'heretical' Arianism. They adopted Islam against the Byzantines but when Islam became oppressive they developed their own liberal forms of that religion. When Arab rulers developed decadent tendencies, the Berbers overthrew them and reasserted a puritan regime.

I learned that certain eminent figures of the Roman Church were of North African and Berber origin: St Augustine was an Algerian. Tertullian, too, a celebrated Father of the Church before he reverted to 'heresy', seems to have been an early pacifist. He recognized only one nation, 'that which has no border but the universe', and only one republic, 'the world'. He denied Christians the right to join any army or institution of the state. He seems to have been the first prominent preacher of 'conscientious objection'.

Pope Paul VI, in his 1967 message to the Africans, recognized the significance of these early Berber Christians. He acknowledged that 'from the second to the fourth centuries AD, there was very intense Christian life in the Northern regions of Africa'. This was faint praise: the Latin Church *was* North African. In the domain of theology, North Africa was the seat of the *avant garde*. From my childhood I remembered the names Origen (who also became 'heretical'), Cyril, St Cyprian, Athanasius, Tertullian and Augustine being droned out in the litanies of Sunday Mass. It was a shock to find that these were all North Africans. The Berber who most intrigued me came later. He was a Tunisian, Ibn Khaldun (1336–1406), who wrote:

> Historians ... have committed frequent errors in the stories and events they reported. They accepted them in plain transmitted form, without regard for its value. They did not probe them with the yardstick of philosophy, with the help of the knowledge of the nature of things, or with the help of speculation and historical insight. Therefore they strayed from the truth and found themselves lost in the desert of baseless assumptions and errors.

This man's practical insights into the history of ancient and medieval thought were unequalled, according to modern historians Philip Toynbee and Hugh Trevor-Roper, until the eighteenth century. Ibn Khaldun had developed a 'science of civilization': he approaches history as a series of geographic, economic and cultural patterns. His *Al Muqaddimah*, the introduction to his world history written in 1377, earned him the title 'Father of Sociology'. I feel that his spirit infuses the works of my heroes, E. Estyn Evans and E.G. Bowen.

I travelled to Casablanca, Tangier, Fez, Marrakech and many places in between, always looking for details but inevitably taking in the magnificent remnants of Islamic civilization. The scale of the architecture of mosques and palaces was beyond petty human pride. The old imperial palace of Meknes, for instance, was so large one needed a taxi to cover the extensive grounds. The intricate detail, the sheer brilliance of the decoration of each door and window, was awesome. A single clear religious belief was the driving force. The unselfconsciousness with which people removed their shoes on entering the Karaouine mosque in Fez, rolled up their sleeves and washed themselves before prostrating themselves in prayer became, for me, not a slightly ludicrous activity but evidence of a sureness of identity and a humility that I regard as a sign of wisdom. I thought sadly of the bored, dutiful approach of Westerners to church on Sundays. No wonder Islam

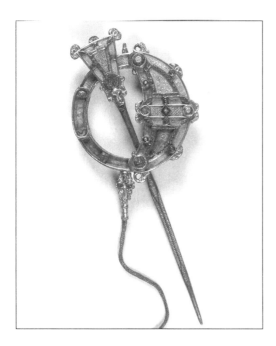

The Tara Brooch
(National Museum of Ireland)

cut like a sword through a flaccid Christendom so many centuries ago.

I had travelled by bus to Meknes. Seated beside me a handsome young woman named Fatima gave me lessons in Berber and said her ambition was to marry a European. 'Moroccan men', she said indignantly, 'do not know how to treat women.' I wished her luck with European men. In a museum of Berber art there, the curator (also French) directed me to objects that she herself felt had an affinity with 'Celtic' art. This led me to the Berber jewellery, astonishing in its sophistication. It consisted of elaborate head-dresses, necklets and bracelets. All of a family's wealth, in the form of coins or precious metals, was incorporated in female adornments. Thus, if two families were contemplating a liaison for their children, they could each tell at a glance the potential for a dowry. From the dates on the coins it was clear that although this was an old custom, it had the distinction of still being practised. It was as if the ancient gold lunulae in the National Museum in Dublin were still being made and sported by the Irish.

The construction of the jewellery and the tiny designs on it struck a chord with me. I took some pictures of it and back in Ireland asked a sculptress friend to comment on the images. Cliodna Cussen pointed out the resemblance to the Tara Brooch and felt sure that, if one looked hard enough through samples of Irish art, one would find at least one of the designs, a distinct four-sided version of the 'triskele'. She described the feel of the jewellery as oriental but said that in the detail there were echoes of Irish art; this applied particularly to the Berber habit of filling every crevice with a design. The 'Celts' shared this *horror vacui*.

Thus everything unusual or distinctive about Ireland seemed to be, consciously or unconsciously, lumped into the category 'Celtic'. The 'Celts' were becoming, for me, a historical cul-de-sac beyond which investigation was almost pointless. It was bad enough that all of the most interesting things about Ireland should be explained away – and thus not truly explained – by reference to some obscure central Euro-people. But this obfuscation had already been applied to the Berbers.

A report from the *Caledonian Medical Journal* of 1908 had the striking title 'Celtic tribes in Morocco'. Dr George Mackey of Edinburgh stated that 'he had learned from a military friend who had made more than one expedition into Morocco that there was reason to believe that there existed there at the present time a race of people of Celtic origin'. The article detailed the various cultural elements that made up the population of the country, and continued:

> There is a fourth and extremely interesting race that is neither Arab nor Jew and that speaks a language having no connection with either. This is the race to which the wild, warlike Berber tribes belong, who inhabit the mountains and table-lands of the interior. They owe allegiance to no-one and although nominally Mohammedan do not practice polygamy. The Sultan does not venture to pass through their territory and actually pays toll to some of them in order to be allowed along their frontiers without being molested on his way from Fez to Morocco [*sic*]. [Gavin Maxwell confirmed this fact for me in his monumental book *Lords of the Atlas.*]

Mackey went on:

> But to speakers of Irish the most interesting fact connected with the Berber tribes is that they speak a language called Shloh or Shluh, which a Irish-speaking medical missionary, who had travelled amongst them in the Atlas mountains and Sus country, told me he at once recognized as Celtic. Although he had no previous knowledge of it and had no conception of its being allied to Irish, he found himself able to understand much of what was being said the first time he went among the tribes solely on account of the resemblance of their language to his own Irish.

The best known have names that closely resemble the clan names of MacTier, MacDougall and MacGhill, namely the famous Berber clans of the M'Tir, the M'Tuga and the M'Ghill, to give them their Arabic spelling. The Arabs speak of them as the Bini M'Tir, but the Bini, which is Arabic for children, is a reduplication of the Shloh or Irish 'M' or 'Mac', having the same meaning.

Dr Mackey added that the Berbers were widely distributed and were essentially mountaineers, the main reason they were able to maintain their independence. He also claimed that the facial type of the Berbers was said to resemble the 'black celt of Scotland', unmixed with Scandinavian stock. 'It did not appear', he said, 'that they had any literature but they had bagpipes.' I have met Breton musicians who are convinced that the Kabyle music of Algeria is identical to their own and they all use bagpipes, the national instrument of Scotland. The Irish, too, have their own bagpipes called the uilleann pipes.

Although respectable scholarship regularly assigns such articles to what they call the 'lunatic fringe' of academe, it is extraordinary how persistent are the attempts to explain what standard scholarship cannot; in this case, certain unusual aspects of both North Africa and the British Isles. The 'Celtic' categorization might be irritating, but at least it admitted affinity between the two areas.

Down the years numerous references similar to the above have been published. In the *Dublin Penny Journal* of 1834 the following appeared:

> About the close of the last century, a gentleman who was superintending the digging out of potatoes in the county of Antrim [Northern Ireland], was surprised to see some sailors who had entered the field in conversation with his labourers, who only spoke Irish. He went to them and learned that the sailors were from Tunis and that the vessel to which they belonged had put into port from stress of weather. The sailors and country people understood each other, the former speaking the language used at Tunis, and the latter speaking Irish. This anecdote was related by a person of credit and must interest the Irish scholar.

This episode would have occurred when the Barbary corsairs were still active, so the presence of a ship from Tunis is quite credible. A.J.S. Buckingham, a member of the Syro-Egyptian Society, meeting in the London Athenaeum in 1845, reported another incident. He declared that a few years previously, in Dorchester, he had met 'a native of Morocco, whose name was Saadi Ombeck Benbei'. The merchant stated that he had visited Ireland and stayed at Kilkenny where

> he went one day to the post office and hearing there for the first time some of the labouring people speaking Irish, he was surprised to find he could understand their conversation; as the language had a strong resemblance to the dialect of the mountaineers of Mount Atlas, in Africa, among whom he had travelled and traded in his youth and learned their language. He addressed the labourers in this language and their surprise was as great as his own to find they understood him. The dialogue was very short and on ordinary topics; but he declared there was not any difficulty in under-standing each other.

Mr Buckingham went on to talk about a woman who had originally come from the west of Ireland, spoke Irish fluently and married the consul of a port in Morocco – which Buckingham thought was near Mogador – and that 'she was surprised to find herself able to converse with the mountaineers of the country who brought in the poultry, vegetables and fruit to the market for sale'.

Independent references corroborate these incidents. One came from a Lieutenant-Colonel Chesney's account of his *Expedition to the Euphrates and Tigris*, published in 1850. Another source was Edward Clibborn, curator of the Royal Irish Academy in 1859, who was not entirely dismissive when he recounted the stories, even quoting Eugene O'Curry: 'He would not be at all astonished to learn that the Irish language was still in existence in Northern Africa.' However, O'Curry attributed the possibility to the number of Irish captives brought there by the Barbary corsairs.

Sophisticated modern scholars dismiss these accounts as fanciful. I find it curious that the same disbelief is not accorded the fifth-century claim, attributed to St Jerome, that the language of the Galateans, in what is now Turkey, was the same as that of the Trevian 'Celts' in what is now France!

Edward Clibborn mentioned the discovery of the wreck of a very ancient ship on the coast of Wexford, containing two chambered cannons

Berber musicians and dancers with 'bindirs', Morocco

made of bars of hooped iron (and said to be exactly of the same manufacture as that of guns fished up in the harbour of Constantinople, and the same as old pieces of ordnance found on the walls of Canton). This tends to raise the possibility that African pirates and/or traders visited the coast as early as the reign of Edward III and possibly before the time of the Danes, whose visits to the Mediterranean may possibly have been intended to keep in check the corsairs, and cover their own piracies in the open seas.

A staff member of the National Museum in Dublin described Clibborn as a very unreliable and unmethodical observer. Further, he said, cannons made of bars of iron were a very common medieval form of construction. Clibborn was actually fairly sceptical of the Irish in North Africa theory. Nevertheless, he wrote:

> I confess I think there must be some truth at the bottom of the old tradition which brings the 'Milesian' population of Ireland from Getulia in Northern Africa notwithstanding that ethnologists claim the language of Ireland as belonging to the Japhetic class of languages. But if Japhetic, its elementary sounds appear to be

more African than European, for an educated African can read Irish manuscript with perfect accuracy as to the sounds of the letters; and thus a good ear, listening to people speaking rapidly both Irish and Arabic, or that had heard one language here and the other in Morocco, being ignorant of both, might readily assume the languages to be identical, the radical sounds being the same.

The man who compiled a number of these stories and opinions in the last century was Robert MacAdam. He seemed to take seriously the old legends of Irish origins too, and summarized his researches thus:

> The old and circumstantial account of a colony established in Ireland from Spain takes us a long way on the Road to North Africa; and if true would render it very possible that the colonists or their ancestors came previously from that country to Spain. In such case it would not be at all impossible that some tribe of the same race may have remained and settled in the present Morocco or Tunis and have been eventually driven to the mountains at the time of the destruction of Carthage or subsequently by the overwhelming pressure of the Moors. Speculation, however, is useless until we obtain more definite information regarding the supposed cognate language existing in that country; and the object of the present article is merely to place the preceding facts together on record and to direct the attention of competent inquirers to a curious subject.

This 'curious subject' would continue to occupy me for years.

Deconstructing the Celtic Myth   8

I MUST ADMIT TO THE HALF HOPE that when I, an Irish speaker, eventually met Moroccan Berbers I might hear some familiar sounds. The hope was ill founded; the tumult of voices in the marketplace in Rabat was to me a chaotic babble. I began to suspect that the study of comparative languages would reveal only, as Simon James so cuttingly described it, 'an expanding universe of mutual unintelligibility'.

Scholarly opinion is probably correct to dismiss antiquarian reports that Irish speakers could converse with Berbers: certainly I found that the late Professor Heinrich Wagner, a linguistic expert originally from Switzerland, was right when he gently warned me that it was 'very unlikely' that I might understand Berber. However, the professor represented a school of linguistics that maintained quite logically that underneath Irish, Welsh and the other so-called 'Insular Celtic' languages, exercising a formative influence on them and still clearly detectable, there lay another language or languages. The disagreements arose when Wagner identified those formative languages as Hamito-Semitic, that is, of the Middle East and North Africa.

The model of one language replacing another and retaining traces of the first is fairly straightforward. English, itself a Germanic language, is

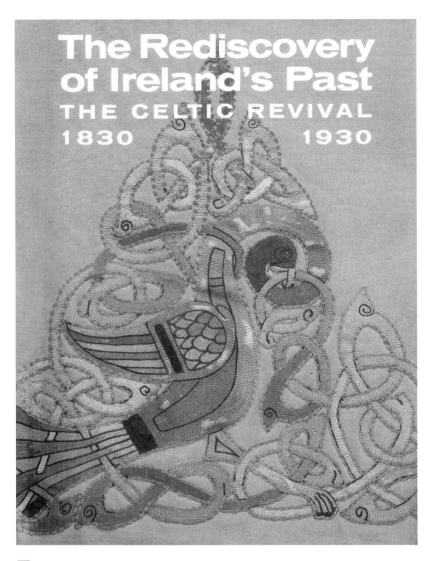

⊠ *The Celtic Revival (jacket design of* The Rediscovery of Ireland's Past: The Celtic Revival 1830–1930 *by Jeanne Sheehy, 1980)*

now the principal language of Ireland, having dramatically replaced Irish over the past two centuries. Conamara is one of the few places left where most residents conduct their business in Irish. But in the parlance of the majority of English speakers on the island, the remnants of Irish syntax – the sentence structure – still resonate clearly. When you hear an Irish person saying, 'I'm after being in hospital,' it is not an indication of quaint thought processes but a direct translation from the Irish: 'Tá mé thaéis bheith insan ospidéal.' It is called Hiberno-English. The syntax of Irish still survives in the speech of many Irish people despite years of English-language schooling and, more recently, exposure to American cinema and television.

This half-life of the Irish language among the monoglot Irish can be described as a linguistic substratum. Just as the English spoken in Ireland has an Irish substratum, it follows that Irish itself, hitherto believed to have spread over the island 2500 years ago, must equally have been influenced by whatever language or languages were *in situ* for the previous millennia. In relative terms, Irish appears to be a recent blow-in too. But not only is it the third oldest language with a literature in Europe, it was claimed by Professor Wagner and his predecessors to have distinct affinities with Berber, Egyptian, Arabic and Hebrew.

This area of linguistic research was initiated as far back as 1899 by Welsh scholar Morris Jones in an article in *The Welsh People*. The idea was further developed by Julius Pokorny, who listed sixty-four Hamito-Semitic features in Irish. Pokorny in turn taught Heinrich Wagner, who came to Ireland in 1946 from Switzerland where, along with Irish, he had studied Arabic and Hebrew. The first thing he did was look up Morris Jones' article in the library of the Dublin Institute for Advanced Studies. To his surprise, he told me, he found that the pages of the book were uncut, which meant that nobody had read the article. David Greene, another eminent scholar, told him that students were discouraged from reading it on the grounds that it was irrelevant and slightly mad. As Wagner pointed out to me, Sir Morris Jones was one of the most respected Welsh scholars. The professor wickedly surmised that the reason for ignoring Jones' findings was that such ideas did not suit the cultural and political ethos that prevailed in revivalist Ireland during the early years of the twentieth century. The professor himself was the target of scholarly sniggering at his own attempts to throw light on Irish. A Harvard contemporary of his, Calvert Watkins, wrote:

> Without sure knowledge of the presence of such substrate populations, and without any notion of the nature of the languages they might have spoken, such a line of speculation is otiose: it is merely a displacement of the problem, a substitution of one unknown for another.

The fact is that, when dealing with languages spoken thousands of years ago, practically nothing is known with certainty. All is reconstruction; the very existence of 'Celtic' or 'Indo-European' as continental languages cannot be proven, only deduced from comparative studies, Pokorny-like, i.e. its roots 'reconstructed' from existing languages. It is, as Greene wrote, 'as if all the records of Latin had been wiped out and we set out to reconstruct it from the speech of French, Italians, Spaniards and Rumanians of today'.

This area – linguistic analysis – was the most difficult and tortuous I had yet encountered. The term 'Indo-European' is simply a description of the assumed earliest recognizable stage in the development of one group of the languages of the world. It does not, contrary to popular belief and ill-informed usage, refer to a race of people. David Greene summed it up well: 'To say that the Greeks or Hindus were Indo-Europeans is like saying that the French or Rumanians are ancient Romans; their languages may be lineal descendants of that of the ancient Romans, but that is a different matter.' The term 'Celtic' is as arbitrary as 'Indo-European'. Neither term has any racial significance and, ideally, neither should be used to describe a particular ethnicity. But increasingly and brazenly they are thus misused.

Wagner described his opponents as 'neo-grammarians' and 'structuralists'. The latter held the view that language developed according to the workings of mechanical and psychological laws, known as the 'sound laws' and the 'laws of analogy'. They tended to overlook the influence of social dynamics or history on the development of language. This suggested to me that if people develop their language 'mechanically', they do it without reference to their neighbours. The ultimate logic of this would be a baby learning to talk without listening to its parents.

Most traditional experts would confine examination of matters 'Celtic' to Europe and eastern points, and would rely on a postulated movement of such a language from central Europe out to the fringes – a parallel to what Dr Joseph Raftery, late Director of the National Museum, dismissed as 'The Thomas Cook school of archaeology'. This school would admit links with Sanskrit (thanks to a Welsh judge called William Jones, who in 1786 proposed that Greek and Sanskrit were related) and, in particular, Hittite, the oldest attested Indo-European language, located in Asia Minor and Syria. But extend the area of study in a southerly direction – to the Middle East proper and to North Africa – and the orthodox shutters come down.

▨ THE ATLANTEAN IRISH

For instance, Professor Wagner told me that ten years after Morris Jones published his ideas, two other major works appeared: a comparative Celtic grammar by Holger Pedersen (pupil of Karl Brugmann, philologist and father of neo-grammarianism), and an Old Irish grammar by Rudolf Thureysen. Both works ignored Morris Jones' findings. As Wagner put it:

> Whenever it can be proved by scholars who do not adhere to the teaching of any rigid school, that a dying language has influenced considerably the growth and development of the language by which it is superseded, the neo-grammarians use the term sub-stratum 'theory', as if the recognition of sub-stratum influence were based on 'theory' alone and not on observations in the field.

Wagner had travelled and worked in Ireland, Wales and the Isle of Man, Brittany, Lapland, Finland and the Basque country, learning the languages and studying them in detail. His linguistic atlas of Ireland is a standard work. 'We are here', he said, 'dealing with a sociolinguistic fact of the highest historical importance.' Essentially, what he was stating was that if in the 'British' Isles, at some dim and distant time, a language loosely called 'Celtic' had been imposed on a people who were 'non-Celtic', then the indigenous inhabitants must have spoken a language or languages unknown and that this must have strongly influenced the development of the new language. The interesting implication is that Irish (and English indirectly) must also retain some syntactical elements of a 'pre-Celtic' language that some reputable scholars now suggest emanated from North Africa. The basic fact behind Wagner's insight was that many features of this alleged new 'Insular-Celtic' language have no parallels in other 'Indo-European' languages. In other words, there were aspects of the evolved Irish that were not paralleled in any other 'Indo-European' tongue.

Further, by using a kind of linguistic archaeology, Professor Wagner had delved through the intervening layers and confirmed that there were grammatical features in 'Insular Celtic' that had affinities with, for instance, Egyptian – the language of the Copts – as well as Berber and Hebrew. These oddities, which appeared consistently in Irish, included the position of the verb at the beginning of the sentence – a feature that is not typical of Indo-European and modern European languages.

According to Wagner, there was a further similarity with Berber in that it 'suffixes or infixes pronominal objects' in a way that is, in principle, identical to the rules governing the use of the old Irish verb.

Several years ago Dr E. Ben Rochd, Professor at Oujda University, Morocco, became familiar with my research and made personal contact, visiting me and also offering hospitality when I was in Morocco. Dr Ben Rochd is professor of linguistics and author of books and articles in this area. Naturally he specializes in Arabic (his first language) and Berber, although he was actually awarded his doctorate by the National University of Ireland. Long ago I brought Professor Wagner's findings to his attention and he enthusiastically supported them, as well as encouraging my own research into related areas and providing a specialist sounding board.

However, Professor Wagner maintained that the language that, he suggested, must have existed in Ireland before Irish, also shared some affinities with Basque, which it is difficult to place in the Indo-European context. Although many scholars contend that Basque is loosely related to Caucasian languages, nobody could explain the existence of this people or how they arrived at the Pyrenees. It was suggested that the Picts of Scotland also spoke a non-Indo-European language. When Irish-speaking missionaries of the early Middle Ages went to convert them, they had to use interpreters. It is also on record that Cormac, an Irish king of the ninth century, described the language of the people of Munster, in the south-west of Ireland, as the 'iron language', presumably because to the king, an Irish speaker, it was impermeable. I myself speak Conamara Irish and have great difficulty understanding the Donegal version.

This of course does not help my tentative suggestion that several quite different languages may have combined to ultimately produce Scots Gallic and Irish, Welsh, Breton, Manx and Cornish. A thousand years hence, scholars may be trying to separate the 125 languages that are presently spoken on the island of Manhattan to try to detail their contribution to whatever will be the lingua franca then.

English has evolved as a compound of Germanic (Anglo-Saxon), Greek, Latin, Norman French, etc. Nowadays some scholars – such as Theo Vennemann of the University of Munich – argue that even Insular Celtic has had a profound structural influence on English. Vennemann has little doubt that the early settlers in Ireland were from North Africa! He also says: 'In my view the case is closed, the thesis of a Hamito-Semitic substratum underlying Insular Celtic being one of the most reliably established pieces of scientific knowledge there is in any empirical discipline.'

Most scholars would agree that the terms 'Celtic' and 'Indo-European' are categories of linguistic convenience and possess no racial connotations. Yet, these terms are still used as descriptions of actual races of peoples. Thousands of books and learned papers – as well as an increasing number of glossy coffee-table tomes and tourist brochures – have been written about the 'Celts'. Most admit, initially, that the term should not be used in any racial sense; all proceed to do precisely this.

How has this terminological abuse survived so long? Herodotus contains the first recorded use of the term. He made a casual reference to people living on the Danube. The Greeks followed suit with the term 'Keltoi' and added the term 'Galatae'. The Romans then continued the process and defined the Gauls. These terms were used with considerable looseness and there is no evidence to suggest that any of these peoples described themselves as 'Celts'. A writer named Posidonius seems to have been the first to popularize the term 'Keltoi'. He thought Europeans were divided equally into two general categories: Scythians and Keltoi. He did not, apparently, allow for the fact that northern Europeans must have been divided into many different tribes and peoples and languages – just as they are today. In fact, we only know Posidonius' opinions through second-hand quotations from Cicero, Livy, Marcellinus, Virgil, Lucan and Italicus. They all got their information from this one writer, and his words exist only in their quotations.

But the man who removed the lid from this Pandora's box was, as noted earlier, a Welsh polymath named Edward Lhuyd who headed the Ashmolean Museum in Oxford at the beginning of the eighteenth century, the same man who in 1699 was the first antiquarian to visit and describe Newgrange. In 1707 he claimed that the above-mentioned fringe peoples spoke languages directly related to that of the resurrected 'Celts' of continental Europe and therefore should also be called 'Celtic'. It is, however, important to remember that Lhuyd was not silly enough to attribute a racial connotation to his findings, although it may have been implied.

The more I investigated the 'Celtic' world, the less it became a reliable means of identifying the Irish, Welsh, Scottish, etc. The whole intellectual construct resembled a house of cards. There is little evidence that would justify speaking of Celtic art – or even Celtic literature – so why a Celtic language? Desmond Fennell has put it well: 'I think we should leave this usage of "Celtic" to foreigners; partly because the description of Irish mental processes as "Celtic" has been an instrument of colonization.'

Even that gentle friend of the Blasket Islanders, Robin Flower, indignantly wrote:

> Another and more insidious enemy of our subject is the popular
> and general use of the word 'Celtic' in literary criticism. Irish literature may be properly described as 'Celtic', if we are to understand by that simply that it is the product of a people speaking
> a Celtic language. But the word is commonly taken to mean
> much more than that ... vagueness and mist and an indefinite use
> of dubiously poetic language has been generally held to be the
> indubitable mark of Celticism.

In 1923 the mist lifted from D.H. Lawrence's eyes on a visit to Sardinia: 'Strange is a Celtic landscape, far more moving, disturbing, than the lovely glamour of Italy and Greece ... But perhaps it is not Celtic at all: Iberian. Nothing is more unsatisfactory than our conception of what is Celtic and what is not Celtic. I believe there were never any Celts, as a race – as for the Iberians –!'

In Ireland, the entire 'Celtic' thesis rests on the belief that in approximately 500 BC, the island was invaded by a continental people who gave the people their language and culture. Dr Michael Ryan, then Keeper of Irish Antiquities in the National Museum of Ireland once said to me that the material evidence for such a 'Celtic invasion' was slight. He added that the invasion thesis could, in the main, be regarded as 'wishful thinking'. Before he died, Dr Joseph Raftery – also of that museum – told me he was not at all convinced by what he described as 'this loose talk' of Celtic invasions. The latter's archaeologist son, Barry Raftery, has written: 'The basic ethnic stability of Ireland during most of the last millennium BC cannot have been greatly disrupted.' Yet, still, writers about Ireland churn out coffee-table books – many published in London – with the C-word in the title.

One of the few realities to which I could cling in all the vagueness is the language called Irish, which my neighbours in Conamara happily still speak, and which must have evolved from settlers who arrived, by sea, at some date within the last ten thousand years, that is after the ice melted.

Even supposing there was a late incursion of an overwhelming linguistic group with a single language called Celtic, it was most probably tightly knit and numerically small. Let us further suppose that by virtue of their technological superiority they cut through the territories of some of the indigenous people on the island. The Angles and Saxons did this in Britain; the Anglo-Normans in the twelfth century are reputed to have had only 600 well-armed knights when they took over Ireland. However, the latter did not materially change the linguistic complexion of this island; in fact, the Normans ended up speaking Irish rather than the natives picking up court French.

One of the ironies of the analogous 'Celtic invasion' theory is that much of the evidence, at least of the literary kind, is found in Northern Ireland – a part of Ireland whose later ruling ideology liked to distance itself from things Gaelic, proudly declaiming its 'Britishness'. Nevertheless, in the huge body of Irish mythology, pride of place is taken by what is called the *Ulster Cycle*, a series of epics that feature quarrels between Connacht and Ulster – between Queen Maeve and a warrior, Setanta, later known as Cú Chulainn.

It is recorded in this epic that when Queen Maeve moved to attack Ulster she stood looking across the river Blackwater at 'an tír aneol' – the strange land. This perceived difference between southern and northern Ireland is one of the longest-running debates in Irish history. It was even believed to have a geological basis in that a line of drumlins, called the Black Pig's Dyke, seems to run like a barrier from Sligo to Carlingford Lough. A distinguished professor of Old Irish, P.L. Henry, commented on this division as 'one of the most deeply rooted, ancient and – from a literary point of view – most productive facts of early history'. However, quite recent aerial research by the Sites and Monuments Record Office has revealed similar linear earthworks in many other counties. The Black Pig's Dyke may yet prove to have been another useful myth.

When I consulted Professor Henry, he complicated things a little further for me. He suggested that the southern Irish were in a category called Q-Celts, from France, whereas the northern Irish, who originated in Wales, were P-Celts and ultimately came from Iberia, i.e. Celt-Iberians. I was then brought full circle by Heinrich Wagner saying that the Iberian element of this relationship probably spoke a Hamitic, that is, a Berber language.

The so-called 'Celtic' languages survive in oral form only on the western seaboard of Europe. The idea that they came from the Continent is based on continental place-names and inscriptions recorded in Greek and Latin alphabets. No spoken Celtic language survives on the continental interior.

Therefore, as they are still relying exclusively on the written word, I conclude that scholars are perpetuating the obsolete neo-grammarian approach to the problem of 'Insular Celtic' languages.

However, in material matters, the position is reversed. In continental Europe there is much physical evidence to suggest technologically well-developed peoples who had a mastery of bronze and iron-working. But artefacts of identical design in Ireland are sparse. In fact, I am assured, such artefacts as have been found on this island suggest more a continuity of design in Ireland than a sudden, dramatic change in the material culture. So it is really only on a linguistic basis that a culture-changing migration from continental Europe is postulated, and a 'Celtic' identity attributed. In other words, it is a Cheshire-cat conundrum: though there is no longer any physical evidence of the existence of the cat, its linguistic smile persists.

At this point in my conjectures, nearly twenty years ago, I had an insight. Was it not possible that the seafaring peoples of the western coasts of Europe had in fact adopted quite an autonomous language and culture with little reference to some imaginary central European race called 'Celts'? Was it not possible that the language spoken in these coastal areas – the so-called 'Insular Celtic' – was simply the evolved language of those areas that had acquired a veneer of central European characteristics and which we now call 'Irish' or 'Welsh' and so forth? After all, if the 'Celts' were such a mighty culture in Europe, was it likely the Romans would have erased all spoken trace of them? Eight hundred years after the Anglo-Norman invasion of Ireland, 300 years after the Tudor invasion, Irish is still spoken in Ireland. Were the Romans so much more efficient as to be able to wipe out completely the 'Celtic' languages in Europe?

What I was suggesting was not that Irish was suspect, but that it was older than any alleged invasion by 'Celts' from Europe and was an autonomous and organic development of Ireland and the Atlantic coasts (including Morocco), perhaps an amalgam of many tongues and many migrating peoples over perhaps 9000 years.

Sixteen years on I came across the following, written by Barry Cunliffe in 2001 in his book *Facing the Sea*:

> It is not unreasonable, therefore, to conclude that 'Celtic', as defined by Lhuyd, was the lingua franca of the Atlantic community. It could further be argued that the *language had developed gradually over*

the four millennia that maritime contacts had been maintained, perhaps reaching its distinctive form in the Late Bronze Age when communication along the sea lanes was at its most intense, and when many aspects of the elite system, technology and beliefs had coalesced to create a broadly similar cultural continuum. [my emphasis]

This was the first time I had encountered any respected historian or archaeologist admitting the possibility that the Irish language spoken by my neighbours in Conamara was not the detritus of a single invasion from continental Europe, but an autonomous language of the Atlantic seaways. Cunliffe's courageous conclusion – the seeds of which I detected underneath the conventional approach in his 1997 book *The Celts* – flies in the face of the scholarly unanimity of the 300 years since Edward Lhuyd first used the linguistic category 'Celtic'.

When I congratulated Dr Cunliffe on his perspective, he responded with refreshing frankness: 'Archaeology,' he responded, 'like most subjects, gets stuck in ruts and it is good to jolt ourselves out of them from time to time.' He also agreed with my suggestion that his years of practical fieldwork on the coasts of England and Brittany had finally forced him to this maritime-based perspective and that I 'had charted his conversion precisely'. I have since learned that in 1987 another respected archaeologist, Colin Renfrew, developed a similar perspective on Irish and Welsh: '… the origins of Celtic tongues are not to be found in the Iron age but six thousand years ago with the first farmers'.

Why not boldly state that Irish itself has its roots in 'pre-Celtic' languages and is an autonomous development of the Atlantic coastal dwellers – as Barry Cunliffe and Glyn Daniel mooted – and let others disprove the thesis, rather than constantly try to cram the language into a respectable European mould? Heinrich Wagner would, with scholarly reservations, have cheered this approach. However, although a few scholars support the Wagner, Pokorny and Jones thesis, they still insist there was a Celtic invasion of Ireland that imposed on its inhabitants a fully formed 'Celtic' language. They may disagree with the methodology used by Wagner, Pokorny and company but they come to the same logical conclusion, that beneath the so-called 'Insular-Celtic' languages lie much older tongues, the same Hamito- Semitic forms. At least two of these Wagner successors, Vennemann and Gensler, believe that the 'pre-Celtic' language of Ireland came from North Africa.

Such a fully formed North African language had to come with people who, millennia later, would have absorbed aspects of the language of the new 'Celtic' invaders but who equally retained the structures of their own tongue. Linguistic opinion is that there was no intermediate lingua franca that could have evolved into such a complex language such as Irish. From my point of view it is enough that reputable scholars should identify the language and people that preceded 'Celtic' as coming from North Africa. This would certainly account for the extraordinary differences in syntax between Irish, Breton, Welsh, etc., and every other European languages.

While within Ireland it is archaeologically difficult to support the idea of a 'Celtic imposition' scenario, the linguists' analysis leans precisely on such an imposition. In 1991 an enormous exhibition in Venice celebrated the achievements of *The Celts*. I acquired the magnificent, and bulky, catalogue of this exhibition in which were published commentaries by the most prominent scholars in this field. Allowing for the highly conscientious work that went into all the essays, there were some that used essentially circular arguments to validate the category 'Celtic'. One illustration shows 'two faces of a travertine marble stele with bilingual inscriptions in Celtic and Latin'. But both inscriptions appeared to me to use letters of the Latin and Greek alphabets and I could recognize some Latin words. I wondered how such loose reference to 'Celtic' inscriptions could be justified. The answer

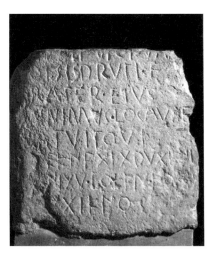

▨ *Travertine Marble Stele, second century* BC, *Gregoriano Museum, Rome (from exhibition catalogue* The Celts [I Celti] *co-ordinated by Sabatino Moscati, 1991)*

▨ THE ATLANTEAN IRISH

the author gave was that 'an a priori Celticity ... *as is logically necessary,* need not be proved'.

In other words, everybody is agreed — based largely on the arguments of Posidonius and Edward Lhuyd — that a linguistically identifiable people now called 'Celts' existed in Europe so there is no need to prove it. They are a given. It seemed to me to be a theological way of going about things: God exists. We cannot dispute that. Therefore let us detect and present evidence for his existence.

On *both* faces of the above marble stele I could clearly see inscribed the words *frater* and *eius,* which my schooldays' memory tells me are incontrovertibly Latin. My impression was confirmed by another essayist in *The Celts,* who declared that the 'Celts' simply adapted the written languages of the people they had contact with, 'all of which were to a greater or lesser extent derived from Phoenician'!

I was left with the feeling that this exhibition and its catalogue were weakened by reliance on a scholarly convention that was at least debatable, yet quite acceptable to and consequently unchallenged by learned minds. At worst, it seemed to me, it was simply an EU public relations exercise to show that all of these early peoples were one homogeneous culture a few thousand years ago and that therefore the modern thrust towards a single European entity, a Euro-people, was a natural organic evolution.

The Aran Islands are the inhabited rocks off the west coast of Ireland immortalized in the writings of John Millington Synge, in the film *Man of Aran* by Robert O'Flaherty, and in the paintings of numerous artists. The islands are within a few kilometres of Conamara and are also Irish speaking. Indeed, because of their extreme westerly position they are considered to be the last outpost of 'Celticism' by those subscribers to the aforementioned Thomas Cook school. If the Celtic invasion theory were true, then these isolated and thus relatively 'unspoilt' islanders should retain biological traces of the invaders.

Unfortunately for this romantic idea, the evidence does not bear it out. The relative blood groupings of the people of Aran are quite different not only from that which is deemed to be 'Celtic', but from the bulk of the population of Ireland. The most fundamental badge of alleged 'racial' origin is, here, not apparent. The anomaly can be explained by invasion, certainly; but it is a little more prosaic than the 'Celtic' scenario. In the seventeenth century the western armies of Cromwell were garrisoned on the largest of the three islands. It appears these soldiers were almost forgotten and, as soldiers will, they stayed long enough to make a considerable impact on the bloodlines of the islanders. When they went AWOL to the mainland they also left their names. In Conamara there is a wide sprinkling of the names Wyndham, Grealish, Griffith, Welsh, Cook, Davy, Bolustrum. In passing – and in line with my general maritime orientation – it is worth noting that Cromwell chose an island to control the western areas; not for him a mainland stronghold, the various danger points were more accessible by sea.

It is surprising how pervasive the Celtic myth still is, when so many Irish scholars are quite sceptical of it. The myth certainly suited the politicians of the nineteenth and twentieth centuries, and provided rich material for Anglo-Irish poets. It was a means of defining – and ultimately defusing – a national identity. It must have seemed a marvellous way of persuading a battered and demoralized people that they had pedigree and potential enough to confront the British Empire. That the tactic partially worked is perhaps sufficient justification. There is little as powerful as an idea whose time has come. But by the same token there is little as embarrassing as an obsolete idea that lingers on. As Brian Friel so beautifully expressed it in his play *Translations*: 'a civilization can be imprisoned in a linguistic contour which no longer matches the landscape … of fact'.

While there is some pragmatic justification for political laws to preserve the Celtic scenario, when scholars support it, however sceptically or even inadvertently, there is cause for concern. In 1981 a huge tome was published in Canada under the title *The Celtic Consciousness*, edited by Robert O'Driscoll. The object, ironically, was to provide a link and common background for French- and English-speaking Canadians. In fairness, the scholars who are sceptical about 'Celticism' but who, nevertheless, contributed to the book, were not responsible for the title. An indication of the book's daring scope was the fact that one long article detailed the prehistoric passage tombs, such as Brú na Bóinne, of the Atlantic regions – a phenomenon that pre-dated even the alleged arrival of 'Celts' by over two thousand years!

One could not, however, quarrel with the standard of most of the scholarship within the book itself. An article by folklorist Kevin Danaher undermined a 'Celtic' basis for Irish folk tradition and culture. He pointed out that the traditional four-season year in Ireland was based entirely on solar reckoning, that in this tradition there was no time-reckoning by the moon and that the predominant element in Irish mythology was the sun. However, the Coligny calendar found in France, now resting in the Gallo-Roman museum in Lyons and attributed to the 'Celts', is lunar-based. Professor Danaher concluded that, in a number of important respects, the Irish tradition was not 'Celtic'. He went on to say: 'We cannot necessarily assume that because something is early Irish it is therefore Celtic'; and, 'We might even go further and ask if we are not straining the bounds of scientific credibility by claiming that the Irish are a Celtic people.' Other writers in *The Celtic Consciousness* echo this point.

It might be considered Celtic cussedness to read, in a book so titled, that the Irish are not Celtic at all. But the demythologizing must start somewhere. It will be a long hard slog, because the myth and the appellation are all-pervasive. I even found a casual example in my old friend John Arden's book, *Silence Among the Weapons*. In it a secondary character named Horsefury is described as a Celt. When he speaks there emerges an accent and syntax that are unmistakably from the West of Ireland. The device is artistically clever and quite supportable. However, it is based on a classical understanding of 'Celticism' that I hope I have undermined. Arden is in respectable company, as Sir Walter Scott applied the term 'Celt' indiscriminately in his fiction.

On 5 May 1984 the Irish Association of Professional Archaeologists held a seminar on the problem of the earliest appearance of Irish-speaking 'Celts' in Ireland. The moderator, J.P. Mallory, had a sense of humour, as his summary of the discussions evidences:

> Object: To discuss the problem of the earliest appearance of Irish-speaking Celts in Ireland.
>
> Basic Premise: To translate an essentially linguistic definition of the problem into cultural-historical terms.
>
> Conclusion: The seminar was unsuccessful at producing an agreed solution to the problem of Irish origins ...
>
> Moderator, J.P. Mallory: 'Through several hours of often heated (sometimes quasi-homicidal) discussion there were occasional moments when the moderator could detect what might pass for consensus among Irish archaeologists, i.e. the absence of violent objection. Although no fully satisfactory solution to the problem could be found, the moderator of the seminar was invited to

acquaint readers with the discussions in a format designed to stim-
ulate further research and comment in the pages of this journal.

If there is uncertainty about the implications of 'Celticism' for the Irish, the same vagueness must apply to the Scots, Welsh, Manx, Bretons, Cornish and Galicians. So what are, who are, these people? If Liam de Paor was correct in describing the so-called 'Celtic' attributes as romantic inventions of the nineteenth century, what are the links that undoubtedly bind these people into some kind of felt affinity?

The peoples of the Atlantic seaways are actually more isolated now by modern communication systems. To visit each other they must travel by secondary overland routes, or via major capital city airports; few travel any-where distant by sea. Yet these areas still form what has already been described as a cultural archipelago, having more in common with each other than with the overcentralized powers that control them – and whose diarists have written their history.

It is difficult and unwieldy to describe these people, their culture and language, without falling back on the vague, if convenient, title of 'Celts'. That is why I have opted for the term 'Atlantean'. At least it has some real-istic maritime connotation, and it suggests a less jaded perspective from which to examine the subject. Logically, though, if the essence of this per-spective is sea-based, then one must extend the catchment area farther north to Iceland and western Scandinavia – areas that have admitted links with Ireland. But – and this is the hard part – it must also be extended southwards, to those other people bordered by the Atlantic, the Moroccan Berbers and Arabs.

Perhaps to add to the 'Celtic' confusion the reader may inspect a physical manifestation of an actual *celt* as discussed by the members of the Royal Irish Academy in 1844. Robert Ball, Esq., 'read a notice of the Means used by the ancients for attaching Handles to the Stone and Metal Implements called *celts* '. Two simple axes were produced. One was described as a stone *celt* from a mine in Mexico; a Captain Adams of the Royal Navy had brought the other, made from iron, from 'Little Fish Bay, Africa'.

In the preface I referred to work by a team of geneticists from Trinity College Dublin, working with colleagues in the universities of Leeds and Cambridge. Their work concerns an intriguing genetic element called mitochondrial DNA, or mtDNA. Scientists have described this form of DNA

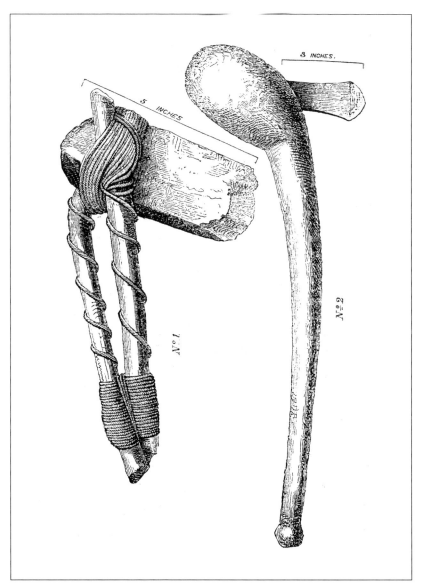

⊠ *Stone 'celts' (drawing by Robert Ball from* Proceedings of the Royal Irish Academy, *no. 43, 8 January 1844)*

as 'the prime molecular interpreter of the human past'. It is transmitted down the generations exclusively through the matriarchal line. In October 2004 they published their findings in the *American Journal of Human Genetics,* of which the following is an abstract:

Celtic languages are now spoken only on the Atlantic facade of Europe, mainly in Britain and Ireland, but were spoken more widely in western and central Europe until the collapse of the Roman Empire in the first millennium AD. It has been common to couple archaeological evidence for the expansion of Iron Age elites in central Europe with the dispersal of these languages and of Celtic ethnicity and to posit a central European 'homeland' for the Celtic peoples. More recently, however, archaeologists have questioned this 'migrationist' view of Celtic ethnogenesis. The proposition of a central European ancestry should be testable by examining the distribution of genetic markers; however, although Y-chromosome patterns in Atlantic Europe show little evidence of central European influence, there has hitherto been insufficient data to confirm this by use of mitochondrial DNA (mtDNA). Here, we present both new mtDNA data from Ireland and a novel analysis of a greatly enlarged European mtDNA database. We show that mtDNA lineages, when analyzed in sufficiently large numbers, display patterns significantly similar to a large fraction of both Y-chromosome and autosomal variation. *These multiple genetic marker systems indicate a shared ancestry throughout the Atlantic zone, from northern Iberia to western Scandinavia, that dates back to the end of the last Ice Age.* [my italics]

Pre-Celtic Place-Names 9

ONE SPRING DAY IN 1991 I was investigating a recently uncovered site at Dog's Bay, Roundstone, a pretty village west of my home along the coast of Conamara.

The storms of February had disturbed the sand dunes to the extent that a very ancient settlement had been exposed. Walls were clearly visible overlooking the strand, plus a huge midden of shells – limpets, sea-snails, periwinkles and others. This physical evidence of their ancestors' diet of millennia ago caused even my youngest children to pause between their tumbles down the sand dunes. For myself, I simply wondered what language these people, our ancestors, had spoken. As we drove home through treeless Conamara I began for the first time to notice the signposted Irish name *Doire*. It means 'oak wood' as in Doire Colmcille, the oak grove of St Columcille, now also known widely as Derry or Londonderry. There is an alternative interpretation of the word *doire*; it is 'a thicket'. But can one seriously imagine one of the more famous Irish saints being commemorated by such an insignificant feature as a thicket? In fact Derry was known as Doire Calgaich until 546 AD, when St Colmcille built a church there.

Many of the places thus named had little vestige of trees, and certainly no mighty oaks. In the western coastal counties of Ireland, where the name proliferates – the greatest incidence is in Co. Cork in the south-west – one sees vast stretches of blanket bog whose horizons are rarely broken by the sight of a tree. According to David Bellamy, the exact equivalent of Irish western lowland bog is found nowhere else in the world. The evidence for one-time arboreal covering is undoubtedly there, but only in the form of huge pine and oak roots. These are buried beneath ancient layers of peat, known as blanket bog, in many places the residue of thousands of years of organic decay. Embedded in these anaerobic layers, often close to the underlying rock itself, is a rich harvest of these petrified tree roots that are locally called *giúsach* or 'bog-deal'; they are even scattered around my own garden. This wood was an important source of fuel, torches and roof beams (as well as the long sharp wood splinters used by salmon poachers) for the ancestors of my neighbours in Conamara. The antiquity of the word *giúsach* is further attested by references in the *Ulster Cycle*. It occurred to me that if a sufficient number of these tree roots had been interred thousands of years ago, and considering that topographical names such as *doire* are the longest-lasting, then the term for an oak wood might be as old as the earliest layers of the blanket bog whose venerable age is readily admitted.

This antiquity was demonstrated to me on a group field-outing led by Dr Michael O'Connell of Galway University, who is satisfied that there were farmers in Conamara as early as 3000 BC. He, a specialist in pollen-dating, pointed to the cross-section of organic layers revealed in one deep bog-cutting and dramatically listed the historical events that might conceivably have corresponded to each layer: at base, the Egyptian pyramids and the building of Newgrange, then the Iron and Bronze ages, the usual 'arrival of the Celts', Caesar crossing the Rubicon and so, fascinatingly, on. As Dr O'Connell breathed life into antiquity, I was reminded of what an exciting pursuit scholarship can be when illuminated by a good teacher. I had a similar epiphany witnessing Dr Pete Coxon of the Irish Quaternary Society identifying interglacial peats in a river bank at Derrynadivva near Castlebar, Co. Mayo. Those were 250,000 years old! He also extracted a core of bog from the bottom of Loch Aisling near Newport, to show us peat that was at least 10,000 years old and marked the rapid melting of the ice that had up to then covered much of Ireland.

The trouble is, if one believes the conventional wisdom regarding the

Giúsach or bog-deal, Conamara

arrival of a 'Celtic' language in approximately 500 BC, the word *doire* could not be more than 2500 years old but, as demonstrated, many of the bogs were much older than that, as the place-names might also be. Desmond Fennell confidently solved the problem by suggesting that *doire* might be 'pre-Celtic', like *Banba* or *Sionna*. This deflated me somewhat, until I became aware of the multitude of Irish words that are conveniently, it seemed to me, demoted to the category 'pre-Celtic'. As Myles Dillon once wrote: 'And in Irish, if we set aside words borrowed from the language of the pre-Celts, *and these may be quite numerous* . . .' [my emphasis]. But he also wrote: 'The Celts found before them in Ireland a non-European people of whose language we know nothing . . . The culture that they practised came to Ireland from the Iberian peninsula.'

The phenomenon of many antique words that do not fit the conventional Celtic wisdom exists in the other 'Celtic' areas too. In Wales there are place-names such as Mynwy, Usk, Eidon, Onneu, Honddu, Senni, Yscir, Sgio – all described as pre-Celtic. In Cornwall there are Tamar, Marazian, Para-Zabulan, Phillack, Menichau, Zepha, Parazeanbeeble, Zannor and Zelah. So many exceptions to the norm of Irish, Welsh and Cornish must at least place a question mark after the term 'pre-Celtic'.

After the trip to Dog's Bay I set out to explore all of the places named *doire* that I could find in Conamara using cartographer Tim Robinson's detailed map of the area. He had listed and mapped approximately twenty-five *doires*.

I eventually added another score to his list, wonderfully graphic names such as *Doire Bhanbh* – the oak grove of the piglet (pigs adore acorns); *Derrynabhreena* – the wood of the queen; *Derrynasligga* – the oak grove of the shell midden. Many took the diminutive, almost affectionate form of *derreen*, 'the little oak wood'.

I hurried into the Galway University library to look up the nationally recorded frequency of the name *doire*. In the 1851 *Townlands Index* there were nineteen pages devoted to the name and variations thereof, including the diminutive *derreen*. Each of the nineteen pages had seventy-two entries. That made 1368 townlands in Ireland named after oak woods! But Co. Galway featured only twelve of the forty-five that I had laboriously inspected in Conamara alone. The rest went unmentioned for the simple reason that they were not 'townlands'. As the name *doire* survived from Antrim in the north-east to Kerry in the south-west, one could therefore reasonably argue that at some stage oak woods proliferated on the island. Nowadays, if you can find even a handful of oak woods you can be sure they were planted within the last couple of hundred years. Not much more than 1 per cent of Ireland's surface now contains broad-leaved trees.

The name may relate to an ancient time when the island was gradually being settled by peoples from all points of the compass. Dr Michael O'Connell has noted that 'woodland prevailed at most sites until the end of the Atlantic period (circa 3000 BC)', but '… woodland had ceased to be the main vegetational element in the landscape by the late bronze age'. The seventeenth-century poet's lament could have been applied thousands of years ago:

> *Cad a dhéanfhaimíd feasta gan adhmaid,*
> *tá deire na gcoillte ar lár*
> *(What shall we henceforth do without wood,*
> *the forests are all gone)*

David Bellamy, among others, held that a climate change towards greater rainfall could have devastated the trees. Allied to this was the early human activity of clearing and burning forests – *landnam* – to make way for live-stock and husbandry. Pollen analysis also suggests a very early incidence of elm disease as being partly responsible. These events can be identified as occurring up to 5000 years ago. The earliest evidence of human intervention

⊠ *Céide Fields Interpretative Centre, Co. Mayo (above); Ancient stone walls in the Céide Fields (left)*

occurs in the Céide Fields in north Mayo, discovered by a school-teacher and lovingly detailed by his son, Professor Séamus Caulfield of University College, Dublin, with Professor Martin Downes of NUI Maynooth. Such activities by well-organized settlers are unlikely to have destroyed all of the woodlands, but would have left groups of trees as distinctive 'features' in the landscape. Distinctive enough, perhaps, to be identified as *doire*, a word I now accepted as 'pre-Celtic'. This would logically mean that the word's root, *dar*, was also pre-Celtic, i.e. 3000 BC! *Darach* means 'abounding in oaks'; *darcain* is an acorn.

The next step was to check the etymology of the word and its root. I first looked at a Sanskrit dictionary. *Darava* means 'made of wood'. *Daru* means a piece of wood. Here was a well-established and non-controversial connection with a pre-Celtic era. Next came a Welsh dictionary: *dar* means, as one would expect from a cousin of Irish, an oak-tree. However, when it came to trawling through German, Polish, Turkish, Basque, Portuguese, Spanish, Dutch, Flemish, Norwegian, Icelandic, Italian, Catalan, Latin, French – every European dictionary I could find – there was no word for oak that was even vaguely similar to *dar* or *doire*. Latin was also a non-starter; however, Pokorny unequivocally specified that the Greek *drus* had an Indo-European root, the single equivalent that, at my first reading, shared only the initial 'd' with my pet word.

I wrote to my friend Dr E. Ben Rochd in Morocco with the request that he use his linguistic skills to search Berber for any equivalent. He replied that the unadorned word *dar* in (Hamitic) Berber merely meant a foot or leg. However, if it was of interest, he wrote, the word means 'elm' and 'ash' in (Semitic) Arabic. This was more than a consolation: traces of elm are also found under the most ancient Irish bogs. The word *dar* in Arabic, I know, also means 'dwelling', as in Dar-es-Salaam. However, in Boston in September 2003 I met an Ethiopian taxi driver and, idly making conversation, I asked him the word for 'oak' in his native language. Without hesitation he said *daro*.

I asked Greek speakers to give me the modern word for 'wood' and they said *ksilo*. I asked them if the word *dar* meant anything to them; the nearest they could come up with was *doro* or *dori*, which means gift. In fact, following Pokorny, reliable scholars are all united in the understanding that Irish *doire* and old Greek *drus* are linguistically inseparable. Hildegard L.C. Tristram wrote to me:

> Irish *doire* and Greek *drus* (and it is Pliny who makes the connection between *drus* and *druids* < *dru-vids*, cf., Irish *fios*, from O Ir *ro-fit-ir*) are of course clearly related etymologically, Greek *deru- os* (Nom Sg) > *drus* with merger of the two syllables and syncope of the first vowel.

That should have put an end to my speculations, but it is hard to stop an amateur scholar with the bit between his teeth. Early Greek is considered by some to be derived from Phoenician, a Semitic language (which may have something to do with Martin Bernal's ideas about the Egyptian origin of Greek civilization).

If it is not yet clear why I am paying so much attention to a single 'pre-Celtic' word, let me quote the following. In a review by Vera Capkova of

J.P. Mallory's *In Search of the Indo-European Languages* I was introduced to Roman Jakobson's insight: 'The archaeologist's data are like a motion picture without the soundtrack; whereas the linguists have the soundtrack without the film. Thus, interdepartmental teamwork becomes indispensable.' As under my other cap I am a film-maker, this makes great sense to me. Silent movies are charming, but synchronous dialogue is an undeniable improvement. This is one reason why the Irish language is so important: it is the principal soundtrack of Irish history. But how ancient? If it could be shown that this language is, at heart, the ultimate and ancient distillation of all the languages and dialects that must have infused the mixed culture of this accessible island and other areas touched by the Atlantic seaways, then the archaeologists would have a unique 'soundtrack' for their inanimate and voiceless images. In the Old Irish *Auraicept na n-Eces* (*The Scholar's Primer*), it is asserted that Irish was created by selecting 'what was best, widest, and finest of every language'. To apply the term 'lingua franca', implying a kind of 'pidgin' patois as distinct from a fully formed language like Irish, may be inappropriate linguistically, but it aids our understanding.

Donncha Ó hÉallaithe has suggested to me that the term 'Old Irish' refers to what I might call 'hoch-Irisch', the standard Irish in which the language was first written down. In the Middle Ages it was the scholarly alternative to Latin, one of the other languages of the Irish literate classes. The ordinary person's speech would have differed from standard written Irish (as it still does today in Conamara) at least as much as Lowland Scots or Geordie differs from standard English. This fact is a reminder that in Ireland there had to be multifarious dialects of the indigenous language we call Irish – probably even some that retained a more substantial trace of pre-Celtic, even Hamito-Semitic, linguistic syntax than others …

Over the years Kenny's Bookshop in Galway, an unequalled source of rare books relating to Ireland, has become familiar with my esoteric tastes. They once presented me with a dusty treatise called 'Irish wizards in the woods of Ethiopia', written by an American as an academic thesis (its alternative title was 'An enquiry into the meaning of God'). The author, Winthrop Palmer Boswell, took the view that many references in Irish sagas had their equivalent in Ethiopian folklore; an ancient Irish hymn, for example, referred to Brigid, an Irish goddess who became a saint, as the Queen of Sheba. Boswell had seen a St Brigid's cross, fashioned in rushes exactly as in Ireland, at Lalibela, an Ethiopian monastic centre. She points out that 'Banba', an old name for Ireland, is also the Ethiopian name for the baobab tree, which is held in great reverence by both Ethiopians and Berbers. As a result, Boswell developed an interesting analogy between the tree culture of that part of Africa and the Druidic interest in yew and ash.

Mrs Boswell's delightful speculations may not have converted me entirely, but she was influential in my subsequent obsession with tree-planting on my poor bog in the heart of Conamara. She reminded me that the Old Irish alphabet was based on the names of trees. However, as her arguments were largely based on comparisons between nouns, I was wary of it. When language changes, the first feature to succumb is the common noun; the syntax, as Wagner illustrated, can linger on indefinitely. An argument based on similarities between common nouns and adjectives in different languages gives the feeling of walking on shifting sands. When etymologists get to work on word roots and endings, it is almost impossible for a non-specialist to follow them through the thickets. All one can do is make an act of faith in their integrity, and hope that their peer group – the equivalent of market forces – will keep a check on flights of the imagination.

Muiris Ó Scanaill spent many years working as a veterinary surgeon in Conamara, in Malta (an old possession of the Arabs) and in Oman on the Persian Gulf. He is also a creator and solver of crosswords, so his ear for the subtleties of language is well honed. On one visit home he, who had hitherto been entirely sceptical of my Irish-Oriental ideas, said, 'Bob, I apologize. You are absolutely right.'

He then gave me a list of everyday verbal coincidences that had occurred to him in his travels, as follows (Arabic/Maltese spelt phonetically):

OMAN

Mwinneh (Arabic girl's name) means 'hope'; *muinín* (Irish) means 'hope' or 'confidence'. *Gyarrah* means 'cut' in Arabic; *gearradh* in Irish means exactly the same. *Kh'ala* is an Arabic port; *caladh* in Irish is a harbour.

OMAN and MALTA

Aire (pron. Arrah) in Irish means 'attention!'; it is the same in Oman.

MALTA	CONAMARA
Barrakke, a small shed	*Bráca, scioból*, small shed
Sikina (also in Egypt), knife	*Scian*, knife
Shkupa, brush	*Scuab*, brush
Xita (Shitha), rain	*Siota*, a gust (as of wind or rain)
Koxxa (pron. Kusha), leg	*Cos/cosa*, leg/legs
Rais, captain or leader of men	*Ros*, a headland

He also told me of a small plant that thrives in the uninviting Arabian sands. As the sand piles up against it, the plant struggles higher. This process results in mounds of varying size and density, composed equally of plant and sand. The mound is called (phonetically) *tullock* in Arabic. The Irish for a small hill or mound is *tulach*, usually anglicized in place-names as 'Tully' or 'Tulla'. The late Brendan Adams of Queen's University Belfast was convinced that the word contained a Hamitic etynom to be linked with Semitic 'Tel' (Tel Aviv, Tel-El-Kebir). Heinrich Wagner contributed the Hittite *tuloiya* to the discussion.

Seán Stiofán Mac Donncha has worked the bogs since he was a child. He took an interest in my research and brought me samples of turf derived from different layers. Each piece had a different Irish name — horsemeat turf, brown turf, spark turf, kneaded turf, etc. — and he assured me that there were many more, right down to the hard compressed *cloch-móin* or 'rock-turf' at the base of a cutting. Each individual sod of turf had to be cut and handled at least seven times before it was eventually consumed in the fire. I was reminded of how deeply embedded in environmental antiquity this turf-cutting activity must be — as is Seán Stiofán's beautiful language.

In the past two decades the Céide Fields in Mayo have been claimed as the oldest, and certainly at 2500 acres the most extensive, evidence for neolithic occupation of this island (incidentally supporting Ruaidhrí de Valera's ideas about the point of entry of the earliest settlers). It has been claimed that the masterbuilders of the Boyne Valley complexes in the east of the island were the design descendants of those pioneering farmers in north-west Mayo.

In the Céide Fields I found useful evidence — in respect of the word *doire* — for my speculations about the antiquity of the language called Irish. There was a headland marked 'Benaderreen' on my map. It means the 'hill' — or possibly, as in 'bun', the 'bottom' — 'of the little oak wood'. It marks

Benaderreen, Co. Mayo, a treeless promontory at the Céide Fields

the northern edge of the area named Glenulra, the Valley of the Eagle. My first visit to the site coincided with the very last day of excavation before construction of a new heritage centre began. The student archaeologists were preparing to leave. They confirmed that Benaderreen was just across the narrow road and that plenty of *giúsach* were to be found in the vicinity.

I picked up a piece of charred pine bark, *pinus contorta*, as I stumbled over the fields. There were no pine trees in sight. Under metres of blanket bog, representing millennia, were stone walls. Few had been fully excavated. The majority were identified only by lines of archaeological probes. Underneath the bog lay much undisturbed *giúsach*. What struck me forcibly was that there was not the faintest remnant of a tree visible on the brown horizon of Benaderreen. The question I was left with was this: who else but those first farmers could have used the ancient word *doire*, applied the name Benaderreen, 'bottom of the little oak wood', to that promontory of presently treeless blanket bog? Would it not, logically, have been so named when the area was covered in forest?

If so, those farmers of 5000 years ago spoke an early, aboriginal version of the language we now call Irish that therefore cannot, by any stretch of the imagination, be called 'Celtic'. The archaeologists have their sound-track. And the Irish have a language at least 5000 years old!

After 300 years of Celtic scholarship, Calvert Watkins conceded in 1962: 'The historical morphology of the Celtic languages remains strikingly obscure', and this encourages me to believe that definitive 'Celtic' conclusions on the subject are impossible. It is, as Theo Vennemann wrote in a related context, a matter as much of belief as of knowledge.

My belief then is that Irish is thousands of years older than is commonly admitted and is not amenable to being parcelled up in an exclusive 'Celtic' or 'Indo-European' category. It is also a language that the Irish themselves have been slowly and painfully discarding for the past century and a half, to the degree that now there are probably less than 40,000 native speakers in the entire island. At the census of the Irish state in 1925, there were 250,000 who claimed to speak Irish fluently.

10 Ireland's Early Maritime History

IN CONSIDERING AN ISLAND'S PLACE in the world, the maritime context is obvious. However, insofar as water covers most of the world's surface, a similar perspective on the rise and development of civilizations is equally useful.

Within an extraordinarily short time of the first Arab expansion in the sixth century, we hear of the Baghdad Caliph Abd El Malek instructing his lieutenant in Africa to use Tunis as an arsenal and dockyard. Later, in 711 AD, it did not take much seamanship to move across the few kilometres from Ceuta in Morocco to Gebal Tarik – Gibraltar. Once they had secured Spain and established the most brilliant civilization in the then-known world, the Arabs could, at their leisure, follow the path of the Phoenicians and investigate the Atlantic. 'Most astonishing of all,' Bernard Lewis wrote in *Politics and War, the Legacy of Islam* in 1931, 'they were able, with the help of the native Christian populations of Syria, Egypt and North Africa, to build and man war-fleets which could defeat the Byzantine navies that had long dominated the Mediterranean waters.'

The Arabs were worthy successors to the Phoenicians, who had paved the way a thousand years before and left an indelible mark on the Iberian peninsula. It was not surprising that by the twelfth century the Muslims had become the most advanced geographers in the world and had absorbed and made their own the best of Jewish and Christian scholarship.

One reference to Irish maritime activity comes from a prominent Muslim scholar named Al-Idrisi, who lived in Spain between 1002 and 1085. He commented on the whaling that ships engaged in off the west coast of Ireland. He also referred to the seafaring activities of the inhabitants of Ireland. His account suggests that the people of this island must have been a little better equipped than those in the single example given by Giraldus Cambrensis, the Norman propagandist who referred to two semi-naked savages paddling out in their canoe to meet the sailors on a Norman ship. They had never heard of Christ, never eaten cheese before. It might be wiser to take the more disinterested Muslim opinion. As they had been in the Iberian peninsula for centuries, and as Ireland had always traded, and still does, with that region, it is likely that the Muslim writers were actually more familiar with the island – certainly with the west coast – than were the neighbouring Cambro-Normans.

The possibility of Ireland rediscovering its maritime past and its Atlantean links has been made difficult by a kind of paper wall that has surrounded the island for the past few centuries. The process of isolating the Irish from their sea-girt consciousness probably began in earnest when Spain, within a century of the eviction of the Arabs, threatened England in the late sixteenth century. Ireland was a useful foothold on England's western flank. The first direct Spanish attempt on England was forestalled by the destruction of the Armada in 1588. Three years later they tried the indirect way by landing at Kinsale in southern Ireland and attempting to link up with Irish chieftains. This also failed. The Spanish then appear to have reverted to peaceful trading with the island. They were replaced by the French who, in the eighteenth century, made two landings in force, one at Bantry in the south-west and the other at Killala in the north-west (not far from the Céide Fields). These attempts also failed miserably. England's increased sensitivity to attack from this quarter was expressed in the building of large granite watch-towers named after their designer, Martello, and turned into a literary metaphor by James Joyce. They still squat on the coasts of Ireland, from Sandycove in the east to Ros a Bhíl in the west.

As late as 1916 the continental rivals of England still perceived Ireland as a stepping-stone to their ambitions. In that year a German submarine attempted to land arms on the coast of Kerry. The operation was a failure; the Irish representative on board the submarine, Roger Casement, was captured and hanged. These incidents say less about the general aspirations of the Irish towards freedom than about the opportunism of the European powers. As one of Queen Elizabeth I's ministers said to her: 'Whoever holds Ireland, holds a dagger to England's heart.' Over those centuries, the activities of Barbary pirates were also a threat to the European status quo. It was obvious to the English and their Dublin agents that the native Irish must be kept from an awareness of the sea as a potential ally.

Under subsequent native rule, the maritime history of Ireland has been all but ignored in national schools. Such a subject appears to have been too materialistic for an education system based exclusively on a literary and religious perception of reality. When Irish schoolchildren were taught that pirates brought St Patrick from Britain to Ireland, they were left in ignorance as to who these pirates were, how widespread was their activity, what other plunder they collected and to which other places they sailed. In my early schooldays the fact that these mariners were Irish and constituted a serious threat to the Roman Empire was skated over.

'Prior to the age of the Vikings,' wrote Archibald G. Lewis, an American scholar of this period, 'the Irish proved themselves to be the most intrepid mariners of the Atlantic.' He is not referring to the innocuous Irish monks, brave as they were in their frail currachs from the sixth century onwards. He had in mind Irish sailors who, as early as 222 AD, had made their first recorded overseas excursion. It began a long period of raids across the Irish Sea to Roman-held Britain. Such were their depredations that the Romans found it necessary to build fortresses and watch-towers on the Isle of Anglesey as well as on both sides of the Bristol Channel, the most important one being situated at Cardiff. They thought it prudent to base a defensive flotilla at the mouth of the Severn as well as several fleets off the Cumberland coast.

Ireland was not always a kind of sponge, passively absorbing the various invaders; there was a two-way traffic, and from the second to the seventh century this appears to have been more outward than inward. How far afield they ranged is hard to establish, but they certainly got at least as far as Bordeaux. They might have anticipated the feats of the Vikings and reached the Mediterranean. It would not have been in the interests of the historians of subsequent periods, or indeed of interest to them at all, to highlight such voyages. By contrast, the history of Irish religious colonization – even in Africa – was painstakingly detailed.

Other groups were similarly engaged in plaguing Roman Britain. The Picts of Scotland were a formidable naval force who attacked both north-east and north-west Roman Britain. Meanwhile, Anglo-Saxon pirates were in control of the east coast.

In 367 AD their three main foes launched a major attack on the north of England. In response to raids like this, both in Britain and on the Continent, the Roman emperor decided things needed tightening up. Theodosius formulated a commercial code detailing precisely where and when people could leave and enter the empire, what goods they could bring in and out and what taxes or duty should be paid on such goods. He eventually brought in passports. He thus hoped to control the barbarian world's trade and counteract the growing anarchy.

One of the last continental tribes the Romans conquered was the Veneti, in 56 BC – ancestors of those modern Atlanteans, the Bretons. The Veneti had their strongholds in that part of Armorica, or Brittany, where Gav'rinis – first cousin of Newgrange – still stands. Nearby is the modern city of Brest, now appropriately the headquarters of the French navy.

Even though the Romans imitated the shallow boats of the Veneti, they could not quite conquer them because the tribe specialized in a form of guerrilla warfare on water. Their strongholds, now called promontory forts, were built on peninsulas and took a lot of effort and manpower to capture. When it looked like the Romans were gaining one peninsula, the Veneti simply boarded their ships and moved to the next, defying Caesar until he could build more sea-barriers, slowly transfer his forces and begin the whole process again. The Veneti were masters of the art of sailing; the Romans relied on banks of oars. The Veneti sails were made of tough hide that could withstand the force of Atlantic gales and their boats were shallow enough to negotiate every creek and rock on this *côte sauvage*. The Romans eventually overcame them, but the Veneti, then the Bretons, continued to be part of the Atlantean maritime world.

Empires might come and go, but the Atlantean peoples have been constantly in contact with one another, trading and exchanging ideas. An Irishman was responsible for the principal method of mussel cultivation in western France. In 1235 an Irish sailor named Walton was shipwrecked in the Bay of Aiguillon, near La Rochelle. He settled down to make a living by trapping birds in a net stretched across the mud flats of an estuary. In order to make the net secure he bedded it deeply in the mud and secured it with poles. Being an observant man, he soon noticed that the poles became covered with mussel spawn, so he switched to growing mussels. This form of fish farming is now a huge industry on the Atlantic coasts of France, Spain and, increasingly, Ireland.

When the Emperor Theodosius proclaimed limited entry and exit points for his empire, he inflated the value of the services of those seafarers on its fringes. In 374 AD the movement of bronze, gold and iron across the frontiers was prohibited and many a smuggler must have giggled in his sea cabin. In 381 the imperial bureaucrats pronounced that 'loyal friendly people' could export to the empire on payment of a customs levy of 15 per cent, forgetting that such qualities as loyalty and friendship have limited application in the world of commerce. And so there developed in these areas what Archibald Lewis described as 'an Atlantic Economic Community in the west, extending far beyond Rome's frontiers'.

While Caesar and his successors were having their triumphs, and promulgating laws, whether obeyed or not, the Irish and Pictish and Anglo-Saxon maritime power grew. Within the economic community of the Atlantic reaches there were movements of people that left their mark. The Irish intrusions on Britain resulted in settlements in Wales and Cornwall; the displacement of the incumbents eventually resulted in the colonization of Armorica. To the north of Britain in the sixth century colonists from Ireland formed a community called the Dál Riada and gave Pictland its modern name, Scotland. The Isle of Man was another Irish colony (the Manx language is still closer to Irish than to Welsh).

In sum, the Roman laws designed to injure economies outside the empire had the reverse effect; they increased the incentives to sidestep those laws through smuggling. They boosted the commerce of the Atlanteans. As we know from the much later period of the Barbary corsairs, this became the pattern of the Atlantic seaways: unorthodox and energetic. Strabo, a Latin writer of the second century, commented on the volume of traffic conducted by the native population – not the Romans – between Clausentum in the south of England and Cadiz in the south of Spain. From the southern areas came wine, salt and olive oil; from the north in return were sent iron, copper, lead, silver, slaves and hides. Some of these items of exchange were also the basis of Galway's traditional prosperity.

THE ATLANTEAN IRISH

I have visited La Coruña in Galicia. A feature of the town is an ancient lighthouse, considered to be the oldest surviving Roman construction of its kind. It is now called the Hercules Tower, but in the fourth century it was known as the Portus Brittaniae, confirming the two-way traffic between Spain and the British Isles. Orosius in the fifth century also referred to the lighthouse and said it was sited 'ad speculam Brittaniae'. It can be assumed that when classical writers referred to Britain, they were aware of the adjoining island of Ireland.

The depth of maritime activity up and down these coasts is also shown by the variety of ships and boats attributed to the various peoples. The Picts used two types: the *coracle*, which was made of skin, and the *ponto*, which was more stoutly constructed. It was flat-bottomed, made of oak, had a high poop and stem and featured leather sails and an iron anchor. Even some of the skin-covered boats used by both Picts and Irish were not the frail craft we always imagine. According to another Latin writer, Sidonius, they were constructed of twenty to thirty hides, three hides thick. They had masts and could carry twenty passengers – possibly in addition to crew. About 550 AD the Irish started building stronger, wooden ships. These included the following: the ocean-going *barca*; a warship referred to as the *navis longa*; the *caupullus*; the *navicula*, a possible antecedent of the present-day *naomhóg* of Kerry; the *navis onera*; the *scapha*; and finally, the domestic *currach*.

Caesar described the ships of the Veneti he imitated, just as his predecessors had imitated the ships of the Carthaginians. The bows were unusually high to enable them to survive heavy seas and gales. Their hulls were made entirely of oak, which rendered them immune to the ramming techniques of naval warfare. The cross timbers, he said, were constructed of beams a foot wide and fastened with iron as thick as a man's thumb. They even used iron chains to attach their anchors.

When the Romans finally extricated themselves from Britain around the year 407 AD, it is commonly assumed that chaos resulted. This is because formal written accounts of subsequent events became scarce. What this really meant is that the normal, pre-existing – or even co-existing – cultural and trade contacts reasserted themselves without the paternal supervision of the empire.

Conventional history dubbed the ensuing period as the Dark Ages, the period when the 'barbarian' uprooted civilization. The Visigoths sacked Rome in 410 and dominated north-west Spain in 419; the Vandals swept down through Europe as far as Gibraltar, crossed the Straits and reached Carthage in 429; the Franks expanded over Gaul in 450; the Huns pushed all before them.

The only people discommoded by this healthy rearrangement of property were subsequent historians: 'barbarians' do not usually leave written records to defend their actions. As a cynical Arab once remarked: 'The soldiers fight their battles; the peoples trade in peace; whoever likes can claim the world.'

With the departure of the Romans, the Irish, who had escaped the heavy hand of empire, reaped unofficial fringe benefits. The flow of trade up and down the Atlantic coasts may have constituted the only cultural continuity in Europe – just as Ireland later preserved a continuity of Western scholarship when, as one historian remarked, 'learning fled to the bogs of Ireland'.

A group of seafarers not yet mentioned in the downfall of Roman Britain were hovering off-stage, waiting for the erstwhile pirates to settle down so they themselves could take over the mantle of marauders. The 'Heruls' originated in Scandinavia and were forebears of the men who, from the eighth century, would dominate the Atlantic seaways and make Ireland their base – the Vikings.

Vikings and Trade
in the Middle Ages

11

THE STORY OF VIKING INFLUENCE ON IRELAND was originally created by monks, who portrayed the invaders exclusively as blood-thirsty destroyers. But the Vikings were not Christian; they could not have been expected to respect the achievements of Irish monasticism. They had no compunction about pillaging great monastic cities such as Clonmacnoise on the Shannon River, any more than did the Christian Irish chieftains.

They were more than destroyers; as traders they developed the first secular towns on the island. After millennia as a modest river crossing, the Town of the Ford of the Hurdles – Dublin itself – was expanded into a Danish Viking kingdom called Duibhlinn, meaning 'black pool'. As mentioned earlier, Wicklow, Wexford, Waterford and Limerick all owe their names and origins to the Vikings. The Vikings' most significant innovation, however, was the introduction of coinage to Ireland; these fine seamen were in direct contact with cultures beyond those of the Atlantic seaways, in this case the Islamic civilization to the east of what is now known as Russia.

In the eighth century a new silver coinage began to appear in the Baltic and thence in the Atlantic regions of the Friesian Islands, Britain and Ireland, Gaul and Spain. Traces of this new coinage persisted for at least another

 *Viking voyages (from E.G. Bowen,* Britain and the Western Seaways, *1972)*

two centuries in regions far beyond its original provenance in the East. The largest British hoard of such coins was found on the north-west coast of England, an area dominated by Viking kingdoms and trading intimately with Dublin. The Cuerdale Hoard is dated to the years 902–20 AD, and contains a large number of foreign coins, of which thirty-one are Kufic Muslim dirhams. It is assumed that they were buried at the time of a quarrel between the Vikings there and their cousins in Ireland. Similar, smaller hoards have also been found in Ireland in places as disparate as Derry, Drogheda, Claremont and Kildare. These hoards also contained Muslim dirhams. However, the preponderance of this wealth is concentrated in the Baltic; 200,000 such coins exist in the Nordic countries, two-thirds of them contained on the island of Gotland. How did the coinage of the Islamic Empire travel so far from the exotic Orient?

Although this coinage is evidence of practical contact with the Near East, most of it did not come via the Atlantic seaways although a portion of Arab silver was mined at al-Abbasiyya in Morocco. But neither did it come overland. While the Norse and Danes were expanding westwards and

◈ THE ATLANTEAN IRISH

From left, above: Abbasid dinar, eighth century; Byzantine miliaresion overstruck on Islamic dirham, eighth century; Saminid silver dirham, Samarqand, ninth century (all courtesy of American Numismatic Society, New York)

establishing colonies in Scotland, Ireland, England, even in Gaul, their fellow-Scandinavians, the Swedes, were opening up trade routes in the opposite direction. They overran the eastern Baltic and penetrated south from Lake Ladoga on the rivers Volkhov and Lovat, meeting the Dnieper, which flows out into the Black Sea. It is common knowledge that the city of Kiev was founded by Vikings and that the name Rus itself is Scandinavian. Another artery, via Lake Beloya, linked up with the Volga and thence to the Caspian Sea in Asia. Over these tortuous routes the Vikings sailed and rowed their longboats, pushing them overland on pine rollers when rivers were too precipitous, fighting and trading alternately. In 921 Ibn Fadlan, ambassador from the Baghdad Caliph to the Bulgars, witnessed the gruesome ceremony of a Viking boat burial on the Volga; his description corresponds exactly with a boat grave from the same period opened at Valsgard in Denmark.

As is so often the case with heroic expeditions, the ultimate goal was material reward. From the southern shore of the Caspian, a land route led to Baghdad, from whence the seemingly bottomless source of silver was controlled and distributed. This was the origin of the Viking silver that, eventually, turned up as far west as Ireland.

The wealth was hard won. In 839 the Byzantine Emperor Theophilus met the Western Emperor Louis the Pious at Ingelhiem, on the Rhine. He was accompanied by a group of Vikings who had lost many men fighting Khazars on the inland waterways of the principalities that later constituted Russia. The battle-worn Vikings had preferred to return home with an escort by a slower route. Some Rus Kagans and Varangian chieftains reached the lower Don in 839 and were sent back to Sweden by way of Constantinople and the Frankish Empire.

But this was exceptional; their normal route was by water, whether on the Atlantic seaways, across the Baltic or on inland rivers. It suggests a picture of Europe that actually equates to early maps of the world, in which a central area is surrounded by a vast river encircling the known world of the time. This river was a much-travelled trade route – up the Atlantic coasts, across the Baltic, down the Russian rivers to the Caspian and Black Seas and thence into the Mediterranean, to link up once more with the Atlantic. But this picture is at variance with the standard image of Europe, which implies civilization always at the centre and chaos at the fringes. It suggests that, without the seaborne and highly structured activity on the perimeter, the centre of Europe would never have acquired its luxuries: spices, silks, wines, etc. – quite apart from progressive ideas – that came from the Orient. This image helps me further to visualize the island of Ireland as less a remote speck in the Atlantic than, as the Vikings demonstrated, an important part of a circular trading network: in fact, Ireland was a trading post, a function to which globalization is now forcing it to revert.

I was reminded of this circular perspective when some years ago a composer friend, David Hopkins, brought to my attention the folk music of Tatarstan, still one of the Soviet republics and now part of the Russian Federation. He found the similarity between Tatar music and that of Conamara quite remarkable.

The indigenous Tatars are Muslim, and suffered as much under the Christian Orthodox Russians as the Irish did under the English. Ivan the Terrible was the first to persecute them in the sixteenth century. He built a wooden fortress in Moscow and floated it all the way down the Volga to Kazan, where he proceeded to baptize the Muslims forcibly. From 1552 onwards the Tatars were expelled from the towns and they could not rent land from Russians. In the three years after 1740 most of their mosques were destroyed (reportedly 418 out of a total of 536). In modern times Moscow was siphoning off most of the considerable Tatar natural resources of natural gas and oil. However, since the fall of the USSR the resurgent Tatars are building new mosques at an extraordinary rate. I and my female camerawoman – short-sleeved – were welcomed effusively into one of them to record an evening service.

The Atlantean Irish

Tatar sean-nós singer, Kazan, Tatarstan

The tape of Tatar singing had made my trip to Tatarstan essential. The similarity between this singing and that of my neighbours in Conamara was striking. When I summoned several musical friends to my home and played them the tape they confirmed that the singing was well-nigh identical to their own; only the language was different. One, Máirtín Jeaimsie, humorously suggested that if I played the tape backwards there would be absolutely no difference. Subsequently I made two trips to Kazan, the capital of Tatarstan, which is bisected by the Volga and also split into two cultures, Muslim and Christian Orthodox. I met numerous singers and dancers, recorded them all and was again struck by the musical parallels. Tatars themselves said that when I played a tape of my neighbour Sarah Grealish singing 'Amhráin Mhuinse', they could detect little difference. A Tatar ethnomusicologist, Ilghiz Kaperov, having listened to the above song, was able to continue the refrain faultlessly with an identical Tatar melody. The only difference he noted was that the Conamara

⊠ *Offa's dinar (British Museum)*

singer 'took the tune for a walk', meaning Sarah's decorations were more elaborate than his.

It was tempting to suggest direct cultural contact (with Viking slaves as culture carriers) between these two peoples at opposite edges of Europe. But I had to concede the principle of polygenesis, i.e. that each musical culture had developed independently. Both forms of singing are based on the five-note or pentatonic scale, one of the simplest and most venerable of musical forms. It suggested that the basis of Conamara sean-nós singing is universal and at least as venerable as the Book of Kells; it has probably changed little over a thousand years. This itself is a remarkable distinction for any living art form; what is more remarkable is that it is treated with utter lack of interest by most urbanized Irish people.

There is a famous coin in the British Museum suggesting that these peripheral trading patterns went beyond simple commercial contact. This coin is a gold dinar – a Muslim coin – with the name 'Offa' clearly stamped on it. Offa is the name of an eighth-century king of Mercia in England, the man to whom 'Offa's Dyke' – a 200-kilometre-long barrier between England and Wales – is credited. What is unusual about the coin is that it has an Arabic inscription: 'God is most Great; He has no companion'. This is a common Muslim sentiment. One explanation for the coin is that it is an imitation of the only gold currency with which King Offa was familiar

– that used by the Muslims in Spain. It is agreed that it is an imitation as there are mistakes in the Arabic that no Muslim would permit. Further, the name Offa is imprinted upside down in relation to the Arabic.

The most prosaic reason for an Anglo-Saxon king striking such a coin is that he needed it to trade with Moorish Spain at the height of its prosperity. But the rest of Europe is supposed to have been at loggerheads with the Muslims. When Offa's dinar is taken in conjunction with the Arabic-inscribed, ninth-century cross found in southern Ireland, together with the various coin hoards mentioned above, it suggests a continuing contact between the residents of these islands and the Muslim world. The idea of a homogeneous Christian Europe having nothing to do with an equally homogeneous, but Muslim, world is a gross nonsense.

At any given historical period one form of currency tends to be dominant and transcends cultural or religious differences. The Greek drachma once held that position. No one disputes the present pre-eminence of the mighty American dollar. In Viking times the Muslim dirham was dominant. It has even been convincingly argued that the successful beginnings of Charlemagne's Holy Roman Empire could be attributed to the influx of Muslim silver, via the Vikings, from the Islamic-controlled east, with the Carolingians melting the Arabic coins down into silver bullion, from which they minted their own coinage. The Belgian scholar Henri Pirenne began to study this possibility in a German concentration camp during the First World War. He argued that, as the Muslim navies demolished the Byzantine control of trade in the Mediterranean, there developed a thriving commercial zone in northern Europe and the Baltic that facilitated the rise of Charlemagne and his empire. Pirenne would eventually coin the slogan: 'Without Mohammed, no Charlemagne'.

The late Professor Sture Bolin from Lund University, Sweden, in 1939 detailed the massive hoards of silver Muslim coins found in the Baltic. He could trace the Muslim-controlled eastern mines from which the ore had come, and even maintained that the Viking traders who brought this booty from places like Kiev in Russia used their new-found wealth to finance their raids on the British Isles. Dr Kenneth Jonsson, the Swedish numismatic expert whom I consulted in 1998 in Stockholm suggested that Professor Bolin was a mere professor of Roman history and did not have the numismatic background to form such judgments. He said that the Bolin hypothesis was plausible 'but maybe not the best'. Subsequently, in the

Copenhagen National Museum the senior curator of coins, Jorgen Steen Jensen, expressed a more positive attitude to Sture Bolin, and confirmed that for at least the ninth and tenth centuries the Arabic dirham was the dominant currency in northern Europe. Ulla Silvegren, the curator of coins in Lund University itself, was equally certain of this.

It was two to one in favour of the Sture Bolin insight. However, as a testimony to Dr Jonsson's erudition I relate the following: as a gift I had brought him a recently printed Irish stamp featuring the head of a Viking king of Dublin named Sitric. The scholar took one glance at it and said 'Why is it printed in reverse?' As soon as I returned home I checked with the Irish postal authorities. They admitted that a mistake had been made in the design of a quarter million of these stamps. They blamed an anonymous — and departed — graphic designer of the private company they had employed to design the stamp. But the stamps were never withdrawn — too expensive, they said. The implication: it's only a stamp, who will notice? Thus is history written.

I was coming to the conclusion that the Muslim conquest of the Mediterranean, combined with their control of silver deposits in the east, could indeed have hastened the ascent of the illiterate Charlemagne to the point where in 800 AD he was crowned in the Vatican as head of the Holy Roman Empire. This idea is based on the fact that throughout history, no matter what happens in politics or war, there is a large group for whom borders, nationalisms and cultures represent only minor impediments to their ambitions: they are the kings, the politicians and especially the men of property, the trading class to whom business is always business. Thus, when the Mediterranean outlets were controlled by the Arabs, affected business people simply moved their attention elsewhere — to northern Europe. And there the traders supreme were the Vikings, a people not confused by ideas of Christian solidarity. They were practical enough to see the advantages of dealing with the Muslim traders who had commandeered the richest silver mines in the known world. The fact that Charlemagne accepted the gift of an Indian elephant named Abu'l-Abbas from Harun El-Rashid, Caliph of Baghdad, suggests that the Christian emperor was also a pragmatist.

In 1989 two British archaeologists, Richard Hodges and David Whitehouse, resurrected the Bolin and Pirenne theses in *Mohammed, Charlemagne and the Origins of Europe*. They argued that rather than the retreat of the Roman

Empire spurring a decline into a Dark Ages chaos, trading actually continued quite normally throughout Europe. They continued:

> We believe that the evidence of Dorestad [site of Charlemagne's mint where the Rhine meets the sea] and Haithabu [Hedeby, a Viking settlement], sharpened by dendrochronological dating, lends new credence to Bolin's imaginative hypothesis. Furthermore, we extend the argument to western Asia to illustrate that events in the Baltic and the North Sea can be correlated – up to a point – with those in the Abbasid Caliphate … A case exists, therefore, for regarding Abbasid silver as a significant source of wealth which … was essential for the consolidation of Charlemagne's massive empire.

Trade primarily flourished on the rivers and the maritime peripheries of Europe. North European commerce largely consisted of hides and slaves (Slavs) exchanged for Arab dirhams and Eastern luxuries – and accounts for the enormous hoards found in Gotland. It is one of the ironies of history that the word 'Tatar' in Scandinavia now has disreputable connotations; the Irish insult 'knacker' would be the equivalent.

▨ *Viking Ship, Roskilde, Denmark*

When I visited Gotland in 1998 I learned more about the significance of Ireland in the trade of these 'peripheral' areas. Dublin had actually operated as an *entrepot*, a distribution warehouse for slaves under the control of the Scandinavians. A quarter of a century ago an oaken warship was recovered from an inlet near the Viking ship museum at Roskilde in Denmark. When dendrochronology was applied to it the Danish archaeologists found that the ship was constructed circa 1060 AD from oak trees grown near Dublin, further evidence that a thousand years ago the island of Ireland was already used as a stepping-stone for global commercial ambitions. *Plus ça change . . .*

Conventional treatments of political and religious developments within Europe throughout the Middle Ages and later have tended to ignore the major dimension that was the Islamic Empire. Its influence is rarely, if ever, mentioned. Traditional European history books have adopted blatant national perspectives. Such parochialism, not to say ignorance, of the Muslim world, bears fruit through a carelessness of which the West is now becoming painfully aware.

Some powerful European intellects have tried to redress the balance. Irishman George Bernard Shaw, an atheist, wrote in *The Genuine Islam* in 1936:

> I have always held the religion of Muhammad in high estimation because of its wonderful vitality. It is the only religion which appears to me to possess that assimilating capacity to the changing phase of existence which can make itself appeal to every age. I have studied him – the wonderful man – and in my opinion far from being an anti-Christ, he must be called the Saviour of Humanity. I believe that if a man like him were to assume the dictatorship of the modern world, he would succeed in solving its problems in a way that would bring it the much needed peace and happiness. I have prophesied about the fate of Muhammad that it would be acceptable to the Europe of to-morrow as it is beginning to be acceptable to the Europe of to-day.

Arnold Toynbee also tried to warn the West: 'The extinction of race consciousness as between Muslims is one of the outstanding achievements of Islam and in the contemporary world there is, as it happens, a crying need for the propagation of this Islamic virtue.'

For seven centuries Islamic civilization dominated a vast area from Samarkand in central Asia, through the entire Middle East, across the Mediterranean southern shores and up to the borders of Spain and France. Charlemagne's Holy Roman Empire was once considered the principal bastion against such a threat. Ironically he might have got nowhere without the silver of his 'infidel' enemies. Let readers consider the utter dependence of today's Western consumer civilization on Arab oil. There is also evidence – especially in Dorestad, where Charlemagne owned a mint – that to diminish the perception of such reliance the emperor had the 'infidel' coinage melted down into pure silver and re-minted as Christian coinage.

Through the Vikings and the Baltic, Ireland was, however indirectly, however unwittingly, materially changed by the wealth and influence of Islam. Insofar as Ireland and the Iberian peninsula were in direct maritime contact – albeit sporadic – from neolithic times onwards, it must be conceded that the 800-year Muslim presence in that peninsula had a fundamental influence on the northern island.

To reiterate: for a few sparkling centuries in the early Middle Ages, Ireland was the Light of the West, the acknowledged preserver of all that was of value to Western civilization. It is no coincidence that this was also one of the periods of brilliance in the Muslim courts of Cordoba, Toledo and Granada.

12 Moorish Spain and Ireland: A Golden Age

THE VISIGOTH KINGDOMS OF SPAIN fell to the Moors in 711–12 AD. The invasion, across the Straits of Gibraltar, was launched by the governor of North Africa, Musa Ibn Noceir (lit. Moses, son of Victory-man) and led by a Berber, Tariq Ibn Zayyad.

Berber soldiers were charged with the defence of the colder northern areas of Spain, while the Arabs sensibly kept the sunnier south for themselves. Moorish Spain became the most advanced and civilized place in Europe; the Arabs brought with them the philosophy and science of Greece, the literary and political wisdom of Persia, and the medicine and mathematics of India. Between the seventh and tenth centuries Spain had a period of relative peace in which learning flourished, and this again occurred in the thirteenth and fourteenth centuries. A culture developed that was unequalled in Europe and frequently outshone Baghdad, formal seat of the Caliphate. Without this Muslim foundation, the age of scholasticism and the European Renaissance would never have occurred.

There was only one other place in Europe that had not sunk into 'barbarism' and in which learning was at a premium. This was the island of Ireland which, between the seventh and tenth centuries, also enjoyed a

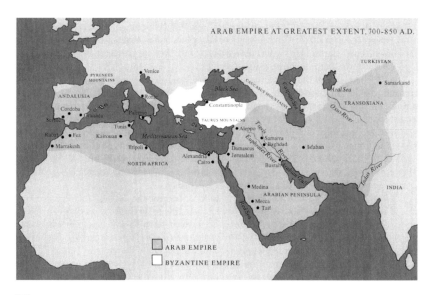

ARAB EMPIRE AT GREATEST EXTENT, 700-850 A.D.

⊠ *Arab Empire, 700–850 AD (from* The Genius of Arab Civilization, *ed. John R. Hayes, 1978)*

golden age. Despite the synchronicity between the splendours of Christian Ireland and of Muslim Spain, it has appeared more prudent to relate Ireland's artistic achievements to Christian Byzantium. This was when Ireland's art and scholarship achieved their pinnacle – when it earned the accolade 'Island of Saints and Scholars'.

The inherent genius of the people expressed itself in illuminated manuscripts, stone carving, metalwork and pure scholarship. Anything that was worth learning – Latin, Greek, arithmetic, geometry, astronomy, natural sciences, logic – could be studied in the monasteries of Lismore, Bangor, Clonfert, Clonard and Armagh. European scholars flocked to the island to learn. The Venerable Bede records English scholars travelling to study under Irishmen. Since the sixth century, Irish scholars had also been travelling to Europe to rekindle the spark of a shattered learning and civilization. More than a century later a Gallic scholar of the year 873 could still describe 'the whole of Ireland with its flock of philosophers, contemning the danger of the sea, coming to Gaul'. These philosophers were also described as manifesting 'a sense of superiority that was held to be irritatingly characteristic of the Irish' and 'a certain exotic use of language also associated with Irish learning'. This description came from the ninth-century court of Charlemagne's grandson, Charles the Bald, who shared the wary view of

The Ardagh Chalice (National Museum of Ireland)

the Irish. One dinnertime he asked the Irish scholar John Scotus Eriugena (810–77), sitting opposite, 'What separates a Scot [Irishman] and a sot?' Eriugena replied: 'Only the table, my Lord'.

Irish scholars travelled as far as Tarentum in the south and Kiev in the east: the Norse attacks of the ninth and tenth centuries increased the flow of prudent scholars taking manuscripts to safety.

People have agonized about how a 'remote' island could have achieved such a degree of sophistication. Traditionally, Irish scholars have put it down to native inheritance from the ubiquitous 'Celts'. The British have implied that, actually, the real development was in Northumbria, whose achievements in art and scholarship were then carried to Ireland, but even the English historian Bede undermines that assumption. Continentals say Gallic scholars on the run from the barbarians were responsible; they escaped to Ireland, bringing their talents with them. The Irish, becoming protective, tended to refuse any credit to outside influences.

In the twentieth century scholars were increasingly forced to acknowledge the presence of oriental influences in early Ireland. These were usually explained by reference to Christian Byzantine art channelled through Rome. But according to Michael Ryan, author of works on the Derrynaflan Chalice and others, there is a significant difference between these Irish chalices and their West European equivalents. The entire Latin West interposed itself between Ireland and the Greek Byzantine Empire, so how could this Christian oriental influence have been mediated so directly to an island in the Atlantic if not via the Mediterranean? And from the eighth century on, the Arabs controlled the Straits of Gibraltar. Hilary Richardson's study of Armenian structures has suggested to her a commonsense explanation, i.e. that the Christian phenomenon was 'world-wide' but that remnants lingered longer in peripheral areas than at the centre.

Prominent among the great scholars of this period was the philosopher John Scotus Eriugena, who left his native Ireland before 847 to settle in the Frankish kingdom of Charles the Bald. He was described as the greatest metaphysician of all time; part of his uniqueness lay in his familiarity with Greek and oriental learning. Usually his talent was explained by saying he must have lived in the East for a long time and received his literary and philosophical training there. One author decided he must even be a Greek because of his knowledge of that school of philosophy. His mastery of Greek, Chaldean and Arabic was also attributed to a long stay in Athens. Nothing I have read on this man alludes to Muslim Spain, the dominant civilization and centre of secular and classical scholarship of the period. Ludwig Bieler has even stated that Eriugena was 'the one and only speculative theologian and philosopher of this time' – the time of Abu 'Uthman 'Amr bin Bahr al-Jahiz (776–879), Hunayn Bin Ishaq (d. 873), Ibn Na'imah al-Himsi (d. 835), Abu Bishar Matta (d. 940), Abu Yusuf Ya'qub al-Kindi (d. 866) and Abu Bakr ar-Razi (d. 925), all of whom shared Eriugena's philosophical concerns.

It seemed a little peculiar to me: I had learned that almost a monopoly of Greek learning could be attributed to the Arabs, acquired in their conquest of the Middle East and especially of Alexandria – long the seat of Greek scholarship. Pagan Greek philosophy was not popular with the established Christian Church, as its emphasis on ethics and reason tended to undermine a system of authority based on faith. A famous school of philosophy in Athens was closed in the sixth century for this reason. Probably the earliest translation into Latin of the works of Aristotle and Plato was not available to Christian Europe until Thomas Aquinas commissioned it in the thirteenth century. In the meantime the Arabs had had the Greek writings translated by Syrian scholars, and these became the foundation of their immense strides in all the sciences. The Arab world was united by language and religion; ideas could travel quickly from Baghdad to Cordoba. Further, because of its distance from the formal centres of Islamic orthodoxy, Moorish Spain soon developed an autonomy that enabled it to encourage independent scholarly investigation. At precisely the same time as Eriugena was impressing the Frankish court with his grasp of Eastern languages, philosophy and cosmology (and incidentally making them nervous with his denial of the existence of hell), Muslim scholars were paralleling his findings in Spain.

Hunayn Bin Ishaq, a medical doctor, was a prominent translator during this period. Before approaching a Greek work, he would collate various manuscripts to establish a sound basic text. He placed the art of translation on a healthy scientific footing. He and his team translated the complete medical works of Hippocrates and Galen, almost all of Aristotle, and Plato. His thorough approach to Greek learning paved the way for other brilliant Muslim scholars. Al-Kindi, like Eriugena, tried to harmonize the findings of philosophy with the teachings of dogma. He subscribed to the idea that 'true religion is true philosophy'. Abu Bakr ar-Razi delved into cosmology and the transmigration of souls — a thesis that Eriugena also favoured and which in Gallic circles was considered daring. This tradition of Muslim scholars of Spain culminated in the work of Ibn Khaldun, a fourteenth-century social-philosopher — the 'Father of Sociology'.

Thirteenth-century intellectual Europe was dominated by a philosophic controversy between the followers of Averroes and Avicenna — both of whom were Muslim philosophers. These two names illustrate the conscious downplaying of Europe's indebtedness to Islamic learning. The names Ibn Rushd, Ibn Sina and Ibn Bajja are unfamiliar in Europe. This is because they have been presented to us in Latin form: Averroes, Avicenna and Avempace. This may be defended as an innocent way of homogenizing the world of scholarship, but it has led to ignorance of the importance of Arab scholars to the Europe. It was not always thus.

As Charles Singer wrote: 'In the Europe of the 11th & 12th centuries ... the westerner knew full well that Islam held the learning and the science of antiquity.' Eriugena's prolific ideas were largely influenced by, and incorporated, Neoplatonism. Later, this came to be a distinguishing feature between East and West; Europe would plump for the cold logic of Aristotle while the East would retain the mystic possibilities of Neoplatonism. The latter perspective took a far kindlier view of man, his potential for good and his ultimate destination. Eriugena followed the belief that people who live according to right reason, be they atheists or agnostics, are capable of salvation. By his reckoning, even a pagan like Socrates could be saved. This had serious implications for the doctrine of original sin, never mind the implicit suggestion that the graces supplied by an Established Church might be superfluous. If a man could be saved by his own efforts, priestly intermediaries were redundant. This was reminiscent of the experience of another reputed Irishman, Pelagius, a contemporary of St Augustine, who in the fifth century had raised the same questions. The Roman Church tried him for heresy and he was acquitted. Incidentally, Pelagius defended himself in fluent Greek learned in the East. History repeated itself in 855 when, at the Synod of Valence, Eriugena's *On the Divisions of Nature* was condemned. The more I learned about these early Irish scholars, the greater grew the impression of men living dangerously, working on the fringe of orthodoxy, trying to bridge the gap between faith and reason which, despite their efforts, ended up as an abyss. The tyranny of orthodoxy always seems to triumph.

Similar tensions existed in Muslim Spain. With its physical distance from the centres of Islamic orthodoxy in the East, there was an openmindedness in their thinking. Occasionally, the strict tenets of Islamic dogma did impinge, when, like the Irish philosophers, they had to work hard at showing there was no essential conflict between dogma and philosophy. One man, Al-Ghazzali (1058–1111), was able to distinguish between aspects of Greek/Arab philosophy that he thought were not inimical to religion; these were logic and mathematics. On the other hand, physics and metaphysics could prove dangerously volatile as avant-garde Irish Christians and the Muslims of Spain used the same intellectual tools to extend their deeply religious, sometimes mystic, ideas beyond the narrow confines of their respective orthodoxies. In his 1982 book, *The Berbers in Arabic Literature*, H.T. Norris wrote: 'The Berber dissenter and the Berber "holy man" or marabout often appears in Arabic literature in a guise and with a temperament not dissimilar to the Celtic saint in Ireland, Wales or Brittany in the Dark Ages ...'

Arab historians say that European scholars were drawn to centres of learning such as Cordoba, Toledo and Seville. In the eighth century, Charlemagne had discreetly forborne from attacking Muslim Spain. The decision was made partly because the various Muslim factions were, for once, united, and partly because word came of a Saxon revolt on his eastern frontier. He may also have heard that the Arabized Christians of Spain, the 'Mozarabes', were prepared to resist him. This indicates that these Mozarabes preferred living in Muslim Spain to the possible domination of a northern Christian emperor. From then on, for many years, there was a stand-off between the Christian north and the Muslim south, with little formal contact between the two cultures. How, then, was European scholarship so influenced by developments in Spain?

From the seventh century on it had been the itinerant Irish scholars who had revived the fragile learning, even Christianity itself, in Europe. They founded monasteries and schools of learning in England, France, Belgium, Germany, Switzerland, Austria and Italy. Their unorthodox form of Christianity was also quite novel in Europe. What is now called, retrospectively, and in my opinion ridiculously, the 'Celtic' Church celebrated Easter on the same date as the Alexandrians, a date at variance with Rome. The Irish monks preserved their own form of tonsure or hairstyle. They were criticized by a pope distressed to find these shabby itinerants so popular with the people. They seem also to have had an independent frame of mind: one, Fearghall (Virgil), became Bishop of Salzburg in 784 and proceeded to announce that there were people with souls at the opposite side of the world. As this had implications for their salvation – had they even heard of Christ? – Fearghall was accused of heresy by the Anglo-Saxon papal legate, Boniface. In the ensuing trial, Fearghall won.

How did Ireland come by this form of Christianity that was so at variance with a conventional Western Church? Fearghall of Salzburg aroused the suspicion of Boniface by teaching the existence of the antipodes; Sedulius Scottus was the first for centuries to study and imitate Horace; the Irish abbot Cellanus modelled an epigram in honour of St Patrick on the epitaph of the other Virgil; Eriugena surprised everyone with his study of Neoplatonism; Columbanus showed a remarkable familiarity with Latin poets. The only other place where such confident scholarship was being pursued at the time was in Muslim Spain; the Carolingian court was just getting off the ground.

This dynamic scholarship lingered on until the twelfth century when the Anglo-Normans, with a papal authorization, crossed from Britain. If my general thesis approximates the truth, Ireland was in constant contact with the ideas and cultures mediated through the Muslim Mediterranean, both north and south, thanks to the convenience of the Atlantic seaways. From the seventh right up to the seventeenth century, events in the Iberian peninsula must have had some, even indirect, effect on the island. The Islamic achievement on the peninsula was impressive. With unparalleled wealth at their disposal – the partial fruits of an empire that stretched 3000 miles – it looked as if nothing could stop the Arabs. Indeed, there was one moment in history when it was in the balance whether, as the author Stanley Lane Poole put it, 'Europe would be Christian or Muslim, whether the future Notre Dame or the future St Paul's would ring to the chant of the muezzin.'

This author described one battle as one of the fifteen most important ever fought. In 733 Charles Martel, the illegitimate son of the Frankish Pepin II, stopped the advance of the Arabs between Poitiers and Tours in France. They had already seized Bordeaux and Narbonne, and would hold the latter for another sixty years. With their tough Berber warriors, superb horsemen and an uncluttered faith, very little could oppose them. As late as 890 they were settling in Provence and making raids on eastern Switzerland. A feature of one of the Swiss cantons is still called 'La Bisse des Sarrasins'. Their presence in France is remembered in the word 'troubadour', derived from *tarab dour*, an Arabic phrase meaning 'house of delight'. From this seminal troubadour musical form grew a tradition that, oddly, has a vestigial expression in both Brittany and Conamara. This consists of an improvised duet, usually humorous, between two singers. In Brittany, it is called *Kan ha Diskan*; in Conamara, they know it as *Lúibíní*. The European tradition of romantic chivalry, with its heroic knights and sighing princesses, derives directly from the Arabs, who adapted the desert Bedouins' horsemanship and code of honour. Cervantes' *Don Quixote* is a wonderful upside-down treatment of this same chivalric tradition.

After Charles Martel's success, the Arabs and their Berber forces retrenched in Spain and concentrated on developing the garden of Spain into a sort of heaven on earth; indeed, their idea of paradise is still a garden, a luxuriance of sparkling fountains and streams. They have not often been as near to paradise as they were in Andalusia. They built palaces, mosques, libraries, hospitals, entire towns. By the tenth century Cordoba had a population of

 *The Alhambra (from* Tales of the Alhambra *by Washington Irving, 1832, re-printed Madrid 1994)*

150,000, served by 700 mosques and 900 public baths. Cleanliness, for the Muslim, was next to godliness. In Christianity, on the other hand, the odour of sanctity attributed to saints was usually due to their not washing. After the fall of Moorish Spain, Philip II, husband of the English Queen Mary, ordered the destruction of all Muslim baths as they were a symbol of the

⊠ *Cordoba Mosque (from* The Genius of Arab Civilization, *ed. John R. Hayes, 1978; photo: Michael Anguti)*

infidels. The Arab engineers had developed irrigation systems enabling fruits and flowers to grow where none grew before – and in some cases where nothing has grown since. Cordoba was the crowning glory of Muslim Spain and its mosque the jewel of that crown. This architectural wonder was begun in 784 AD by Abd Er Rahmen, the Ummayad Caliph, who spent 80,000 pieces of gold on it, the proceeds of battle with the Goths. His son completed the work in 793 with loot from the sack of Narbonne. The building was described by Stanley Lane Poole in 1900:

> Each succeeding Sultan added some new beauty to the building, which is one of the finest examples of early Saracenic art in the world. One put gold on the columns and walls; another added a new minaret; another built a fresh arcade to hold the swelling congregations.
> Nineteen is the number of the arcades from east to west, and thirty-one from north to south; twenty-one doors encrusted with shining brass admitted the worshippers; 1293 columns support the roof, and the sanctuary was paved with silver and inlaid with rich mosaics, and its clustered columns were carved and inlaid with gold and lapis lazuli.

The pulpit was constructed of ivory and choice woods, in 36,000 separate panels, many of which were encrusted with precious stones and fastened with gold nails. Four fountains for washing before prayer, supplied with water from the mountains, ran night and day. Hundreds of brass lanterns made out of Christian bells illumined the mosque at night. [These bells were taken from Santiago de Compostela and carried south on the shoulders of prisoners. When the Muslims were defeated the bells were returned, this time on the shoulders of Muslim prisoners.]

Three hundred attendants burnt sweet-smelling ambergris and aloes wood in the censers, and prepared the scented oil which fed the ten thousand wicks of the lanterns. Much of the beauty of this mosque still remains. Travellers stand amazed among the forest of columns which open out in apparently endless vistas on all sides. The porphyry, jasper and marbles are still in place; the splendid glass mosaics, which artists from Byzantium came to make, still sparkle like jewels on the walls.

As one stands before the loveliness of the Great Mosque, the thought goes back to the days of the glories of Cordova, the palmy days of the Great Khalif, which will never return.

Centuries later a Christian church was crudely placed in the centre of the mosque. It was described by Titus Burckhardt (1908–84) as 'like a giant black spider', which, he said, was 'in marked contrast to the clear and innate harmony that emanates from the form of the Islamic structure'.

The influence of Byzantine artists on Muslim art and architecture resulted from diplomatic exchanges in 839. It shows that at least half of Christendom – the eastern half – was able to communicate with Islam. If one bears in mind the propensity of Irish Christians for Eastern attitudes, as exemplified by Eriugena, and the fact that their greatest artistic achievements have Byzantine echoes, the position of Muslim Spain becomes more significant for the island. There had been a schism between Rome and Byzantium in the sixth century. It was never completely healed and was formalized in 1084. The earlier iconoclastic row, during which artists were forbidden to make human representations, drove many out of Byzantium.

An attack on Seville by the Vikings – only five years after Cordoba's diplomatic exchange with Byzantium – shows that the Atlantic seaways were functioning very well. It is also recorded that soon after this attack the Caliphate of Cordoba sent a diplomatic mission to the Norsemen, in Zeeland. There can also be no doubt that contact, whether aggressive or friendly, was still maintained between the island of Ireland and Spain.

There were many examples of clear cooperation existing between members of different religions during the Moorish reign. The Jews were among the scholars employed by the Muslims and they enjoyed, according to Burckhardt, their finest intellectual flowering since their dispersal from Palestine to foreign lands. The two Semitic peoples, Jews and Arabs, when they cooperated in Spain – under an Islamic authority – were a powerful scholarly combination. The most prominent Jewish scholar was Moshe Ben Maimon, or Moses Maimonides, born in Cordoba in 1135, who produced works like the *Guide to the Perplexed*. This occupies as important a place in Judaism as the works of Thomas Aquinas in Catholicism. Maimonides followed the example of Eriugena and many others in incorporating the philosophy of the Greeks in his work.

The Mozarabes – the Arabized Christians of Spain – were so integrated with the Islamic state that when Abd Er Rahmen wanted an emissary to visit the Franconian court of Otto I at Magdeburg, as well as Constantinople and Syria, he chose a Mozarabe bishop, Rabi Ben Zaid, known to Europeans as Recemundus. Christians had, for centuries, been divided on the doctrine of the Trinity; it was the root cause of many 'heresies' and excommunications. With its insistence on the divinity of Jesus Christ, it was infinitely more inimical to Muslims and Jews, whose basic tenet was one incomparable God. In an effort to ease theological tensions between Arab, Jew and Christian, Archbishop Elipandus of Seville proclaimed in 784 a doctrine of 'adoption' for Jesus. In doing this he showed that his beliefs were much closer to Eastern Christianity than to that of the West. Predictably, his idea was condemned in Rome and at synods throughout northern Europe. An Asturian monk named Beatus composed an illustrated commentary on the subject; this was copied many times by Andalusian monks who had emigrated to the Christian north of Spain.

According to Burckhardt, these pictures 'are a curious blend of early Christian, Mediterranean and Asiatic elements, proving that despite their affiliation with Rome the Mozarabic communities were in closer contact with Christian communities in Palestine, Syria and Mesopotamia than with western Europe'.

When investigating Muslim Spain and the Mozarabic Christians, I was tempted to attribute all the best of this flowering of Irish art to direct contact with this overlooked civilization. But there was a problem. The Arabs did not bring the aesthetic and intellectual treasures of the East to Spain until 711. By then, the earliest formative influences on Irish art were already at work on the island. So, although contact with Muslim Spain had later and significant repercussions, it could not explain the beginnings of the golden age of Irish art.

I believed there had to have been an even earlier Eastern influence.

Myths and Storytelling
13

WHEN NIALL FALLON BEGAN RESEARCHING HIS BOOK on the Spanish Armada in Ireland, he was struck by the accuracy with which local people could pinpoint the site of a particular wreck; in not one instance was the locals knowledge of the precise position of a 400-year-old ship proved wrong. He suggested that 'Too often historians have downgraded the accuracy with which these wrecks are remembered; it is a curious aberration of judgment that ignores the fact that native folklores and memory have a long recollection of local events, and while it may distort, it cannot alter the kernel of truth which is the centre of such legend.' This is a perfect rejoinder to the idea that the label of 'myth' immediately removes a phenomenon from rational discourse.

The monks who recorded the words of the Irish epics – and, as we know, rearranged them – had in the first instance copied them down from story-tellers who had memorized them from others. The presence in a story-teller's house of people familiar with a tale might be an encouragement to embellish the narrative, but they would also be a deterrent to gross distortion. As David Greene has said: 'We must beware of seeing the old stories primarily as a form of entertainment ... if stories were told, it was because they were believed to be true, and not from any conscious desire for literary expression.' In view of this I felt it to be a good idea to be at least aware of the stories, beliefs and mythologies that support the idea of a connection between Ireland and the Orient.

A Welsh chronicle relates that Britain was first colonized by Hu the Mighty, 'who came over the sea from the Summer country'; in Brittany, the long lines of menhirs became the remains of an army of southern invaders; in Ireland, a particularly long upper lip was proof positive of a Milesian background; in North Africa, the existence of red-haired, blue-eyed people was attributed to the Irish. Stonehenge in England was reputed to have been built by Merlin the magician, who used stones from Naas in Ireland that had originally come from Africa! In the Friesian islands, also part of the Atlantean area, there is a Santa Claus who is believed to come from Spain and travels with a servant called Black Pete, who is a Moor. The Friesians also dressed young boys in skirts to ward off the fairies, who were apparently not interested in girls, a tradition exactly duplicated in the Aran Islands.

A Semitic origin is attributed to the original workers of the Cornish tin mines, i.e. direct descent from the Phoenicians. These Semites were banished in a pogrom by King Edward the Confessor in the eleventh century. In 1833 a man named Joachim de Villaneuve wrote a book called *Phoenician Ireland*, which maintained that Irish druids were the snake priests of those seafarers. Their god, Baal, can certainly be connected with the Irish 'Balor of the Evil Eye' as well as with *Bealtaine*, Irish for the month of May and meaning 'the fire of Baal'.

An Irish clergyman, the Rev. Robert Walsh (1772–1852), who spent some time in Constantinople and who travelled widely in the Mediterranean in the nineteenth century, made some notes on a visit to Carteia in Spain:

> Tartessus was probably the first city ever erected by a civilized people outside the Mediterranean, when the Phoenician Hercules rent asunder the mountains and opened for his enterprising companions a passage into the Atlantic.
>
> My companion was very fond of Irish lore and had no doubt of the Phoenician origin of the Irish people. He therefore was assiduous in pointing out to me many circumstances about this town as confirming his opinion. We met several of the peasantry;

the men rode always two on a horse or mule with the face of one close to the back of the other; the women sat on the offside, with the left leg to the neck of the beast. The head-dress of the females consisted of a scarf, or shawl, drawn over their caps and tied behind in a knot, the corners of which fell between their shoulders – all of which peculiarities are still to be seen among the peasantry about the Milesian or Phoenician town of Galway at this day.

They have also many opinions in common which have their origin antecedent even to the time of the Romans. They imagine for instance that a sick man's life depends on the state of the tide, and that he never dies until it begins to ebb. This notion, which is mentioned by Aristotle and referred to by Pliny, is common in the west of Ireland and entertained by many physicians there. These usages and opinions, he asserted, were proofs of the identity of the two peoples, not to say anything of the nondescript animal at the cistern, whose tail twines round its legs exactly like that of the extraordinary beast to be seen in the front of Cormac's very ancient chapel on the rock of Cashel. I have no doubt if our worthy friend, General Vallancey, was still alive, he would make out a very respectable theory from these data.

The Rev. Robert Walsh had a healthy scepticism about these suggested links, but at least his account indicates that these impressions existed in Spain, too. Actually, the rich designs on the Galway shawl are derived from Spain; I miss the old lady who every Sunday for many years passed by my door in Carraroe wearing one of the last of these shawls. At least I recorded her on film. The Rev. Walsh did not mention the cloak worn traditionally by women of West Cork; it was called *an fallaing Mhuimhneach*, which means 'Munster cloak', and has frequently been likened to the Arab burnous.

Such speculation is not confined to the nineteenth century. In 1937 J. Foster Forbes presented a series of lectures on BBC radio entitled 'The unchronicled past'. The subject was the archaeology of the British Isles and referred to the Iberians who 'sailed up from Spain and Portugal and moved in [to Britain] from the Atlantic. But they can be traced much further afield than Spain and Portugal; they came, it is now confidently believed, from Egypt.' He then quotes Sir Norman Lockyer, who 'was led by his astronomical enquiries to conclude that the people who reached Britain four thousand years ago had evidently communicated to them a very complete Egyptian culture'.

Foster Forbes continued,

> So you must imagine these ancient Egyptians sailing down the Mediterranean or pausing for a while on the Northern shores of Africa, and so on, out through the Straits of Gibraltar, in their search for precious stones and metals. It must surely have been these people to whom mythology refers as the Ancient Mariners who passed through the Pillars of Hercules in search of the Garden of the Hesperides.

The tradition of an Egyptian connection with the British Isles frequently recurs in folk tales. Between Ireland and that area there seems to have been much coming and going. In the *Book of Invasions* of Ireland there are details of the voyage of the early 'Irish' from Egypt and Libya to Crete and Sicily, thence to Spain and onwards to Ireland. Perhaps Forbes was relying on this concoction of legend. Still, according to Henri d'Arbois de Jubainville — author of *Cours de Littérature Celtique*, begun in 1883 and comprising twelve volumes — the Irish were called 'Egyptian' both by themselves and others during the Middle Ages. This may have been simply a way of distinguishing their brand of Christianity from that of Western Europe. The prehistoric invaders of legend, the Fir Bolg, were said to have spent two centuries in exile in the east after being driven out of Ireland by the Fomorians: the Fir Bolg returned to overwhelm the Fomorians and were again driven out by another invader, again from the east, the Milesians.

It is understood that the sophisticated modern reader — if at all interested — will read such titbits with a tolerant air, confident that only today's rational interpretations of history are valid. Until, that is, they are replaced by tomorrow's. Still, as late as 1953, that observant traveller among Romanies in Spain, Walter Starkie, could write: 'On that Easter Tuesday morning I knew for the first time that Ireland, my island home, was Mediterranean, but like the magic island of Delos it had escaped from the inland sea and gone wandering, towards the fabled West in the wake of the Hellenic wanderers.'

I approach all historical accounts as selective, written to support the perspective of the culture the writer represents and therefore not definitive. However, the frank presentation of accounts from many sources and perspectives may, if ruthlessly distilled, produce some tiny approximation of truth. It seems to me a more rational approach than presenting a collection of worn precedents, in the legal sense, as dogma. 'Innovations' in archaeology, for instance, have been described as moving old bones from one grave to another. The overall aim should be, as the poet said, 'to disturb the indolence of the mind'.

Folk tales or folklore are, by definition, accessible to everybody. They also remind us of the fact that metaphor has been, for a million years, a perfectly acceptable tool with which to illustrate human truths. E.L. Ranelagh, in her book *The Past We Share* (1979), went to immense trouble to show the close relationship between Eastern and Western folk tales. One particular example of interest to me depended less on the truth or myth of the stories than on their essential similarity. These were accounts of the exploits and background of the two greatest heroes of, respectively, Arabia and Ireland: Antar and Cú Chulainn.

They both spring from their respective 'heroic ages', although Antar is customarily given a historic reality as having existed in 600 AD. Cú Chulainn is simply ascribed to pre-Christian, pagan Ireland. They are both located in a cattle economy where the main activity appears to be rustling (Ranelagh humorously suggested that the frequency with which cattle were on the hoof must have made for very lean beasts in early Ireland). The *Táin Bó Cuailgne*, in which Cú Chulainn is immortalized, translates as the 'Cattle raid of Cooley'. Antar and Cú Chulainn have both distinguished themselves in their childhood by killing ferocious dogs. The Irish hero, whose original name was Setanta, actually derived his title 'Hound of Culann' from the exploit. Both men were reared by single women – Antar by Zebeedah and Cú Chulainn by Scathach. Both have arms given to them by close male relatives. Each of them can terrify the enemy with his eyes alone: Antar's can grow monstrously red and protuberant with rage; Cú Chulainn draws one eye into his head and causes the other to stick out like a cauldron.

It is in their deaths that they are particularly distinguished. Antar, badly wounded, deceives the enemy by sitting motionless on his trusty steed, Abjer, keeping himself upright by leaning on his spear. He thus guards the pass and allows his companions to escape. Cú Chulainn, also at the point of death in the Gap of Ulster, ties himself to a post and remains upright even though mortally wounded. It is only when a raven alights on his shoulder that his enemies know he no longer threatens them. A statue by Oliver Sheppard, commemorating this as well as the 1916 Rising, stands in

⊠ *Cú Chulainn bronze by Oliver Sheppard, 1912*

the General Post Office in Dublin. Ironically the image is also used by paramilitary loyalists in the North of Ireland. Meanwhile both Antar and Cú Chulainn's steeds behave similarly: they charge the enemy to discourage any approach to their masters.

Generally speaking, these are archetypes of all heroes; it is in the detail that significant similarity lies. As a footnote to Ranelagh's researches, I discovered that another Irish story – of Nuada of the Golden Arm – had its exact equivalent in an Arabian epic. The latter featured a famous pre-Islamic rain god called Hobbal who, like Nuada, lost an arm. It too was replaced with one made of gold.

Ranelagh regarded these similarities as worthy of note because the early stories did not appear to have been mediated through normal Greek-Roman-Latin channels, i.e. through continental Europe. Further – and this particularly pleased me – not only was the Irish corpus of stories agreed to be the ultimate source of British epics such as the Arthurian legend, but the early literatures of Ireland, Britain and Iceland were considered to be independent of European heroic literature.

The European adoption of Muslim modes of chivalry and romance, in which are embedded so-called 'heroic' elements, did not occur until the Middle Ages. Long before that there existed in Ireland the epic of Cú Chulainn and in Arabia the epic of Antar. If these stories were not mediated through Europe, by what route were they exchanged? This and similar matters continually puzzle those students who assume that everything in Ireland and Britain had to come direct from the continent of Europe.

These stories existed before Christian monks began to write them down in the seventh century. What is in dispute is whether the oriental and classical references were brought in by the monks or were already present. Robin Flower stated one side of the case well:

> These men of the new learning set themselves from an early date to consider how the Irish history which they had received from their predecessors, vivid in detail, but regrettably loose in chronology, might be fitted into the scheme of universal history which ruled the Latin Church. This scheme had been laid down once and for all by Christians in the Chronicles of Eusebius ... The theory at the base of this remarkable compilation was that the great world kingdoms – Assyria, Egypt, Palestine, Greece – had all

by a divine providence led up to the Roman Empire which in its turn by the peace of the Church under Constantine had become the empire of Christ and had given the world constitution its final form. The actual arrangement of the chronicle corresponded to this conception. The whole history of the ancient world was set out in a series of parallel columns, one for each kingdom, and the events of each kingdom were synchronized so that the advance of history, century by century, could be followed at a glance for each kingdom and for all kingdoms.

It was a simple matter to add another column for Ireland, but much less simple to settle the chronology so that the Irish kings might appear in the succession and in a right relation to their contemporaries in the great world kingdoms. These early historians and chroniclers were consequently known as 'synchronizers' or *Fer Comgne*, and it is clear that their version of history included references to the Middle East.

A body of historical material and stories must have existed before the monks appeared, to which the major European heroic epics were at least partly indebted; in these there were classical, oriental, even Indian echoes, more likely to be accounted for by direct contact with North Africa, Spain and the Middle East than by any European 'civilizing' intervention.

In rereading these stories, there was another aspect that was very satisfying: a large proportion of them were acted out in a maritime context. Indeed, one of the most prominent of the gods in these stories was Mananann Mac Lir, the equivalent of Neptune:

> *Their ocean-God was Mananann Mac Lir*
> *Whose angry lips in their snowy foam*
> *Would oft inter great fleets of ships.*

It is appropriate that this god should be recalled in the name of the Isle of Man, Oileán Manann, located in the middle of the Irish Sea, presumably so that he could keep an eye on his Welsh, Irish and Scottish subjects. Mananann is first encountered by an Irish voyager named Bran who is, typically, searching for the Isle of Joy. Suddenly he sees a strange figure riding the crest of a wave in a chariot. The stranger sings:

THE ATLANTEAN IRISH

> Bran thinks this is a marvellous sea.
> For me it is a flowery plain.
> Speckled salmon leap from the belly of your sea;
> To me they are calves and sprightly lambs.

Mananann carried a bag made from the skin of a crane that purportedly contained the alphabet – an echo of the Phoenicians. The unfortunate crane had been his wife, Aoife, who earned his wrath by trying to steal the god's secret knowledge and tell it to the world.

This story of the seventh century is healthily pagan. There are no pious monks braving all for the love of God; a simple hedonistic way of life is celebrated. But by the ninth century it has been expanded to become the voyage of Maél Dúin, in which the hero has become pious enough to praise the Lord for his various deliverances. It still retains some lechery, as when Maél Dúin's companions try in vain to persuade a woman to sleep with their leader. However, towards the end they find a church and a grey-haired incumbent, a priest to whom Maél Dúin defers. Christianity has arrived! Predictably, not long after Maél Dúin, the same story becomes solely the vehicle for an account of a saint's wanderings. This is the 'Voyage of St Brendan', the culmination of all Irish maritime escapades of the period.

References in many other stories show that the Irish, Welsh and Scots were not only familiar with the vagaries of the sea but that it was a large part of their consciousness:

> The ocean is full, the sea is in flood, lovely is the home of ships;
> the sandy wind has made eddies around Inbher na dá Ainmheach;
> the rudder is swift upon the wide sea.

The coastal folklore of Ireland is rich with encounters between seals and humans, sea-horses, huge eels, magic islands, mermaids, even sub-marine butter-making. Most of these stories are highlighted by pithy verses and sayings:

> The three swiftest things in the sea are the seal, the mackerel and
> the ray; the three that leave the least trace are a bird on a branch,
> a ship on the sea and a man on a woman.

In one story a man named Connla falls in love with a fairy woman and sails away in her crystal boat; in another the hero mounts a fine steed behind his lady love and they both fly away over the sea. In a third fantasy, a sailor named Ruadh is on his way with three ships and ninety men to meet the Norsemen near Scotland – the details are always necessary to give verisimilitude – when his ship is becalmed. He immediately knows what to do: he goes over the side and swims deep down until he meets nine women. He has to sleep with each of them before they will lift the spell that has immobilized his craft.

The frequent surrealism of these stories reaches its peak in an account of what happened to some monks in Clonmacnoise as told by Kenneth H. Jackson in *A Celtic Miscellany* (1951). They were praying in their chapel when they looked up and saw a ship sailing overhead, its anchor trailing. The anchor caught in a door and one of the crew descended, going through the motions of swimming. He released the anchor and was about to swim up when a priest caught him by the ankle, causing him to screech out: 'Let go, for God's sake, or I'll drown.' Released, he calmly swam up through the air, taking the anchor with him. The ship sailed smoothly away.

Even when they were beach-combing there was an imaginative touch: when a woman was washed up on the shore in Ireland she was an androgynous giantess, 50 metres tall but with breasts unformed; in Scotland, in the same story, the woman becomes 92 metres in length. There are 17

Scene at Badajos, Extramadura, Spain (photo: I. Roisin, Madrid)

metres between her breasts, and her nose is 7 metres long. But 'every limb of her is as white as the down of a swan or the foam of the sea'.

Centuries after the dutiful hand of ecclesiastical scribes had converted most of these stories into parables leading the faithful to God, the power of the original could still seep through. The richness and variety of Irish folk tales is one testimony of the tradition of the *filí* or poets who disdained writing for fear their memory might atrophy. The noting down by clerics of these stories did not suddenly make these storytellers redundant.

One of my first encounters in Conamara was with a well-known seanchaí, the late Beartlaí Ó Conghaile. He was sitting in a tiny shop in the middle of the day, a child on each knee, reciting a story in Irish. It had the exaggeration, the repetition of phrases, the flowing phrases of the true storyteller. The tradition was still alive, a thousand years after the monks encountered it, and Beartlaí's son Éamonn maintains the tradition. The latter, after rearing his family, became a priest and is still invited to tell his tales all over the world.

An account of another storyteller in Kerry is full of pathos. This man had finally run out of an audience; they had been seduced away by cars, radios and television. But the craft of storytelling was important enough for him to try and preserve it. So he could be seen driving the cattle home on a summer's evening, reciting his stories to the midges and the unheeding backs of the cows. Fortunately, his stories and those of the other Irish seanchaí have been largely preserved on tape and in notebooks in University College Dublin so that a future, more appreciative, generation may enjoy them.

Possibly the most important myth in the context of the Irish Atlanteans is that of Atlantis itself, the drowned continent. I agree with Robert Graves that it is a pity the term 'myth' has come to mean 'fanciful, absurd, unhistorical'. The poet maintained that myths are all serious records of ancient religious customs or events, and reliable enough as history once their language is understood. *Once their language is understood*: that is the key phrase. Our recently acquired rationalist dialects make us quite illiterate in the important language of myth.

Atlantis is as mythical as the Land of the Blest, Hy Brazil, Tír na nÓg (Land of Youth), the Isle of Joy and all the descriptions in which we dress our dreams. In outline, the argument runs that a continent once existed in the place where the Atlantic now is; that it disappeared under the waves, for whatever catastrophic reason, and that the survivors fled east and west.

In the west, they formed the higher civilizations of South America; in the east, they became the Sea Peoples who plagued Greece, Egypt and the Mediterranean.

This was the basis of a book written in 1882 by Ignatius Donnelly, an American senator, called *Atlantis, the Antediluvian World*. A century later an

Irish author, P.A. Ó Síocháin, could still say that Ireland was the last remnant of this civilization and that its peoples were directly related to those lost people. The megaliths on the Atlantic coast were the evidence of the outskirts of that territory in the ocean, as were the mighty stone fortresses, for example Dún Aonghusa on the Aran Islands, whose builders have never been identified but which can be traced at least as far back as the Bronze Age. Professor Etienne Rynne of Galway University always maintained that this was exclusively a ceremonial structure. His former student, Michael Gibbons, has recently, with the aid of aerial photography, shown it to have been a functional fortress in the Iron Age, and a symbol of a great maritime power.

The Irish Atlanteans, who are still in tune with the sea, retain a folk memory of their original common heritage: even the Berbers have it. Indeed, the latter may have the best claim to be called Atlanteans because part of their home territory is the range of mountains known as the Atlas. They, too, have their Atlantis myth. There is a Sumerian legend of a drowned civilization, which Ouzzin, a modern Berber scholar, found contained names that were familiar to him from his own culture. In this legend there is a princess called Tangis, from whose name Tangier is derived. The story goes that she is one day overtaken by a storm at sea and drowned. Her distraught husband begins a search for her and attacks an island called Atlantis by means of an underground cavern. The force of his attack triggers an earthquake that causes the island to disappear. The husband becomes a hermit and spends his days sitting on a rock overlooking the sea, hoping his wife will somehow return. At last the spirit of Tangis calls to him, he is overcome with joy and throws himself into the sea to join her.

The name of the husband was Lugal, a name that constantly crops up in 'Celtic' mythology. Indeed, Lyons (Lugdunum) in France is reputed to be named after him although in the Roman-Gallic museum there it is translated as Raven Hill. A major pagan feast in Ireland was *Lughnasa* – the Irish name for the month of August and the god Lu. When Lyons was called Lugdunum, it was the scene of one of the murders of the Roman Emperor Caligula; his victim was the last king of Mauretania, home of the Berbers. No doubt, on the basis of the Lugal story, a scholar could erect a common Sumerian ancestry for both 'Celt' and Berber.

Some years ago I was contacted by an aeronautical engineer from Peterborough in England called Nigel Corrigan. He and his friend, an airline navigator, had stumbled on the following coincidence: the Atlantic Ridge, from which it is traditionally supposed that the Atlantis myth emerged, is situated exactly equidistant from, and on precisely the same latitude (30°) as, both the Giza Pyramid in Egypt and a place called Cumpas in the Sonora region of Mexico. The men worked out that at the moment when the sun is setting on the Giza Pyramid it is rising on Cumpas where, they speculated, there may also be a pyramid or ziggurat. What they also found intriguing was the word 'Cumpas', which seems too close to 'compass' to be regarded as a coincidence. There is no etymological basis for the universal word 'compass'. I have never had the resources to investigate the questions raised by my friend's hypothesis but a computer-literate nephew in Paris put it to the test. They had gauged the simultaneous rising and setting of the sun alright, but the computer proclaimed that the morning equivalent of night-time Giza was not Cumpas in Mexico, but New Orleans.

Mr Harry Bourne a London historian who studies 'African' sculpture in the Americas, writes:

> On what was said already, the arrivals at Panco [Mexico] came from the rising sun and the colossal heads of Africans at La Venta [Mexico] also face the east. The pyramid at La Venta seems to have been built on a north/south orientation apparently unknown in the Americas before the rise of the Olmecs and relevant here must be that on the very platform of this temple were the African colossi just noted.

La Venta is due south of New Orleans across the Gulf of Mexico. But I must return to the living evidence. I found more of this in Egypt.

North African Influences on Early Irish Christianity

14

St Antony's monastery in Egypt, located in a desolate spot in the desert hinterland of the Red Sea, has been in continuous occupation for the past 1800 years. It is now some twenty years since a sympathetic Irish ambassador to Egypt, Brian Ó Ceallaigh, and I enjoyed the hospitality of the monks who maintain the tradition.

A few kilometres away is the Coptic monastery of St Paul. It is agreed that these two foundations mark the places where the first anchorites or solitaries lived. Antony was quite sure he was alone in this wilderness until he accidentally stumbled on Paul, who had been there for years before him. From this barren place emerged the saintly madness that fuelled early Irish Christianity and made it unique in the West. In trying to find pointers that would suggest a direct connection with Ireland, I was, of course, hoping for Arabic and Islamic clues, but the Copts impinged on every lead I followed.

I had done the normal touristic things: I sailed a felucca on the Nile and confirmed that it had, indeed, the rig of a Conamara púcán; visited the Tutankhamen exhibition in Cairo and noted the Osiris pose of crossed arms, which is a particular detail of Irish illuminated manuscripts; saw the gold lunulae or necklets that were also common in Ireland over 2000 years

Sign for St Antony's monastery (top); St Antony and St Paul (above)

 *St Antony's monastery (left); St Paul's monastery (right)*

ago. I even found the source of the shamrock, the national emblem of Ireland. This tiny, three-leafed plant bears the weight of an amount of traditional Christian mythology, not to mention theology. People traditionally believed that it grew nowhere else but the green isle of Erin. It is said to have been the plant used by Ireland's national apostle, St Patrick, to introduce the pagan Irish to the mystery of the Holy Trinity.

In the Islamic Museum in Cairo I came across some beautifully carved wooden doors in whose design was integrated the unmistakable three-leafed plant. When I enquired about this design the curator said it was described as a 'shamrakh'. Any trefoil plant, he said, is called in Arabic a *shamrakh*. Later a friend supplied a supporting quotation from the section on St Patrick in *The Book of Days*: 'but it is certainly a curious coincidence, if nothing more, that the trefoil in Arabic is called shamrakh, and was held sacred in Iran as emblematic of the Persian Triads'.

In the same museum there were other pieces of wood dated to the third century that bore the imprint of designs in leather, long perished. The designs, to my eyes, were strongly reminiscent of those on some pages of Irish illuminated manuscripts.

Coptic cross incorporating Egyptian ankh symbol

The phenomenon of desert monasticism was not an invention of Christianity; it had existed long before in ascetic communities such as the Katechoi recluses at Memphis in Egypt. The Essenes, writers of the Dead Sea Scrolls, were a Jewish desert community. The Jordan Valley once teemed with saintly eccentrics. Even John the Baptist emerged from a solitary life in the wilderness. The term anchorite comes from the Greek *anchoresis*, meaning departure. Monk simply means, in the same language, 'alone'. The Christian adaptation of this flight to the desert happened in the third and fourth centuries. It sprang mainly from the belief that the end of the world was nigh, the Second Coming was imminent and one should anticipate this by renouncing the world of the flesh. And so, a variety of saintly retreats developed: caves, holes in the sand, hollowed-out trees, the tops of desert stalagmites and wherever else might satisfy the equation of discomfort with sanctity.

In the desert of the Wadi Natrun, between Cairo and Alexandria, it was estimated that in the early years of this activity there were at least 5000 of these individuals trying to achieve 'solitary' communion with God. It is likely that they were not all successful or even serious in the attempt to become bona fide saints. The conditions of the peasants of Egypt were so grim that monastic life must have seemed quite attractive by comparison, particularly when a successor to St Antony, named Pachomius, organized the monks into communities. These embryo monasteries were self-sufficient, which meant that an erstwhile peasant stood a good chance of getting fed without the usual hardship.

While not wishing to deprecate the drive for sanctity that must have informed most of these early ascetics, it is also proper to mention another pressing incentive to abandon the world: persecution. The Year of the Martyr in the Coptic Church is 284 AD, when the Emperor Diocletian organized a systematic persecution of Christians. Even after he stopped, even after the Roman Empire itself adopted Christianity, the persecution of Copts continued. As the empire became Christian, the Church became imperial.

In the main these native Egyptians of the Christian persuasion spoke neither Greek nor Latin. They clung to their own Egyptian language, which singled them out from the sophisticated Christians of Alexandria. The Synaxarium of the Coptic Church records considerably more martyrs for the period up to the seventh century, when Christianity was dominant, than for the years following, when Islam was in charge. This is not so much an indication of the fact that Islam was tolerant – which, relatively speaking, it was – as of the bitter in-fighting among Christians themselves. By the fifth century they were divided into Diophysites, Monophysites, Arians, Donatists, Nestorians, Manichaeans and many other competing sects. The Council of Chalcedon, in 451 AD, put the seal on the fate of the Copts and many other Eastern and North African Christians. The latter could not accept the Council's complex formula defining the position of Christ in relation to God; it seemed to diminish the uniqueness of God, His essential Oneness, and they therefore retreated into what has since been termed a Monophysite position. The Egyptian Copts, for good or ill, continued to share this perspective with their Muslim and Jewish fellow citizens.

A mischievous English ex-Benedictine whom I met in Cairo put a different complexion on the matter. Perhaps assuming that my Irishness would welcome such a reading, he claimed that it was because of their ultra-nationalism that the Copts were excluded by the Council of Chalcedon. The finer points of theology were just an excuse. Such nationalism was an attitude that could never fit snugly into the universalist ambitions of a growing Church. Indeed, to me there was something vaguely familiar about this thesis – it reminded me of the excommunication of extreme Irish nationalists in the past century.

The survival of the Copts is like a miracle. Rejected by the Orthodox Church for two centuries, until the take-over by Islam made such a rejection academic, they not only preserved their beliefs but also the Egyptian language in which their liturgy is still partially expressed. They also kept faith with their forefathers by integrating into their liturgical art the very symbols of the pharaohs. The ankh, symbol of life, was transformed into a Coptic cross; the custom of portraying human bodies with animal heads was directly borrowed from tomb illustrations and incorporated in their icons. The Tau Cross and the Antony and Paul figures are represented on Irish high crosses such as those at Monasterboice, Co. Louth, and Kilfenora, Co. Clare. The term Coptic simply means Egyptian. It is derived from the Arabic *Qubt*, a corruption of the Greek *Aigyptos*, which in turn is a derivation of the ancient Egyptian *Hak-ka-Ptah*, i.e. the house of the temple of the spirit of Ptah.

Western Christianity lost sight of this unique Church until 1860, when a Presbyterian mission 'discovered' it and tried to convert its members – to Christianity! The Coptic Archbishop of Assiut was understandably irritated: 'We have been living here with Christ for more than 1800 years,' he said, 'How long have you been living with him?'

Lest I give the impression of a Rip Van Winkle sect barely hanging on for life in the deserts of Egypt, I should report that there are an estimated 7 million members of the Church of Egypt (a compromise between the state's estimate of 4 million and the Copts' estimate of 11 million); and that, in Cairo, it has its own 'Vatican', with a pope, schools of theology and fine libraries.

In one conversation a Coptic deacon mentioned a solid link with Ireland. He knew, he said, that the Copts had influenced early Irish Christianity because at least seven of their monks were recorded as martyrs there. These were the Seven Monks noted in the *Martyrology of Tallaght* as having been buried in a place called *Díseart Ulidh*, the Desert of Ulster, not known in Ireland. The Copts believed that the monks were buried in Ballymena, which is in Ulster, because one of their known saints is St Mena. However, the real name for Ballymena is – in Irish – *Baile Meánach* (middle town), which has nothing to do with saints, Coptic or otherwise.

Díseart is a common place-name in Ireland; it means desert and commemorates the early Irish monks' acknowledgment of the influence of oriental Christianity. The number seven also gives the matter a vagueness, because it is a standard figure to indicate perfection or holiness.

However, in Co. Clare I came across an old church at a place called Dysert O'Dea. The Irish form of this name (at least on the signposts) is

Egyptian icon of St Mark with Tau sceptre (left); Kilfenora Cross showing Antony and Paul with Tau sceptre (photo: Office of Public Works) (right)

Díseart Tola, meaning Desert of the Flood. Now, if one pronounces this name rapidly, elision causes it to emerge as 'Diseartola' – which is as near as makes no difference to *Díseart Ulidh*, at least to the tenth-century scribe who first mentioned the Egyptian exiles. In another churchyard at Kilfenora I saw a sculpted stone cross (the Doorty Cross) with a strange emblem on it. This featured two sceptres – one the normal shape of a shepherd's crook, the other an odd T-shape. The historian Peter Harbison has associated this iconography with St Antony and St Paul. The last time I saw such a T-shaped staff was in the chapel of St Antony's in the desert. There it is referred to as a patibulary. An old monk was using it for support during the long service. It was also a common feature on the Coptic icons. I further learned it was the standard form of ecclesiastical staff in Ireland up to the ninth century. There are other three-dimensional stone representations of this sceptre in Ireland. The two best known are on Tory Island, 15 kilometres off the coast of Donegal, and at Killinaboy, Co. Clare.

While talking to Father George, my informative Coptic deacon, I noticed a leather cross worn by another priest. It had an ingeniously woven pattern whose broad interwoven bands seemed close in spirit to a design carved on a stone called the Fahan Mura, also in Co. Donegal. These broad bands are also to be seen, in colour, in the Book of Durrow. Father George

⊠ *Coptic leather cross (left); Fahan Mura Cross, Carndonagh, Co. Donegal (photo: Office of Public Works) (right)*

told me that the Coptic form of his name was actually Girgis. This saint was credited with slaying Satan in the form of a dragon, which suggested that the Copts had also given the English their patron saint! The cumulative effect of discovering these odd little details gave focus to the following idea.

The development of Irish Christianity has always been something of a puzzle. Nobody knows exactly by which route early monasticism came to the British Isles. Any direct continental evidence that exists gives no hint as to the source of the original contact with Christianity. Oddly enough, the earliest direct references to the existence of Christianity in these remote islands comes from two North Africans, Tertullian and Origen, in the third century. The pattern of persecution in the Middle East and North Africa produced a breed of Christian who thought all the 'world' was evil and that one should distance oneself as much as possible from it. The desert is an ideal place for such an exercise but, with 5000 other people having the same intention in the same place, its value as a 'wilderness' decreases. With many of the refugees aspiring more to the security of a monastery than to the true ascetic spirit, the coinage is debased; the atmosphere in these desert enclaves must have become slightly suburban.

Where could the true believers go? They were accustomed to seeking oases, the islands of the desert. Why not even more inaccessible islands, those of the sea? The farthest place you could go at that time was the edge of that world. The Greeks had described a Holy Isle; Ptolemy the Alexandrian had charted it; the Carthaginians had explored it in pursuit of tin. The Ancient World had, as we have seen, many beliefs about places called the Fortunate Isles in the far west, a paradise beyond the setting sun, the Continent of Kronos, Ogygia, the Garden of the Hesperides, Atlantis, etc. But, more important, there were legends of a northern sea called Marimorusa, i.e. *mare mortuum*, the sea of the dead. The culture of the anchorite aimed at being 'dead to the world'. In the light of their belief that the world was inherently evil, a sea of the dead must have seemed highly appropriate.

Coptic and Syrian refugees are known to have 'relocated' in substantial numbers to southern Gaul. They formed a distinct community there in the fourth and fifth centuries. Their existence must have been precarious, representing a branch of Christianity deemed heretical by both Eastern and Western orthodoxies.

The early form that this religion took in Ireland appears to have been much closer to the desert solitaries. The earliest monastic settlements were tiny, crude, scattered and numerous – more like shrines than monasteries. The Skelligs Rock – twelve kilometres off the coast of Kerry – is sheer enough, rugged enough, cruel enough to satisfy the most masochistic ambitions of any anchorite. The stone huts of these ascetics still survive on the rocks. The early literature quotes endless examples of such anchorites in remote places like the Skelligs. Like Egyptian monasticism, which was a revolt against ecclesiastical organization and the episcopal system, the later Irish Church developed a base firmly rooted in the tribe. A leader or 'abbot' could inherit his role from his father, and bishops were under his thumb. But this development was later than the initial phenomenon of the solitaries.

In the fourth century the Emperor Theodosius clamped down on movement into and out of the empire. This had as much application in the religious as in the commercial sphere. The Copts and many other North African Christians were 'outside the pale'. That is why most of the Coptic missionary activity that is recorded was in a southerly direction, in Nubia and Ethiopia, in areas avoided by Greeks and Romans. It would account for an

Irish nun writing to me some years ago and enclosing samples of Ethiopian art that she felt sure had affinities with the Irish forms. 'Ever since coming to Ethiopia in 1974,' Sister Mary T. Ryan wrote, 'I have wondered about the likeness between Celtic design (as we call it) and Ethiopian-Coptic design.'

I have already suggested that the tightening of restrictions on travel through the now-Christian empire must have produced a stimulus to travel on its borders. It has also been shown that sea travel was a normal way of covering large distances. There was no reason why the phenomenon known as early Irish Christianity should not have come directly from North Africa, bypassing continental Europe and making 'pit-stops' along the Atlantic coasts.

While in Cairo I noticed some women with a 'lozenge' or diamond-shaped mark on their foreheads. These marks reminded me that the Berber practice of tattooing was universal throughout North Africa. The more traditional Copts also had a cross tattooed on their wrists. Those who pretended to sophistication, and did not wear this sign of faith, explained that 'they carried the cross in their hearts'.

A manuscript in St Gall, Switzerland, records that Irish monks, known as wanderers for Christ, also used tattoos and painted their eyelids. Where did they get this custom that, along with their unorthodox appearance, so irritated the clerical authorities on the Continent? Pope Celestine wrote on the danger of appointing 'wanderers and strangers' to local episcopal office: 'They who have not grown up in the Church, act contrary to the Church's usage ... coming from other customs ... clad in a cloak with a girdle round their loins.' He must have been talking about the Irish; they were certainly unorthodox, if not heretical. The disputes over hairstyles

Berber woman's tattoo (Tribus Berbéres *by André Bertrand, 1977)*

and the date of Easter were so vehement at the Synod of Whitby in 664 AD that the northern Irish Christians decamped back to Iona in Scotland and thence to Ireland.

The efforts to integrate this awkward thing called 'early Irish Christianity' into a respectable European mould have been energetic. They range from the explanation that the Coptic/ Syrian influence in southern Gaul accounts for its idiosyncrasies, to the possibility that St Patrick himself brought back oriental touches from the North African-influenced monastery of Lérins, off the south coast of Gaul. I saw for myself the modern plaque on the exterior wall of this monastery that optimistically commemorates that famous visitor. St Patrick was British, which coincided with the belief that all the efforts to civilize the Irish came from that quarter. There is no written reference to the saint until the seventh century, two hundred years after his supposed conversion of the Irish. It is very odd that he is not mentioned at all by prominent scribes such as Gildas, Bede, Adamnán or Columbanus.

The date of St Patrick's arrival in Ireland, 432 AD, is clearly a 'mythological' number. In the Icelandic sagas, Valhalla has 540 doors through each of which 800 warriors pass. Multiply the two figures and the result is 432,000. In the Chaldean legends of Babylon, the interval between the building of the first city, Kish, and the disaster of the Flood is also 432,000 years. Astronomically, the number of years in one complete cycle of the procession of the equinoxes is 25,920. If that is divided by 60 — the basic multiple of the most ancient Mesopotamian mathematical system — the

⊠ *Isle of Lerins monastery, Cannes*

answer is 432. Even in the Puranas, old Indian epics, there is a great cycle referred to as the Day of Brahma estimated at 432,000 years. This date, 432 AD, appears to have been chosen for its metaphysical and allegorical dimension, to mark what was simply a clerical take-over of Irish history. Just as the scribes of the early Middle Ages fitted the pagan Irish tradition into a

Isle of Lerins, plaque to 'Saint Patrice'

classical chronology, so also must they have assigned a cosmological number like 432 as a date to a significant event, such as the alleged coming of Christianity in the form of St Patrick. Fortunately, we know that there were Christians in Ireland before him, if he existed at all. He was sent 'to those Irish believing in Christ'.

The story of Patrick driving the snakes from Ireland is also mythical: there were never any snakes in Ireland, at least not since the last ice age. Professor Aodhagáin O'Rahilly once suggested that there were two St Patricks. This would certainly satisfy those Egyptians and Lebanese who believe that they each sent a St Patrick to Ireland.

As I have tried to emphasize, it is better to try to understand the meaning of a myth than to dismiss it altogether. As noted earlier *shamrakh* is an Arabic word – in fact, its first mention in relation to Ireland was written in the twelfth century, the period of the Crusades. The charming allegation of its use as a teaching device by Patrick – to explain the three-in-one concept of the Trinity – may be significant because this 'Trinity' was precisely the point of friction between 'orthodox' Christianity and the schismatic Copts, Syrians and all the other Monophysite religions.

The story of the snakes is so bizarre that it, too, must have a meaning. It happens that in the North Africa of this early period there was a Christian

Snakes slink to Naas

KILDARE County Council has succeeded where St Patrick failed and has banished the serpent from the County. But the reptile is keeping his cobra-like grip on Naas where he will continue to coil himself around the town crest's sword.

The snake, which has represented the county of Kildare since the original crest was designed in 1888, finally met his doom on the grassy plains of Croke Park where councillors flinched at the sight of the county team bearing a reptile on their chests before the eyes of the nation.

"I just don't think that a snake really represents Kildare as it is today," said Councillor Jimmy O'Loughlin, chairman of the council and head of the protocol committee which

By Ken O Shea

signed the death warrant for the snake.

"Personally I never liked the snake and we used to get a terrible slagging over it on the council," he added. "People used to say that we were the snakes! But then again, the snake also represents cunning and wisdom so that's not too bad."

One of the most ardent enemies of the much-maligned creature in Kildare is Councillor Michael McWey.

"I think it's a terrible yoke!" he said with all the disgust of a man dead set against slimy creepie-crawlies.

"I was very alarmed to see the Kildare county footballers wearing a snake on their

jerseys in the National League final against Dublin. It's very bad for the image of the county to be associated with a horrible animal like that!"

The council promptly commissioned a new coat of arms, sans snake, from the Hearladic office in Dublin featuring a horse's head, oak leaves, a harp and a St Brigid's cross on a shield quartered by a Fitgearld cross with crossed swords. A new county motto was also chosen with a suggestion from County Secretary Harry Lyons being adopted in the end. It reads: "Meamna agus Misneach" - spirit and courage.

The new crest will be used on all official documents and on a series of new road signs planned for the county's boundary.

Snakes newspaper cutting; snake symbol on the old Kildare coat of arms (Kildare County Council)

sect called the Ophites or Naasenes, who worshipped God in the form of a serpent. This was because they believed the god defined by their orthodox enemies and persecutors must be evil; consequently, that god's enemy – the serpent – must be the real God. Therefore they worshipped the serpent.

There is a town in Co. Kildare called Naas; the symbol of that town – designed in 1898 – was the serpent. Alas, no more; the county council recently decided that the pejorative connotations of a snake on their footballers' jerseys could no longer be endured, and they voted to change the symbol. They may have been unaware that they were repeating history, emulating the action of St Patrick. It is a good example of how history may have its serious, even tragic, origins, but its repetition often ends as farce. By such whimsical imperatives, the personality of the island of Ireland is increasingly being sanitized.

St Patrick's reputed success with the snakes is a rich metaphor to illustrate the ultimate triumph of orthodoxy over a pre-existing form of Christianity in Ireland, which consisted of sects like the Ophites. Even a sensible observer like Michael Viney agreed that the snakes 'could actually have been a metaphor for the pagan druids and the symbols of their rival religion'. However, this triumph was not totally achieved until the twelfth century when the Normans arrived. And so it seems that the conventional account of early Irish Christianity as an offshoot of respectable European orthodoxy might have been an invention of this late period. If the early clerical scribes could 'synchronize' pagan stories with classical history, it would not have been difficult to bring the early development of the religion

Egyptian 'pearl' found at Plouhinec, Brittany (photo: Henri Cabillic); grave where it was found (photo: Henri Cabillic)

on this island into line with an idealized account of the Great Western Church.

In 1958 V. Gordon Childe wrote that the activities of 'Celtic' saints might be compared to the spread of megalithic tombs in Western Europe. As he maintained that the idea for these tombs originated from the Eastern Mediterranean and spread west, through the Straits of Gibraltar and up the Atlantic coasts, I take this as a supportive analogy. Glyn Daniel himself wrote: 'It cannot be disputed that a powerful religion of East Mediterranean origin informed and inspired the builders of the megalithic tombs as they spread throughout Western Europe.'

The later, still ancient, wine routes from the Mediterranean to the north were presumably not disrupted by theological squabbles. Pieces of pottery found in Garranes, Co. Cork, as well as in Cornwall, were identified as having come directly from Alexandria in Egypt. A cache of 'pearls' shown to me in a grave at Plouhinec – not far from the megaliths of Morbihan in Brittany – were identified as Egyptian and dated to the fourth century, the period when persecution was a strong motive for travelling. Similar 'pearls' (actually faience beads) were found in excavations on the Hill of Tara and were dated to 2100 BC. These miscellaneous items might explain 'The Book of Adam and Eve', allegedly composed in Egypt in about the fifth century and known in no other European country except Ireland, where it became the eleventh-century *Saltair na Rann* ('Psalter of the Quatrains').

In Cairo I met a journalist, a Jesuit priest, who had studied the relationship between the Copts and what he understood to be 'Celts' (the Bretons) for seventeen years. He was convinced there were solid grounds for suggesting such a connection. He based his opinion not only on liturgical and monastic similarities but on the semi-pagan rituals that still underlie many practices. He instanced the processions for the dead in Brittany (of which he was a native) and those in the Egyptian deserts, which also took place in November. He told me that on the 2nd July each summer in the village of Lannion, east of Brest, a traditional religious *Pardon* is still celebrated that commemorates *La Sept Saint* and the dim memory of Muslim pilgrims of long ago. Visitors to the *Pardon* in 1984 noted:

> It was Louis Massignon whose scholarship established the connection between Christianity and Islam that makes this Pardon unique. The Seven Sleepers were revered in early Christendom and continue to be in Islam: they are mentioned in the 18th Sura of the Koran. The foundation of their cult in this distant corner of Brittany presumably dates from the sixth century AD, when it was brought by Eastern Christians following the tin merchants' route from the Aegean to Cornwall and the Scilly Isles.

In Cairo I also met an American musicologist, Dr Martha Roy, who had spent nearly fifty years living in Egypt. I played her a tape-recording of the sean-nós singing of Conamara's revered Seán Jack Mac Donncha. She listened attentively and then said its pentatonic form was not necessarily Arabic but was characteristic of Nubian singing and of African countries in general. But could such a musical form have travelled all the way to the west of Ireland, I ventured? She by no means dismissed the idea and mentioned an example that Bela Bartok had discovered of the transmission of music over many kilometres and many years. He had found a community in the Caucasus who had emigrated from Hungary 600 years previously but who still retained the precise melodies and words they had brought with them from the home country. I have since then realized that Bartok simply reversed the direction: the Hungarian musical modes were actually influenced by the eastern Turkic forms brought by the Islamic Seljuk empire. However, Dr Roy's information so pleased me that I went to a Nubian wedding to celebrate. There I heard the amazing sound of the *zagharit* – the fierce, tongue-rolling yodel of the women. I knew that this could be experienced in any country of North Africa: another example of how a distinctive vocal expression can be shared by people 1600 kilometres apart. Bearing in mind the monks of the desert of Egypt, I thought of what another

Conamara sean-nós singer had told me about the origin of her music: she said the old folk thought it came from 'the monks'.

To summarize: the structure and ethos of the early Irish Church is so suffused with Eastern and North African characteristics that to attribute it to second-hand influences begs too many questions. The Copts of Egypt, as living evidence of similarity, are an obvious group on which to base the maritime argument and the feasibility of influence along the Atlantic seaways.

Carthage, with its historically recorded contact with the British Isles, was also a prime locus of potential. It was here that the major heresy of Donatism developed. Like the Copts, the Carthaginian Christians were completely integrated with local cultures and languages. The Carthaginians were Punic and Berber. They were not just a minor tributary to the mainstream of Christianity, nor were they a minor sect; one of their bishops, Timgad, left the largest and finest cathedral in North Africa. The history of Carthaginian wars with the pagan Roman Empire – the Punic Wars – was not forgotten. In time this spilled over into a mistrust of the imperial Roman Church. These people were anti-authoritarian, independent-minded and ascetic. They thought that the Church's alliance with the empire was disastrous in that it had become too worldly. Christianity, which had come to Carthage early in the second century, retained there an early idealism that refused to compromise with a world seen as evil.

The Carthaginians were highly organized, with as many as 500 bishops on whom they kept a tight rein, ever watchful for signs of arrogance or decadence. They coined the title 'Communion of Saints' for themselves, one later taken over by the imperial Church. Their obsession with personal perfection started the row. The Carthaginians maintained that if a bishop was a sinner – specifically if during earlier persecutions he had collaborated with the Roman imperial Church – this invalidated his sacramental role. Things came to a head when eighty Numidian bishops objected to the appointment of Caecilian as Bishop of Carthage, on the grounds that the celebrant of the rite was a 'sinner'. They appointed a man named Donatus in his stead. The resulting conflict expressed itself in a war between sophisticated, urbanized, Christians – the neo-liberals of those days – and a nationalistic, indigenous people. The Emperor Constantine naturally backed the former – those who supported the Roman point of view.

Persecution of the native Church lasted for the next sixty years. Orthodoxy had the weight of the secular empire on its side, but the

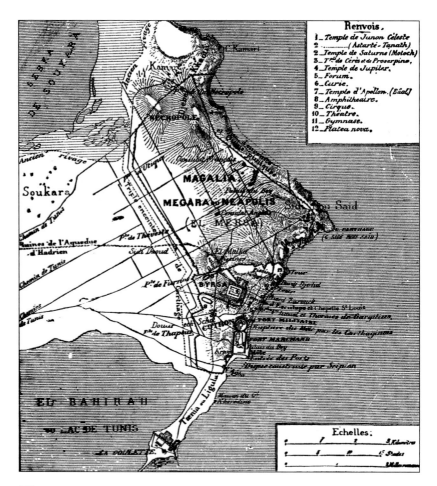

⊠ *Plan of Carthage (from* Hannibal, Soldier, Statesman, Patriot *by William O'Connor Morris, 1897)*

Carthaginians were well organized and were fighting on their home territory. They even developed private armies of 'circumcelliones' who carried cudgels to make sure their own bishops were not tempted to capitulate on the issues. Absentee Roman landlords maintained large estates in North Africa – a legacy of the original conquerors of Hannibal, the destroyers of the original Carthage. The Donatists became a kind of guerrilla force who made sorties against these estates.

The Orthodox Church, in alliance with the physical might of the empire, conducted a campaign both political and physical to destroy the Donatists. A number of councils were held, ostensibly to try to resolve the dispute, but in the end Donatus was excommunicated, and his followers more intensively persecuted. The chief architect of this victory was also a North African – a man born in Algeria of a mother called Monika and a father called, interestingly, Patrick. He was the famous St Augustine of Hippo – a man described as 'the dark genius of Imperial Christianity, the fabricator of the mediaeval mentality'. For the first thirty years of this famous saint's life he belonged to a heretical sect called the Manichaeans; apparently this was unremarkable in a man of his family in those early years of Christianity.

Paul Johnson, on whom I have perhaps relied too heavily, describes the end of Donatism:

> Even after a long bout of imperial persecution, inspired by Augustine, the Donatists were still able to produce nearly three hundred bishops for the final attempt at compromise at Carthage in 411. Thereafter in the course of two decades, before the Vandals overran the littoral, the back of the Donatist Church was broken by force. Its upper-class supporters joined the establishment. Many of its rank and file were driven into outlawry and brigandage. There were many cases of mass suicide.

North Africa seemed to me to be the last refuge of the ancient traditions of asceticism, non-conformism and general independence of mind. Rome and Constantinople became 'orthodox' and imperial; North Africa stayed nationalist and became schismatic. It sounded, to me, like a perfect receipe for what I had learned of the early Irish Church. What became of all these North Africans, with their passionate religious beliefs? They could not all have conformed to the Augustinian idea of total religious uniformity. The majority that stayed in North Africa must have submitted very reluctantly, but even they were overwhelmed by the Vandals who are considered to have hammered the final nail into the coffin of the Church in North Africa. The ease with which Islam took over two centuries later – it had no priests, no pope, just a clear belief in one God – demonstrates that. But what of those who refused to serve?

Is it not likely they would have searched for a place beyond the reach of the imperial Church, a place well known by reputation, a place the empire had never touched? The coming of Christianity to Ireland certainly happened within thirty years of this North African turmoil. When, centuries later, Irish missionaries began to spread their wings and travel abroad, when Brendan and the others began their voyaging, there was no apprehension about long sea trips. What is solely in question is the length of the voyage the first Christians undertook to get here in the first place.

A voyage from North Africa to these northern islands in those early centuries of religious strife and persecution must have seemed, not a frightening prospect, but a welcome chance of escape. There actually existed a green and pleasant land free of interminable theological quarrels, of rapacious bishops, of an increasingly bureaucratic – and corrupt – Church, of the pagan Vandals. There was no need to travel overland 1600 kilometres through territories where in one you were in danger if you were Arian, in another you were accused of Donatism, or Montanism, or Manichaeanism, or Nestorianism, or even Pelagianism – any of the hundred and one 'heresies' to which, in fact, you might actually be proud to adhere. Furthermore, as Máire and Liam de Paor wrote: 'The old sea-route to Western France and the Mediterranean – the route of the wine trade – almost certainly remained open in some degree in spite of the barbarians and it seems most likely that there were some direct contacts between Ireland and Egypt.'

Indeed, reading of these many 'heresies', on what narrow ground could orthodoxy possibly reside? Heresy was not a description of an objectionable innovation. It was precisely the opposite. A church adapting to political reality in its many forms was forced to drop some ancient practices adopted for the time being from older religions. It was mainly these older practices and beliefs, retained by some Christians, that were condemned as heretical. In the year 390 there were 156 distinct 'heresies' in full flight. In the fifth century at least a hundred official Church statutes opposed such deviancies. So much for the idea of a monolithic, united Christianity.

Increasingly, it seemed possible that the early Irish Church owed little to continental Europe – that, in fact, this religion travelled by a circular route, following the earlier trading routes, westwards along the Mediterranean, up the Atlantic coasts, hibernating in Ireland for a while, before moving onward through Scotland and England into Europe. I found more support for this idea in arts and crafts.

Irish and Eastern Illuminated Art   15

FOR YEARS WESTERNERS WITH FAT WALLETS have collected Coptic books and textiles. Impoverished monks cooperated reluctantly. The best examples were reputed to be in New York, but I wanted to see one of these books in its natural context, in the monastery of St Macarius in the Wadi Natrun Desert, Egypt, to get a sense of the holy intensity that, more than a thousand years ago, enabled men to meticulously copy sacred texts and illustrate them with designs derived from a rich Middle Eastern tradition of art. I hoped to find in these illuminated books some evidence that they might have predated the Book of Kells and Book of Durrow in Ireland.

The earliest manuscript Father Johann of St Macarius had was a Book of the Office, called the 'Katameros', made in 1052; the Irish books were designed in the seventh and eighth centuries. I learned that the physical age of such books was no measure of the antiquity of the designs. When a monastic scribe was copying a book, his belief that it was the word of God made him reproduce it precisely. An Irish scribe put it like this: 'I beseech all those who may wish to copy these books, nay more, I adjure them through Christ the judge of all the ages, that after careful copying, they compare them with the exemplar from which they have written, and emend

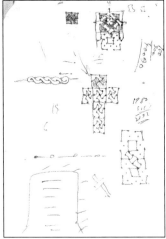

Coptic monastery, Egypt; sketches by Dr Lazar showing the construction of Coptic illumination

them with utmost care.' Hence a design executed in the tenth century could easily be a close representation of one conceived centuries before.

This principle was suggested to me by Dr Pat Donlon (then assistant-curator of the Chester Beatty Library) and demonstrated by a Syrian doctor, Dr Lazar, in Gloucester, England. Lazar learned the technique from his father, who had, in turn, learned it from his father. The doctor sat at his kitchen table and drew a pattern of dots that he then connected with lines, producing a design identical to those I had seen in Father Johann's books. The function of the dots was to ensure that the designs could be transmitted mechanically by people of little natural artistic skill. The same technique was used in some of the more prosaic designs of the Irish books.

The fact that these Syriac and Coptic designs had lost much of their original dynamism did not detract from the fact that some of their elements were echoed in the Irish books. They were complex and beautiful, but there was something inert about them, as if frozen in time. Unlike the Irish designs, they did not 'move in their stillness'. They had little of the life and flow of the books of Kells and Durrow — nor of the Koranic designs that have been compared to them. But what else could one expect from a church that had literally been isolated for more than a thousand years; in order to preserve its identity, it would have had to retreat into repetition and conservatism.

▨ *Design from Harklean Gospel book (Chester Beatty Library)*

Further, it was obvious that when a schismatic church produced such books, they must be odious to the Orthodox authorities. They would have been the first casualties of persecution. Who knows how many thousands of Coptic and Syriac manuscripts were destroyed by Rome and Constantinople, even by Islam when it arrived? Fortunately, there is some evidence that this art of book illumination was once alive and vibrant, in the Syriac

Design from Makarios monastery book (left); detail from Harklean Gospel book (Chester Beatty Library) (right)

Gospels in the Chester Beatty Library and also in the Glazier collection in New York. In fact, in the Harklean version of the Syriac Gospels in Dublin, which is a tenth-century copy of a seventh-century book, there are resemblances to the Irish designs. At the bottom of many pages is a tiny design of interlace that I would at one time have described as 'Celtic' and one image of a fisherman displays the same humour found in the Book of Kells. In the Glazier collection there is a design, from no later than the fifth century, that uses a broad yellow and red interlace pattern similar to a carpet page in the Book of Durrow — a book produced at least a century later.

As Titus Burckhardt wrote:

> There is a curious parallel between the flowering of an art with geometric motifs like interlacement, double spirals, triple vortices, continuous swastikas and so on in Northern Europe, and particularly in the British Isles, and the almost simultaneous appearance of these forms in the nascent art of Islam ... This ... is directly perceptible in the Christian art of Ireland.

◩ THE ATLANTEAN IRISH

⊠ *Virgin and child; page from the Book of Kells (Trinity College Dublin)*

The similarities between Irish and Eastern illuminated manuscripts are both stylistic and concrete. Early Christian pictures of the Virgin and Christ-child depict the adoration of the Magi: the Virgin is shown holding the child facing outwards, presenting him to the wise men. This image – so often found on sarcophagi from early Christian Rome – is quite distinct from the Book of Kells' Virgin and child, in which the Virgin holds the child facing inwards as if nursing him: the Magi are absent. It represents an important development in Christian art, as it shows the Virgin and the child outside a scriptural context – the picture is an icon, not an illustration to accompany part of the Gospel. The Virgin and child is the only illuminated page in the Book of Kells that does not serve as an illustration to the narrative.

The change from narrative to iconic illumination may well have taken place in Egypt, where the Coptic Church was influenced by the Pharoanic cult of Isis. The image of Isis suckling Horus is frequently found, the Divine Goddess being represented with human attributes. This image easily converts to Christian tradition, with the Queen of Heaven showing maternal affection as the earthly mother of Jesus. The legacy of the Isis image provides a starting-point for the art of the Virgin: it is worth noting that the Christ-child in the Kells' illumination does not have a halo, and that the focus is on the figure of the Virgin. This is more appropriate to Isis and Horus, where the mother is the superior figure, than to Mary and Jesus, where the child is more important.

The Book of Kells' Virgin is flanked by four angels. The lower right angel carries a split foliate staff, the other angels each carry a *flabellum* – an Eastern instrument for keeping flies away from the communion table. (I brought one from Egypt and it hangs over my desk as I write.) The archangels Michael, Gabriel, Raphael and Uriel are especially honoured by the Coptic Church, but the Kells' Virgin is unique in being flanked by four angels – in the Saqqara manuscripts, found in Egypt, there are two angels beneath the Virgin and two local saints above. There are four angels flanking Christ in the Ascension scene in the Syriac Rabbula Gospels (dated 586) and again in the Ascension icon from the monastery of St Catherine at the foot of Mount Sinai.

The colouring techniques used in the books of Kells and Durrow encouraged me to seek further analogies with North Africa. Natural pigments and dyes were the only ones available at the time of their creation. The colour red in both is derived from red lead mixed with a substance called kermes, which, it transpires, was made from the pregnant body of a Mediterranean insect called the *Kermococcus vermilio*. Purples, mauves and maroons came from a plant called *Crozophora tinctoria*, also from the

Mediterranean. The shades of blue were reputed to come from lapis lazuli, mined in the foothills of the Himalayas!

Those who consider such connections to be 'botanoromantic' should consult the naturalist Michael Viney, who has written in his column, *Another Life*:

> Many of the Painted Ladies [butterflies] reaching Ireland in May or June of most years have descendants from migrants which started out from North Africa. The Painted Lady caterpillars feed on thistle and mallow plants on the coast from Morocco to Egypt, where huge populations build up, and the butterflies reaching Ireland lay eggs on similar plants (Red Admirals head for our stinging nettles).

In conversation with Father Johann, I noted the similarity between the designs on his books and Islamic manuscripts I had previously seen. In view of the fact that the books in his custody mainly postdated, for instance, the Ibn Bawwab Koran in the Chester Beatty Library, I innocently wondered if the Copts might not have learned from the Muslims. He pointed out that the Arabs who emerged from the desert might have had great faith and a wonderful oral tradition, but they had little art and less literature. They learned from the peoples they conquered, including the Egyptians, who had a proven record in art and – in the case of the Copts – textiles.

The fact is that book illumination was developed in the Middle East and particularly Persia, long before Christianity came to these islands. Secondly, although the earlier illuminations such as in the Book of Durrow are non-representational and are thus in the iconoclastic tradition of early Eastern Christianity (and Islam), soon other influences crept in. Byzantine faces and bodies and Anglo-Saxon or Viking animals were cleverly integrated into the native Irish tradition. The latter undoubtedly gave these designs their energy and is their most striking characteristic. Other features showed an openness to influences from as far as Constantinople and Scandinavia. But the Irish design can be traced back through centuries before, and is a clear argument that these books were produced by scholars and scribes trained in the island – perhaps by 'economic migrants' from the Middle East!

In seeking the provenance of the individual design elements, there is always a temptation to ignore the larger question: what inspired this relatively sudden explosion of talent on the island, an event not parallelled in Europe? What fused these disparate elements together into what Francoise Henry has described as 'the most satisfying and most perfect form of non-representational art which Europe has ever known'? This art developed and flourished in a place traditionally considered to be on the periphery of civilized human affairs but which, on this evidence, clearly was not. The art later transmitted to Europe by the wandering monks can be found in Irish-founded monasteries throughout the Continent. It is a graphic illustration of the process of culture-spread, the model of circular diffusion that had become very real to me: seaborne, carried by people outside the control of centralized religions or empires, in a constant traffic on the edges of Europe, moving ideas and artefacts along the coasts and islands of the Mediterranean, the Atlantic and the North Sea, occasionally taking root and blossoming in the most unlikely places, later to expand into darkest Europe.

As James E. Doan said in 1982 at the Harvard Celtic Colloquium:

> Far from being cut off from the Mediterranean world during the seventh and eighth centuries, artists in the British isles were in an extraordinarily good position to observe post-classical art and to incorporate it, with changes appropriate to the new context, into their own productions.

One stopover on the circular trading routes must have been the Aran Islands, off the west coast of Ireland, where I came across a curious connection with Coptic Egypt. The people of Aran are famous for the unusual quality of knitted garments produced there. A small industry on the middle island, Inis Meáin, has developed this home craft into a major exporting business. The women of these islands still knit at home and perpetuate the fine designs that distinguish this knitting. The patterns are memorized and transmitted to the children, who continue the tradition. Each woman has her own repertoire of designs. In former times, it was said that if an island fisherman was drowned, the most reliable means of identification was the sweater he was wearing.

When initially speculating on Conamara, its music and its sailing tradition, I learned that Aran knitting was originally a male occupation, developed by sailors on long voyages and by fishermen waiting for the fish to bite: again, the maritime dimension. It was natural that seafarers should have evolved a 'cable stitch'; but what kind of sailors could have developed the other more elaborate patterns: the 'diamond', the 'trellis', the 'zigzag', the 'tree of life', the 'Trinity' stitch, the 'honeycomb', the 'spoon' stitch? One could imagine a hardy island people producing some functional patterns, as they did in Jersey and Guernsey, but these Aran ideas were complex, luxuriant, a celebration. They had to be a manifestation of more than basic needs; perhaps there was a profound, even religious, motivation? This would fit the title: Aran of the Saints. Archaeological evidence on the islands indicated a thriving religious community a thousand years before. The customary explanation of these monastic remains, that they had been built by monks who were drop-outs from larger foundations on the mainland, was too much like the landlubber thesis of diffusion, whereby everything has to originate on a mainland. What was to stop monks coming directly from the south, by sea?

Then I met a man called Heinz Edgar Kiewe – a specialist in knitting. He had even written *The Sacred History of Knitting*, in which he maintained that the islanders of Aran had received their design inspiration from the Coptic monks. Those knitting patterns were, according to him, an illiterate people's way of expressing profound religious ideas. He gave credit to

 *An Aran knitting pattern*

 *Heinz Edgar Kiewe (left); ANI knitting shop, Oxford (right)*

the indigenous flair for what he termed 'Celtic' design, but maintained that the order, the way in which these native designs achieved their formal Christian expression, even in the Book of Kells, came from the Copts:

> Folklorists have a habit of becoming too enthusiastic about insular tradition. Since they usually live in big towns and take the importance of political geography too seriously, they often mix up nationalism with the migration of symbols and designs. The latter are usually inspired by faith and superstition rather than by local genius. Abstract folk designs of Europe generally came with the pilgrims, the missionaries, the pirates and/or favourable trade winds to the northern countries from the Eastern Mediterranean where the three great religions were born.

Kiewe first encountered Aran designs in Dublin in the 1930s and was amazed by their complexity. He sent one sweater to a knitting specialist in London who thought the garment was a 'sampler', a virtuoso display of all the stitches available. At that time there was only one interlace pattern in the knitting vocabulary of the British Isles, the cable stitch used by the Jersey and Guernsey islanders. The Aran sweater far exceeded these in the profusion of its patterns.

Kiewe was not only a technician in this area; he had developed a philosophy about the simple craft that seemed to summarize the permanent tension between the classical trappings of the Great Church and the tenacious witness of an earlier, more humble Christianity: 'Graeco-Roman classical art became the golden measure for a millennium,' he said, 'but craft which furthers the continuity of ancient cosmopolitan, abstract symbols, lingers on, not in urban regions but rather along the coasts, on the isles, with the sailors of the seven seas.'

He was suitably sceptical about the nineteenth-century revival of romantic interest in folk art but, at the same time, was quite definite about the Aran islanders' knitting skills and their religious origin:

> The beginnings of civilization, of craft on the islands was in the hands of the monks who brought with them to the North patterns of the Coptic designs, with which they created formal abstract interlace patterns in their illuminated bibles, missals, crosses, croziers and carved stone crosses. No doubt the local population toiled with the monks in building, maintaining and beautifying the church and were thus inspired by the character of style which in the eighth century displays three elements in Irish art: Coptic, Anglo-Saxon and native Irish.

When I met Mr Kiewe in his textile shop in Oxford, he decided that he had been too generous to the Anglo-Saxons and he removed the reference to them.

He showed me the relationship between the broad ribbon interlace of the Book of Durrow – 'derived almost certainly from Coptic sources' – and the Aran pattern that he called the 'caduceus', the intertwining 'Jacob's Ladder', which he said originated in the signs of Hermes and Mercury, originally the symbol of healing. He concluded:

> It is true that the Aran patterns belong ... to the international faith of the Gospel in all lands, to the apostles, the missionaries and the pilgrims who carried with them as signs of the Holy Land some scrap of textile as an amulet – a thing easily carried, easily hidden ... the Aran patterns ... are symbols of the divine geometrical speculations of the Near East.

The people of the Aran Islands retain a skill that may link them with the genius of design in Ireland in the seventh and eighth centuries, as well as

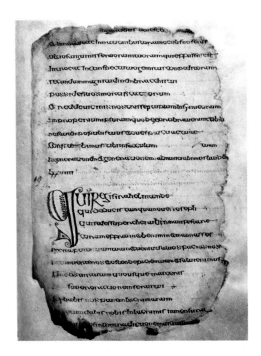

with the early Christianity of Egypt and North Africa.

Kiewe found an illustration in the Book of Kells that he was convinced supported his ideas. This image is usually referred to as 'Daniel feeding the Dragon', but Kiewe saw in it a figure wearing a knitted garment. It took years for the expert Françoise Henry to confirm her opinion that it was, indeed, a figure wearing 'a sort of tightly fitting knitted costume'.

One item of apparel on the islands, the *crios*, is a hand-woven, multi-coloured sash made of wool. The word itself is derived from *Criosdaí*, Christian in Irish. The only other place I have heard of this particular design is in Portugal, also worn by fishermen, on the Atlantic seaways.

The earliest known Irish book that experiments with graphic embellishment is the Cathach. This sixth-century marvel can be inspected in the Royal Irish Academy library in Dublin. The first known ruling on the law of copyright was made on its behalf; St Columba, who had copied the book without permission, refused to hand over the copy. King Diarmait Mac Cerr-Béil was called on to arbitrate and he pronounced judgment thus: 'To every cow its calf and to every book its copy.' Columba, in a high dudgeon hardly befitting his alleged sanctity, became an exile.

In the Cathach one finds the first example of a distinctive Irish script, usually called the 'Celtic' half-uncial. Here is the first Irish expression of the elaborate initial letters that was developed wonderfully in the Book of Kells and the Book of Durrow. As I searched through the Syriac and Coptic books in the Chester Beatty Library, among them three little Coptic books described by Dr Pat Donlon as 'the best preserved vellum books of such an early date – 6th century – that have been discovered in

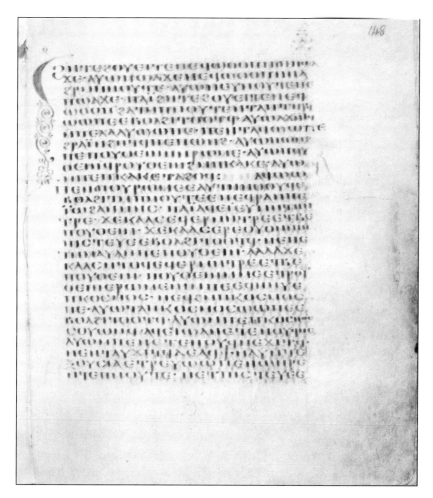

Initial page of Saqqara manuscript (Chester Beatty Library)

Egypt', the Saqqara manuscripts, I found initial letters that could easily have been drawn by the monk who wrote the Cathach. G. Frank Mitchell later confirmed this when he wrote, 'Eastern Mediterranean influence also appears in the Cathach: another initial shows a fish or dolphin bearing a cross, a motif familiar in Coptic Egypt.'

Gradually, I learned about other similarities between Coptic and Irish books. They both had the same method of binding the pages; they both used dots liberally to outline figures; they only partially completed the framing of some of their designs; their use of red, yellow and green coincided closely; a lozenge design on the Virgin and child in the Book of Kells

Egyptian boat-builders

was popular with the Copts — it may have been cognate with the tattoo I noted on the faces of women in Egypt. The Irish use of these features was unique in Western Europe. Once more it seemed that this island was directly in touch — through a maverick Church — with North Africa.

Before I left Egypt, I came across a group of musicians and dancers performing a strange ritual in a public park in Cairo. Two men faced each other like Robin Hood and Little John, each wielding a long wooden staff. In their long, flowing djellabas they danced round each other, clashing their staffs in rhythm with the drums and pipes. It was obviously a ritual enactment of battle. This stick dance is performed throughout North Africa, and Conor Cruise O'Brien has remarked on its similarity to an Irish custom performed by the Wexford Mummers.

These Mummers dress in a kind of bishop's garb and face each other in a line. They use shorter sticks than the Egyptians and produce a greater noise, accompanied by the fiddles and flutes of traditional Irish music. It is also a ritual of battle — military ranks in contrast with the man-to-man combat suggested by the North Africans — but it has religious overtones. The term 'mummer' is derived from 'Mohammedan', itself a pejorative description used by some Westerners to describe the religion of Islam. 'Mummery' is consequently defined in Western dictionaries as 'an absurd, superstitious rite'. The Wexford Mummers unconsciously mimic the stick-dances of

North Africa and thereby commemorate the sorry history of clashes between Christians and Muslims. The same is true of the Morris (Moorish) dancers of England, specifically those I witnessed dancing with blackened faces through the streets of Bacup in Lancashire on an Easter Saturday morning, many years ago.

I conclude these impressions of Egypt with an example of the extraordinary conservatism that imbues traditional crafts and arts. In 1954 the preserved timbers of a 40-metre boat were found neatly stacked in a limestone-pit beside the Giza Pyramid. The timbers proved to be 4500 years old and the thousands of pieces took thirteen years to reassemble into a funerary vessel that was named the Royal Ship of Cheops. Archaeologist Paul Lipke wrote that the method of its construction – stitched-planking – was identical to that still being used by Nile boat-builders in the late 1950s.

◼ *Nile fishermen*

16 The Sheela-na-Gig

SHEELA-NA-GIG FIGURES HAVE BEEN DESCRIBED in various ways: the 'Irish Goddess of Creation'; an 'obscene female figure of uncertain significance'; 'a fertility figure, usually with legs apart'; and finally, 'a female exhibitionist figure — one of the many representations of lust in Romanesque carving'.

Well over a hundred of these extraordinary stone figures have been found in Ireland. The entire attention of the observer is directed at the female genitals. The carvings owe nothing to classical ideas of beauty; indeed, they seem to go out of their way to be crude. Sheela-na-Gigs are somehow associated with religion as they have been found built into the walls of churches and convents as well as castles. Their very explicitness suggests that hundreds more may have been the casualties of righteous assaults by puritans, Victorians and clergymen. As long ago as 1631, in Tuam diocese, statutes were issued ordering priests to hide away these ugly figures. Thirteen of the finest and the most explicit are held in the basement of the National Museum in Dublin. When I first filmed them in 1975 they had never been exhibited to the public; the Sheela-na-Gigs were an embarrassment. It was feared that some old lady might attack them with an umbrella. How could

THE ATLANTEAN IRISH

⊠ *Sheela-na-Gig (National Museum of Ireland)*

they fit the chaste image of the Ireland of Saints and Scholars? On my last visit to the National Museum in Dublin I was glad to see that one of the Sheelas was finally exhibited publicly.

These stone carvings are found in a broad swathe of country stretching from Co. Louth in the east to Kerry in the south-west, with the greatest concentration in Offaly – near the river Shannon – and in Tipperary, near the river Suir. There is graphic evidence of the reaction of Victorian antiquarians when they first encountered these figures. In some of their sketches they tried to diminish the sexual explicitness, in others they deliberately altered the position of limbs to turn the figures into innocuous contortionists. That they mentioned the Sheelas at all is an indication of the figures' widespread existence: they could not be totally ignored.

They existed in an age when sexual prudery was not the norm in Ireland. To imagine such an age now is difficult, so deep was the nineteenth-century impact of Jansenism and other narrow continental ideas on the island. The seventeenth-century destruction of Gaelic culture – which was bawdily healthy, as evidenced by the literature – opened the doors to Puritanism, pessimism and anti-intellectualism. In a country that later made itself a laughing-stock with its censorship laws, it was stunning to discover that the Irish had been producing 'erotic' carvings many centuries ago.

The reason the Sheelas could be dated at least that early was that some of the churches and castles into which they were incorporated were built in the twelfth century. There is a strong tendency in Ireland to attribute their first appearance to Anglo-Norman influence: Sheelas were seen as part of a European development of exhibitionist carvings that were commonplace on the pilgrim routes to places like Santiago de Compostela. In a National Museum booklet issued in 1996, Eamonn Kelly stated that 'they

appear to date to the period of the Norman invasion', although there was a concession towards 'an earth goddess attested in many parts of Europe who is of primitive Celtic or even Indo-European derivation'. The writer's predecessor, Michael Ryan, said they were merely 'a footnote to history'.

The object of the Sheelas' continental Romanesque cousins was to warn the pious away from occasions of lust. They featured angels, devils, men and women in the most imaginative possible range of acrobatic positions. Indeed, what strikes one is the sheer dirty-mindedness of the medieval carvers. In the most splendid Gothic and Romanesque cathedrals you have an impressive array of male and female anal exhibition, phallic display, genital assault, beard-pulling (a euphemism), androgyny, breast display – all of the practices that we associate with pornography. It is possible that these activities reflected the amusements of the ordinary people of the time, including clerics, which a medieval Church – originally inspired by St Augustine – wished to eradicate. Pilgrims on their way to amend their lives might wish to have one last sinful fling on the long and hard road to the holy shrines. All along the routes prostitution was big business. The obscene carvings were the antidote, a means of frightening people into a state of piety, rather like the Redemptorist sermons of my youth.

In placing the Sheela-na-Gigs exclusively in this context, writers like Jorgen Andersen and Anthony Weir have been exemplary, but have also left a few loose ends. The first is the assumption that the carvings mostly date from the twelfth century onwards. It is impossible to date stone as a material; a carving made yesterday will have much the same date as a stone taken from the same quarry a million years ago. The only loose dating methods are stylistic and typological, i.e. locating the stone in a particular historical context, one that has a known date. Because of the provenance of Sheelas in buildings of the Anglo-Norman period and later, it is assumed they were carved not earlier than that period. A Sheela functioning as a cornerstone in a building was clearly put there when the building was first erected. But the carvings in the National Museum in Dublin, for instance, are on stones so awkwardly shaped that it is hard to imagine them fitting comfortably into any well-built structure. With the possible exception of the Lavey stone, they are stand-alone figures. As James A. Jerman wrote, 'the evidence is very shaky for whatever theory one wishes to propound'.

Very few examples of Sheela-na-Gigs, in the precise form so widespread in Ireland, are to be found in Britain and continental Europe. The idea of exhibitionism certainly exists, and in a definite style, but the specific unwieldiness of the female imagery of the Sheela seems to be a speciality of Ireland. Even their crudeness cannot be used as evidence of a lack of stone-carving skill on the island; the brilliance of Irish stone crosses is enough testimony to a fine tradition of stonemen. It has been suggested that the crude Sheelas are a poor insular attempt to imitate the custom of fine exhibitionist carving on the Continent but, even allowing for such a thesis, if Irish carvers were slavishly copying a continental example, is it likely that they would have confined themselves to this grotesque female form? Rarely is there an example of the continental acrobatics, rarely a decent phallus. The daring range of imagery listed earlier does not find its expression widely in Ireland; the Sheelas seem to be unique. Admittedly, it is easier to destroy a phallic figure's distinctiveness. But phallic figures are rare in Ireland – although the famous stone the Lia Fáil was known in local parlance as *Bod Fhearguis* (Fergus's penis), by contrast with Britain or Europe where the Roman Empire ensured widespread familiarity with the cult of Priapus. I found a fine example of such a phallic figure in a tiny museum attached to Margam Abbey in South Wales.

One positive feature of the Anglo-Normans who came to Ireland was that, unlike subsequent conquerors, they integrated so well with the natives that eventually they adopted the Irish language and became 'more Irish than the Irish themselves'. This suggests that they may also have adopted some ancient local customs. It seems probable that the natives already practised the custom of erecting talismen in the form of a female figure on their buildings. What if, when the newcomers went to build their keeps and castles, they had sensibly used the stones of ruined buildings – including

Sheela-na-Gig, Kilpeck Church, Herefordshire

those already fashioned into Sheelas? The Sheela-na-Gigs have been found in so many different locations – in castles, churches, fields, streams, as gateposts or parts of stone walls – that there is no way of establishing their antiquity. Their widespread distribution points to an integration with the tradition of the people, a normality of usage that counters the idea of a passing fashion imported from the Continent.

When attention was first paid to the figures, in the mid-nineteenth century, they were considered to be ancient pagan artefacts. This opinion was revised towards a more manageable Romanesque perspective in the early twentieth century. But the interpretative pendulum seems to be swinging again – as in McMahon and Roberts' little book, *Divine Hag of the Christian Celts*, in which they attribute the origin of the Sheelas to the pagan Iron Age and, of course, the Celts. In 1987 Etienne Rynne expertly rehearsed all of these arguments in a monograph called 'A pagan Celtic background for Sheela-na-Gigs'.

There is a middle ground between the indigenous pagan and the imported Christian Romanesque approaches that might be considered: one could actually turn the argument upside down. Some centuries before the period to which the Sheelas are conventionally assigned, Irish monks were responsible for the revival of learning in Europe. Could they not also have brought an exotic concept of the role of the female in religion to the Continent? Instead of the Sheela being the echo of a continental custom, could the grotesqueries of medieval Western Church architecture have been inspired by the Irish? The early Irish monks were not uniformly celibate; that odd restriction was not enforced in Ireland until many centuries afterwards. What if these wanderers also brought with them into Europe the germ of an idea that the medieval Church would later incorporate into its gruesome iconography? One of the best examples of the Sheela in Britain

Egyptian Baubo figurine (Danish National Museum, Dept. Eastern Antiquities)

is in Kilpeck Church, Herefordshire. It is reputed to have been carved by Irish craftsmen.

While males are painfully aware of the enormous sexual power of the female, it will probably be women who will definitively unearth the true background to the Sheela-na-Gigs. Mary Condren has written a fascinating history of the successful attempts to control the power of an older, female-centred religion in Ireland. A Finnish writer, Britta Sandqvist, has studied old Finnish culture and especially the culture of the Samojed peoples (hitherto pejoratively known as Lapps) of Scandinavia and northern Russia, with particular reference to the Finnish epic, the *Kalevala*. She informs me that 'the first explorers that came to these areas found that the Shamans, or the most important of them, were women, and the peak of their magical ability was during their period of menstruation ... She communicated with the universe through her body. She was the singer and the Shaman.' Ms Sandqvist also wrote that she had learned that American Indian male Shamans believed that during her period the woman was 'able to take all the magical power (whatever that is ...) and that was the reason the male shamans shut them out of the society'.

Possibly the males felt that such was the unbridled perception of the menstruating female it was necessary to invent the custom of purdah to control their ungovernability, at those intervals. It would be disruptive of the tribe and, they could argue, might endanger its cohesiveness and safety. Ms Sandqvist continued: 'People practising tantra have, for example, always known that a man should try to have sexual contact with a menstruating woman to become a tantric, and in alchemy and sex magic the blood was believed to contain "elixiris rubeus", a very potent ingredient.'

In Ptolemaic Egypt, women in childbirth had the habit of keeping by their sides a female figurine called a Baubo, with the same posture as a Sheela. Its precise function is unknown, but as it was a well-fleshed figure it is assumed to have some fertility connotations. I enquired about such a figure in every museum in Cairo, but nobody had ever heard of it. This may have been partly because no such daring figure would have a place in Islam; perhaps, also, because German scholars at the turn of the century brought many of the available figurines home with them. The best examples, I am informed, are in Berlin. Goethe was aware of the name. In the 'Walpurgisnacht' section of *Faust* he wrote: 'Here comes Baubo, the ancient crone / Riding a sow, and all alone.'

For me, the rounded figure of the Baubo provided a strong contrast to the emaciated Sheela-na-Gig, whose breasts are usually flat or non-existent, the reverse of what one imagines as a fertility symbol. A healthy buxom figure such as the Baubo or the limestone Madonna from Willendorf, Austria, or even those found in the palaeolithic Gravettian culture (22,000-18,000 BC), seem more appropriate as an image of fruitfulness and reproduction. However, in the Sheelas the position of the hands directs attention to the organ of reproduction. It is like an invitation which is, at the same time, repellent. What could it possibly signify?

⊠ *Willendorf Madonna, Austria (from* Prehistoric Societies *by Grahame Clarke and Stuart Piggott, 1965).*

The name itself is not understood. If rendered in Irish it would be *Síleadh na gCíoch*, i.e. 'the shedding (of liquid) from the breasts'. In the absence of breasts, *cíoch* might be taken as a misrepresentation of *gíog*, meaning hunkers. This word is much more apposite, as it fits with the squatting position of the figure. But a shedding of liquid from the hunkers? To take this as meaning urination is a little prosaic. Could it possibly refer to menstruation?

At this point in my musings, I came upon a North African reference that was like a beam from a searchlight on the subject: this was the phenomenon of the Christian Gnostics. *Gnosis* means 'knowledge' or 'insight'; the word is applied to those Christians who relied on their own spiritual resources, their personal insights, to discover their relationship with God. This automatically placed them in conflict with the authority of the Established Church, which, naturally, wished to maintain a monopoly of the 'truth' and the graces by which people could achieve it. Gnosticism was at the extreme end of a spectrum of belief; it profoundly disagreed with the idea of the 'Church' as the sole mediator between God and man. Gnostics considered the world to be essentially evil. Their aim was to separate the 'divine spark' from the material world. Among the Gnostic sects were the Manichaeans, the Cathars, the Mandeans and many others described as heretics. Their rituals suggested a direct connection with the Sheela-na-Gigs.

I first came across a description of them in *The Dead Sea Scrolls and the Christian Myth* by the late Professor John M. Allegro. This scholar had been one of the first Western observers invited to study the Dead Sea Scrolls when they were discovered in a cave at Qumran in 1947. I spent some invigorating hours with him at his home in the Isle of Man, listening as he described the 'cover-up' imposed by the Great Church on the early days of Christianity. He quoted Clement of Alexandria, writing in the second century: 'Not everything that is true need necessarily be divulged to all men.'

Professor Allegro brought to my attention a fourth-century bishop who had described the rituals of a Gnostic group called the Phibionites:

> The shameless ones have sexual intercourse and I am truly abashed to say what scandalous things they practise ... following coitus in uninhibited lust, they proceed to blaspheme Heaven itself. The man and woman take the ejaculated sperm in their

hands, step forward, raise their eyes aloft and, with the defilement still on their hands, offer up prayers ...They then proceed to eat it in their infamous ritual, saying: This is the Body of Christ, and this is the Pascha (Passover Meal) through which our bodies suffer and are made to acknowledge the passion of Christ. They behave similarly with a woman's menstrual blood: they collect from her the monthly blood of impurity, take it, eat it in a common meal and say: This is Christ's Blood.

Accounts like this were written by orthodox bishops who would naturally paint as lurid a picture as possible of their opponents' activities, but there were many accounts of *agape* or love-feasts, in which the male semen and the female blood would be mixed into a kind of cake and eaten.

Predictably, orthodox scholars now dismiss the late professor's opinions. However, I could easily imagine the male sexual function being included in religious ritual; phallic worship is one of the most ancient forms of religion. Was it possible that this function was what the Sheelas symbolized: the idea of the female producing her contribution to the sacred ritual? Blasphemous though it might sound, perhaps this was the Christian way of integrating the ancient practice of female shamanism – as suggested by Ms Sandqvist – into the new religion?

The logical import of Professor Allegro's argument was that sex and religion are always intimately tied together. 'That is why,' he said, 'the Church is afraid of sex and has been for the past two thousand years.' He traced the rise of Gnostic belief through the Essenes – the authors of the Dead Sea Scrolls – right back to the Canaanites of Palestine. This was where, he said, the Phoenicians had come from, the same people who founded Carthage and sailed north to the British Isles. He thought it quite possible that they would have brought with them the secrets of their mystic cults.

In the first centuries of Christianity, Carthage was a stronghold of Gnosticism. North Africa was the centre of such cults right through the early Christian era. If my speculations were correct and these outlawed sects sought refuge along the Atlantic seaways, they would have brought some of their customs with them to Ireland. 'St Patrick' might have banished or converted Christians who subscribed to serpent worship, but it would not be as easy to destroy the stone evidence of a cult that incorporated women into their rituals.

Every successful Church absorbs the customs of the people it is evangelizing. Christianity has shown a genius for this process. The Sheela-na-Gigs must have represented a deep-rooted belief for such a strange idea to be adopted and incorporated in the Orthodox Church's own buildings.

Conventional accounts overlook the point that women were integral to the monastic scene in Ireland; that even in saintly Clonmacnoise there is a carving of a Sheela-na-Gig; that the Old Irish for a nun is *cailleach*, which can be translated as 'witch' or 'hag'; that the original description in Irish of a 'nun's chapel' is 'temple of the hag'.

In these matters Irish monasticism was clearly to be distinguished from the great monasteries of Europe, where celibacy was introduced quite early. In the East, on the other hand, celibacy was not and is not mandatory for other than the very highest church dignitaries. Once again, Ireland seemed to have more affinity with the East than the West.

Even the objection that, apart from the Egyptian Baubo, there are no examples of Sheelas apparent in North Africa did not discourage me from this idea. The Irish manuscript illuminations and stone crosses all incorporate Eastern ideas, but emerge as something unique to the island; the islanders took these ideas and made them their own. In cultural as well as economic aspects of Christianity, they were much closer to the East than the West. It would not have been beyond the scope of craftsmen on the island to render the Phibionite ritual, as described by the Bishop Origen, into something as solid as a stone Sheela.

It is probable that if the Sheelas ever had a fundamental significance in the belief systems of this island – be they Gnostic, Orthodox, Christian, pagan or semi-pagan – the memory of such a device would gradually have been eroded by the ministrations of an officially celibate Western Church. What happens in a case like this is that the memory and meaning of such practices enter the people's folklore; this is then assumed to be of purely secular or pagan origin. But up to recent times everything in life, particularly peasant life, was articulated in a religious context. Every aspect of folklore has a religious resonance, be it pagan or Christian.

There is an old belief that the way to stop a charging bull is for a woman to expose her buttocks to him. This is a polite form of an older belief that a woman could drive away the devil by exposing her genitals. In Ireland one of the 'pishrogues' attached to the Sheelas was that it was a means of averting the evil eye. This was rooted in the idea that a man who had suffered the attentions of this evil eye could call on a woman to expose herself and thus cure his affliction. A belief in the curative properties of the Sheelas is evidenced by the custom of rubbing the limbs of those carvings located at holy wells or the scene of 'Patterns', local community celebrations. Significantly, some of these Pattern Days fall on the feast of Brigid the Goddess. In some cases the sign of the cross is made on the figure, an action that is the counterpart of the early Christian custom of carving crosses on existing standing stones. The latter had clear phallic implications in pre-Christian Ireland.

In general the attempts to locate the origin of the Sheelas in a recent European context have been as unconvincing as the efforts to gloss over all other awkward details in the personality of Ireland. In the light of recent feminist adoption of the figure, it is ironic that two Irish women, Edith M. Guest and her researcher Helen M. Roe, seemed to copperfasten the Irish interpretation of the majority figures as a relatively recent alien idea in the 1930s (with, as Andersen reports, a certain restraint in description, i.e. Guest referring to hands clasped on 'the lower abdomen'). True, Guest conceded that the single Sheela example on Boa Island in Fermanagh might date to the seventh or eighth century but, as far as I know, it is only as recently as 2001 that the theory of pagan antiquity for these figures has been revived in Ireland by Joanne McMahon and Jack Roberts. They speculate that the custom dates back to as early as the third century BC.

However, in May 2003, in a second-hand bookshop in Paris, the image of a Sheela stared out at me from a shelf and, examining it, I was confronted with the proof that not only are the Sheelas are far older than any of us realized but that their provenance is even wider than suspected. The image was on the cover of a 1979 catalogue issued by the French Museum of National Antiquities to mark an exhibition of Serbian archaeology dating from 6000 to 2500 BC. The stylized figure on the cover was unmistakably a Sheela-na-Gig. The symmetrical position of the hands in relation to the vulva was clearly echoed in the Irish Sheela from Lavey, Co. Cavan, and the face was that of the Sheela from Kilpeck Church in Herefordshire. The Serbian stone had been unearthed in the 1960s at an extensive neolithic site in the section of the Danube River called Lepenski Vir. The site is thought to be between 4500 and 800 years old. The inhabitants were fishers and boat people, occupations reflected in the fish/humanoid aspect of the sculptures they left behind. The stone is now held in the Narodni Museum in Belgrade.

Sheela-na-Gig found at Lepenski Vir, now in the Narodni Museum, Belgrade (catalogue of the 1979 exhibition at the French Museum of National Antiquities)

The existence of this ancient Sheela in Serbia – especially at a site on one of the greatest waterways in Europe, the Danube – opens up a field of speculation vast enough to justify greater attention than I can presently give to it. I leave the subject to some better-equipped scholar. It certainly renders questionable the suggestion that the Sheela figure is (a) a minor footnote in history, (b) a relatively recent phenomenon or (c) belongs to the Romanesque gargoyle tradition. The settled people who created their Sheela-na-Gigs at Lepenski Vir clearly paddled their boats up the Danube from the Black Sea and brought their gods and goddesses with them, probably from as far away as Anatolia. The existence of the figures in Ireland is another instance of this so-called peripheral island sharing antique folk customs with countries far away. It may be noted here that the name 'Danube' commemorates a goddess of Irish mythology: Danu, after whose breasts (paps) two hills in Co. Kerry are named. The fact that Eastern influences have always penetrated Europe by river and sea is once more underlined.

In the coastal region of southern France the heresy of the Cathars flourished right up to the thirteenth century. That heresy directly descended from the Eastern Manichaeans, whose profane rituals Augustine condemned in the fifth century. As we have seen, 'heresy' can be a time-honoured custom, ritual or belief that is no longer convenient for an ideology to sustain. The Sheela tradition, now a feminist icon, undermines millennia of both secular and ecclesiastical patriarchy and until now has been necessarily dismissed as little more than a quaint irrelevance.

Before the Anglo-Normans came to Ireland, a major crusade was preached against the same Cathars or 'Albigensians'. The heresy was finally crushed when the town of Beziers in Languedoc was torched by the crusaders. When it was pointed out that they could not all have been heretics, the response was: 'God will know and save his own.' The entire population, men, women, children, heretics and faithful, perished.

La Tène Culture

17

As I came across these disparate aspects of Ireland, Europe, the Middle East and North Africa over the years, the image of crazy paving kept recurring. All the pieces were present but the manner in which they were assembled, the accepted historical and geographical perspective, did not have an aesthetic that accommodated the details. It worked only when viewed from an airy height, from an imaginary point of view: the conventional European and classical perspective.

From any other place, such as Conamara on the edge of Europe, the pieces seemed to have been assembled by a child: some had the edges frayed awkwardly; there were, on closer examination, many pieces missing, many more guessed at. Could the jigsaw be reassembled to make any more sense? Was Ireland always marginalized, and Conamara itself marginalized within Ireland as a desolate place of rock and mountain? To quote the poet Les Murray, 'Only a flat earth has margins.'

Where, for example, would you place the centre: London, Paris, Athens, Rome, Madrid, Munich, Moscow or, increasingly, Washington? What did the world look like when Alexandria was its acknowledged centre? How did northern Europe appear to the Persian or Chinese or Aztec empires?

Bust of Hannibal (Hannibal, Soldier, Statesman, Patriot *by William O'Connor Morris, 1897*)

Relatively unimportant, I suspect. The centre is always a shifting perspective, its movement directly related to power, or to the prejudices of whoever currently assembles the jigsaw. As Les Murray elaborated: 'All the same, equality cannot coexist with the metaphor of centre and margin. Neither can justice. The metaphor will always be the victor over revolutions, though at the same time it provokes and abets them, making them all the more murderous.'

The achievement and maintenance of power was, until a few centuries ago, directly related to mobility by sea – the British Empire between 1750 and 1850 is a classic example. Larger movements of armies are still made by sea and 90 per cent of all goods that enter and leave Ireland do so by sea. The Spanish, French, Portuguese, Dutch and British, all used the sea to acquire new territories and wealth with which to finance their squabbles in Europe. As history has tended to concentrate on these local squabbles, most Westerners have been educated to assume that they constitute the sum total of significant history.

From a defiantly peripheral standpoint, I have chosen to view Europe from 'the outside'. From here, Europe itself retreats into an appropriately marginal position on the globe.

What conception, for instance, did Hannibal have of Europe, to see it as a target for an expedition from North Africa in 218 BC? His exploits are still a cause of wonder. He, a Phoenician/Carthaginian, whose people had conquered and held for centuries half of Spain, could conceive of attacking Rome from the north, the long way round via the Pyrenees and the Alps, through France, Switzerland and Italy. He could muster an army 102,000 strong: 90,000 infantry, 12,000 of the famous Numidian cavalry, even 37 elephants, and bring them through the Pyrenees and the Alps, piercing the heart of the Roman Empire. He was so familiar with Europe that he could recruit local tribes (especially the Swiss mountain men – when they were not actually ambushing him) on the way. Having arrived in Italy and failed to

La Tène swords (Latenium, Parc et Musée d'archéologie de Neuchâtel)

take Rome, he could still spend the next twenty years dominating the coun-tryside and harassing the towns – and this was after Rome had allegedly crushed the Carthaginians twice in the Punic Wars.

How powerful was the growing Roman Empire if it could not evict such a nuisance as Hannibal from its own sphere of influence? Our classical concept of empire may be more porous than we have been led to imagine. Such an empire must rely on slave labour as well as mercenaries who, by definition, have allegiance to nothing except payday. The success and main-tenance of empire ultimately and absolutely relies on how it is perceived, on how convincing is the image it projects to friends and enemies – a phe-nomenon with which modern man is now quite familiar. A simpler truth is that all empires believe their own propaganda, which may be the reason they decay from within. In the context of the Roman Empire, our historical impression relies on the fact that the Romans left records and Hannibal left few – unless, I might mischievously suggest, these are found in a hoard of weapons and other artefacts in a place called Neuchâtel in Switzerland. Lake Neuchâtel lies in the cradle of the Swiss Alps near Fribourg, at a point of crossing between the Rhine and Rhone valleys.

This is where the Celtic invention of Edward Lhuyd achieved what was proclaimed to be its ultimate material support: the La Tène culture. It is

quite possible that Hannibal was one of the original tourists to pass through this pretty canton just north of the Alps. Nobody is sure what route he followed, and indeed a sensible tour schedule might have had him floating his troops and elephants the length of Lake Geneva or Lake Neuchâtel rather than assailing the mountains. When I visited Neuchâtel in 2003 the lake and town were shrouded in fog. Fortunately the museums were open.

Laténium is a superb modern museum displaying evidence of continuous human settlement for the past 40,000 years in the small area now known as Switzerland. The bones of Neanderthal and Cro-Magnon hunter-gatherers peacefully share space with Greek, Roman and medieval artefacts. The 'Celts' have a fine room to themselves. Much of the La Tène collection was discovered by accident in the 1870s, when the level of Lake Neuchâtel was six feet lower and a mass of wooden poles were noticed protruding above the surface. Initial amateur groping by hand produced at least forty weapons. In the following years professional excavation produced evidence of extensive lakeshore settlement, an immense hoard of abandoned goods, and a wonderful tourist industry.

On two swords in the modern display I could clearly see traces of that curving 'trumpet and spiral' design on which is partly based the idea that the Irish are Celts. The fact is that pitifully few such La Tène objects have ever been found in Ireland. The few that exist seem to have dribbled into the island over a long and indefinable period. As archaeologist Barry Raftery has said: 'La Tène archaeological finds [in Ireland] are all "strays"' (although, confusingly, elsewhere he has written that 'Britain and Ireland have an abundance of weapons and other artifacts comparable in style to these mainland materials'). Besides, the spiral, circle and triskele design belong as much to the Magdalenian period of 40,000 years ago (also represented in the museum) as to any 'Celtic' culture. They are also clearly to be seen on Minoan and Mycenaean artefacts. A thousand years after La Tène, they were brilliantly and uniquely incorporated into Irish illuminated manuscripts.

In Laténium, 'Celtic' coins were also displayed. But the designs on them seemed to me to be clearly derivative of the tetradrachmas of Philip II of Macedonia as well as later Greek, Punic (i.e. Phoenician) and Roman influences. The ubiquitous horse representations were a feature of early Phoenician coinage. Nowhere was such a provenance admitted. The names of tribes and chieftains seemed to me to be inscribed in Greek and Roman letters. On checking sources later, my impression proved to be well founded. Writing on the coins described as 'Celt-Iberian' was in some cases obviously derivative from – if not actually consisting of – early Greek and Phoenician. (The early Greeks had actually derived their alphabet from the Phoenicians.) Nowhere in the world exists a coin that names a tribe called 'Celt' or 'Keltoi'. The absence of mention of the contemporary and equally powerful Phoenician influence suggested that even here, the pure Aryan 'Celtic' image must not be tainted with a North African source.

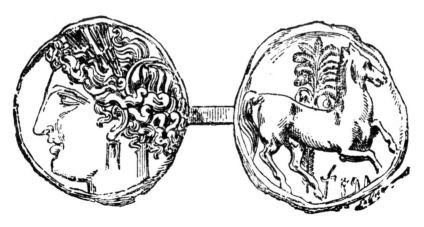

⊠ *Carthaginian money (from* Hannibal, Soldier, Statesman, Patriot *by William O'Connor Morris, 1897)*

Later research also showed me that although southern British tribes produced similar imitative coinage, the Irish did not; they continued to eschew minting coins and clung to their ancient, cattle-based barter system. It would be a thousand years before the conservative Irish would abandon that tradition and accept the Viking introduction of coinage.

So how could Neuchâtel and La Tène possibly support the idea that the Irish were 'Celts'? The figment of imagination that is La Tène Ireland is based on incomplete, singularly biased, evidence. Whatever about the possible absurdity of my idea that Hannibal left an arms cache on the shores of Lake Neuchâtel, is it any more rational to believe that people such as those in Neuchâtel moved *en masse* across the forests and rivers of Europe to invade and transform the indigenous cultures of Ireland? I think not, and my visit to La Tène itself finally convinced me of this. But my reasons were not based exclusively on the exhibition itself. In the fine library attached I found Paul Jacobsthal's 1944 book *Early Celtic Art*, republished by Oxford University Press in 1969. In 1935 Hitler dismissed Jacobsthal from the Chair of Archaeology at the University of Magdeburg. The scholar was given refuge by Oxford University and devoted the rest of his life to studying 'Celtic' artefacts.

His conclusions were interesting, not least because in this book he ignored the evidence in Britain, Spain and that most 'Celtic' of all places, Ireland. His reasons for these omissions were (a) the Second World War and (b) that Iberian art 'modifies its models so deeply and peculiarly that the student of Celtic art as a general European phenomenon might well leave Spain on one side'. I liked this frankness. He might well have said the same about the artistic evidence in Ireland, which is equally idiosyncratic. Jacobsthal promised to devote a future separate study to such areas.

Jacobsthal's first conclusion was that continental 'Celtic' art had a triple root: (a) Italian, (b) Hallstatt (in Austria) and (c) the Orient. He painted an amusing picture of a kind of Celtic heritage centre that he nicknamed Laténopolis, with shelves full of imitation Etruscan, Greek and Roman souvenirs. The master craftsman and his apprentices would be studying the latest fashionable object from, say, Italy or Greece, and deciding how to copy or adapt it to their customers' tastes – their clients being the local chieftains, the robber-barons of their time who would share tastes with their supposed enemies – the chieftains of the neighbouring tribes.

The antagonism between élite groups is always feigned; they have more in common with each other than with their own subjects. The manipulability of the many and the rapacity of the few are no novelty. Among these élites the coinage of the time probably had little more than prestige or gift value – and of course it was used to pay mercenaries, whose foreign escapades made them familiar with the idea of cash and who would have demanded their blood money in hard currency.

Paul Jacobsthal wrote that the early Iron Age Hallstatt style of decoration (which preceded La Tène) was geometric and that Greece and Italy were the first to free themselves from these 'geometric fetters', as he put it, 'By taking over forms of the more advanced art of the Near East, they created the Orientalising Style.' He then listed some of his observations on this oriental style:

Celtic animal and mask styles were of Oriental origin.
A gold bracelet from Rodenbach copied Scythian animals.
A bird on a fibula from Jungfernteinitz had a Persian model.
The Glauberg torc copied Persian rings, as did handles of Lorraine
    jugs.
The animal-type handle of a Salzburg flagon had a Syrian prototype.
The torc was the ornament of men in Persia.
Trousers were borrowed by the Celts from the Orient. Posidonius
    – quoted by Diodorus – had spoken of the 'bracae' of the Gauls.
Polychromy was an Oriental feature.

Jacobsthal wrote that 'in (at least) two cases it could be established that foreign artists were employed in "Celtic" workshops: a Venetian, who engraved a sword from Hallstatt, and a Greek who made jugs with lionesses'.

In a companion volume Jacobsthal supplied photographs and diagrams of every single object to which he referred, and mentioned that 'some motifs have their only analogies *not* in the arts of Scythia proper but in the Altai mountains, Siberia and China; a fact that defies explanation'. He would not have known of the treasures of Urumchi, found in 1994 in the extreme west of China, on a major silk road north of Tibet. Mummies with Caucasian features were discovered wrapped in magnificent textiles. These mummies were shown to be contemporary with those of the Egyptians, 3000 BC. Jacobsthal also might not have been familiar with the Tokharian language from the same location to which, in the nineteenth century, 'Indo-

⊠ *Spiral designs on pottery from Ban Chieng, Thailand, painted in* 300 BC *(from* Civilization on Loan *by Heinz Edgar Kiewe, 1973)*

European' similarities were attributed. Above all, I believe, prudence would have discouraged him from emphasizing the Phoenician, i.e. Semitic, influence.

What I gleaned from Jacobsthal was that the fashions of even those north European tribes, the latterly named 'Celts' – or at least their élite groups – were thoroughly 'orientalized' via Italy and Greece. It makes sense when one considers the extraordinarily rich civilizations that antedated them by thousands of years and that thrived in the Near East and North Africa. Oriental and African (e.g. Egyptian) ideas always seeped northward. Consequently, to suggest that the island of Ireland, more easily accessible from the south by sea, was similarly – but separately – orientalized, must surely not seem far-fetched now. 'Civilization' traditionally lay to the south and east.

Hilary Richardson said that 'no one has written better on Celtic Art than Jacobsthal'. I think I understand why he lost his position in Magdeburg. Not only was he Jewish; he had the temerity to suggest that the origins of (Aryan!) Greek, Roman and – for this book's purposes, 'Celtic' – artistic genius lay in the *Untermensch* origins of Persia and the Middle East.

I now believe that the threadbare 'Celtic' ethnonym has been, for the past 300 years, based not only on a romantic but on a fundamentally racist interpretation of history. In this exercise traditional Irish and British scholarship, from Lhuyd's *Archaeologica Britannica* of 1707 through Edward Ledwich in 1790 and onwards, as well as general European scholarship, must stand accused of at least inadvertent collaboration. They ridiculed Vallancey, who championed the Semitic (Phoenician) influence, and Jacobsthal are two of the exceptions. I am sure there are others equally scorned by orthodox classical scholarship. Martin Bernal's *Black Athena* again comes to mind.

The fundamental misapprehension, I believe, was that, mainly thanks to invasions, there is always progress in human affairs, that people can only get better and better and that artistic and technological advancement is a mark of superior humanity. This is one of the self-delusions on which centralized power is always based. It usually coincides with the conversion of innocuous terms such as 'local', 'parochial', 'rural' and 'provincial' into epithets for barbarism.

When W.B. Yeats observed that 'things fall apart, the centre cannot hold', he was for the moment concerned, like any member of the comfortable class, with the consequences for a status quo in which he was comfortably ensconced. His delightful celebrations of peasant life were predicated on the man of the soil remaining eternally up to his oxters in dirt. What Yeats may actually have been apprehensive about was the rise of sansculottes above their station – momentarily forgetting that some members of the lower orders inevitably improve their station to the point where they learn from and become just as corrupt as their predecessors – who have, of course, themselves originally ascended from the 'lower orders'.

A man of his time, Yeats gloomily predicted that the result of a relaxing of centralized power would be a blood-red tide loosed upon the world. But he, of patrician mould, must also have known that centralized-power structures have always been more responsible for blood-letting than any peasant rebellions and must, like Ozymandias, inevitably return to dust. One can sympathize with his Burkean dread of authority giving way to 'anarchy' – the French Revolution was always the hovering nightmare. Aggressive central powers and their apologists usually attribute the disorganization of a subject people to some fault inherent in their 'racial' makeup, so they can be deemed unworthy of autonomy.

In 1796, summarizing his tour of Conamara, de Latocnaye wrote:

> It is not to be believed that the inhabitants of this country are more wicked or barbarous than elsewhere; they seem indeed to be better clothed than those who live near the capital. It is very easy to call them savages and to make sport of their misery. Will you believe it, readers and good people, if I tell you where I have really found savage and barbarous men? I tell you it was in Paris, in London, in Dublin, in Edinburgh – in fact in all the large cities.

All power corrupts; all governments and their *apparatchiks* lie; all empires are myopic. None are redeemable. I am reminded of Kurt Vonnegut's account of an incident that occurred while he was writing *Slaughterhouse Five*. When a Hollywood producer assumed that he was writing 'an anti-war' book, Vonnegut admitted that this was probably so. The producer said: 'You might as well write an anti-glacier book.' So it goes.

The interrogation of a centralized historical orthodoxy always stimulates some heart-searching, perhaps even heartburn. In the end, the risk must be taken. There is no historical alternative.

At the beginning of the twenty-first century a worm's-eye view of history has emerged again, as the world is once more gathered into large blocks called areas of influence. Those outside the 'civilized' blocks are referred to as Third World. The cultivated injustice of such an arrangement is constantly exposed, to little avail despite the heroic efforts of non-government organizations. As George Bernard Shaw said about the nineteenth-century nature poets: they only started to appreciate the beauty of the world when it was threatened by industrialization.

Ordinary citizens of the West find themselves having to adapt uneasily to a globalized consumer world – the rest of the planet being considered merely grist to its mill. The ancient land of Ireland recently attempted a balancing act, vacillating between assuagement of a great industrial/military power and lip-service towards an ethical stand. As a result the island has reverted to being a trading post with few core values and no 'noble lies' remaining: it is now merely an interesting economic laboratory. We are once again forced to look for evidence of our uniqueness as individuals and peoples. Western youth properly expresses this in an anarchic stance towards all authority. This should not prevent citizens, indeed it should encourage them, to proclaim at all times that every nation, big or small, is a rich mix of many cultures and peoples, each of whose constituent parts is indispensable to the overall flavour of a universal humanity.

Should that truism survive the débris, time will not have been wasted.

Conclusion

IN THE PRECEDING PAGES I have presented the evidence for a continuity of seaborne contact between Ireland and the entire Atlantic coast, from Scandinavia to Senegal, taking in the Mediterranean, the Middle East and North Africa, from Neolithic times.

Such contact ranged from wandering prehistoric exploration driven northwards by the gradual desertification of the Sahara region and the concomitant melting of the northern ice sheets, through to the targeted voyages of Phoenician/Carthaginian tin-miners. The Atlantic seaways facilitated North African Christian refugees' escape from religious persecution, the activities of Irish and Algerian pirates and smugglers, and the ancient wine trade from North Africa and Spain. Modern Iberian fishermen followed the shoals northwards as far as Iceland and reached the cod banks of Newfoundland. Distance has rarely been an obstacle to sailors.

From the Moroccan structure known as M'Zora to its equivalent in Newgrange; from the evidence that neolithic inhabitants of Ireland spoke a North African language to the modern reality of Hiberno-English; from antique Conamara sean-nós singing to its exact equivalent in Tatarstan; from Egyptian stick-dancers to Wexford mummers; from the Arabic *shamrakh* to the myth of St Patrick's single-handed conversion of Ireland to Christianity; I have emphasized that the island of Ireland was, essentially, a traffic island. The sea did not distance this island people from the grand movements of history.

It can no longer be respectably maintained that the island or its people are, or ever were, culturally or ethnically 'Celtic', a narrow historic – and touristic – strait-jacket, essentially imposed by outsiders. The notion of a 'Celtic' invasion is largely based on a linguistic fallacy unsupported by the archaeological evidence. This philological approach relied on comparing isolated words taken from inscriptions rather than from a living language – a practice now held in question by modern linguists.

When I first publicly rehearsed these ideas, they were treated mostly with good humour leavened by curiosity. In the intervening twenty years such speculations have become popular, almost respectable, and are supported by the findings of reputable scholars. My perspective is that of common sense observation, informed by field archaeology rather than by desk archaeology, by living rather than by dead languages.

Traditionally, the sea did not divide peoples: it united them.

Being poorly equipped to do so I have avoided trying to give a scientific basis to those ideas. However, with my last word I must return to mitochondrial DNA.

Professor Bryan Sykes of the Institute of Molecular Medicine at Oxford University has studied this substance for many years, during which he has proved that the Polynesian islanders did not – as Thor Heyerdahl believed – go west from the Americas but came east from South Asia (Taiwan, etc.).

Most modern Europeans hitherto believed that their genetic ancestry lay in the post-Ice Age Mesolithic farmers who rapidly spread out from the eastern Mediterranean to overwhelm European *Homo sapiens*, the hunter-gatherers of the Palaeolithic era – who had themselves replaced Cro-magnon people.

However, Professor Sykes has, by studying seven clusters of this mitochondrial DNA, established that approximately 80 per cent of modern Europeans – including the mysterious Basques – actually retain their Palaeolithic genes; the remaining 15–20 per cent of genes being traceable to people who arrived within the last 8000 years. This latter group, he discovered, shared their mitochiondrial DNA with the Bedouin of Saudi Arabia. The professor's findings were ultimately supported by the pioneer of demographic movement studies, Luigi Luca Cavalli-Sforza, in the November 2000 edition of the journal *Science*.

Professor Sykes further established (and detailed his findings in *The Seven Daughters of Eve*) that the seventh cluster of this special DNA had split into two groups: one gradually spreading north through the Balkans and the Hungarian plains and along the river valleys of Central Europe to the Baltic. The other portion of this cluster was confined to the Mediterranean coast as far as Spain, then could be tracked around the coast of Portugal and up the Atlantic coast to western Britain and Ireland. This process began 8000 years ago and, as Sykes points out, is supported by the existing archaeological evidence.

When the ice sheet retreated these farmers would have been the first settlers to bring their seeds and their animals, their language and culture, all the way from the Orient to the small island of Ireland.

They were the first Atlanteans.

Sources

Introduction [pp. 9–18]

John M. Allegro, *The Dead Sea Scrolls and the Christian Myth* (Abacus 1981).

John Blacking, personal communication, annotations to my first script outline (1980).

Sture Bolin, 'Mohammed, Charlemagne and Ruric', *Scandinavian Economic Review*, 1, 1 (1953).

E.H. Carr, *What is History?* (London 1983).

C.W. Ceram, *Gods, Graves and Scholars: The Story of Archaeology* (London 1952).

Con Costello, *Ireland and the Holy Land* (Alcester, UK 1974), p. 7.

Elizabeth Butler Cullingford, *Ireland's Others: Gender and Ethnicity in Irish Literature and Popular Culture* (Cork and Notre Dame 2001).

Barry Cunliffe, *Facing the Ocean* (Oxford 2001).

Glyn Daniel, *The Megalith Builders of Western Europe* (London 1958), p. 131.

Liam de Paor, 'The art of the Celtic peoples' in R. O'Driscoll (ed.), *The Celtic Consciousness* (Laois 1981), p. 121.

E. Estyn Evans, *The Personality of Ireland: Habitat, Heritage and History* (Dublin 1992).

Orin Gensler, 'A typological evaluation of Celtic/Hamito-Semitic parallels', dissertation to be published by Oxford University Press as *The Celtic-North African Linguistic Link: Substrata and Typological Argumentation* in 2005.

Françoise Henry, *Early Christian Irish Art*, trans. M. MacDermott (Cork 1979).

P.L. Henry, personal communication (1980).

Richard Hodges and David Whitehouse, *Mohammed, Charlemagne and the Origins of Europe* (London 1983).

W.S. Howell (trans.), 'Alcuin: The Rhetoric', *Princeton Studies in English*, 23 (Princeton 1941).

Simon James, *Atlantic Celts: Ancient People or Modern Invention?* (London 1999).

G. Frank Mitchell, reference to the Latin Church of North Africa in review of Michael Ryan (ed.), *Ireland and Insular Art AD 500–1200: Conference Proceedings* (*Irish Times*, March 1987).

Lillis Ó Laoire, 'Sean-nós singing and exoticism', *The Journal of Music in Ireland*, 3, 2 (Jan.–Feb. 2003).

Seán Ó Riada, *Our Musical Heritage*, RTÉ Radio Lectures 1962 (Laois 1982).

Henri Pirenne, *Medieval Cities* (Princeton 1925); *Mohammed and Charlemagne* (New York 1939).

Bob Quinn, *Atlantean: Ireland's North African and Maritime Heritage* (London 1986).

Le Mystère des Voix Bulgares (Sofia 1982).

Colin Renfrew, *Archaeology and Language* (London 1987); see also his 'Essay on culture, migration: Models in prehistory', *Antiquity*, 42 (1968).

Hilary Richardson, 'Observations on Christian art in early Ireland, Georgia and Armenia' in Michael Ryan (ed.), *Ireland and Insular Art AD 500–1200: Conference Proceedings* (Dublin 1987).

Michael Richter, *Medieval Ireland: The Enduring Tradition* (Dublin 1988).

Michael Ryan, 'Bookview', *Archaeology Ireland*, 2, 2 (Summer 1988); 'The Derrynaflan Chalice and other early Irish chalices: Some speculations' in *Studies in Medieval Irish Metalwork* (London 2001).

Hildegard L.C. Tristram, 'Celtic in linguistic taxonomy in the nineteenth century' in Terence Brown (ed.), *Celticism: Studies on Cultural Identity* (Amsterdam 1996).

Heinrich Wagner, 'Near Eastern and African connections with the Celtic world' in O'Driscoll (ed.), *The Celtic Consciousness, op. cit.*

1: *Historical Origins: Vallancey and Ledwich* [pp. 19–32]

F.M. Barnard, *Herder's Social and Political Thought: From Enlightenment to Nationalism* (Oxford 1965).

Martin Bernal, *Black Athena: The Afro-Asiatic Roots of Classical Civilization* (New York 1987).

Martin Brennan, *Boyne Valley Vision* (Laois 1980).

Hubert Butler, 'Lament for archaeology' in R.F. Foster (ed.), *The Sub-Prefect Should Have Held His Tongue and Other Essays* (London 1990).

Giraldus Cambrensis, *Topographica Hibernica* (1186), trans. J.J. O'Meara (Laois 1982).

Colin Chapman, *Whose Promised Land?* (London 1983).

Daniel Corkery, *The Hidden Ireland* (Dublin 1970), p. 10.

Judith Cuppage, *Suirbhé Seandálaoíchta Chorca Dhuibhne* (Ballyferriter 1986).

Chevalier de Latocnaye, *A Frenchman's Walk Through Ireland, 1796–7*, trans. John Stevenson (Belfast 1917, 1984).

Liam de Paor, in an RTÉ interview (re-broadcast 31 Jan. 2004).

Séamus Delargy, *The Gaelic Story Teller*, quoted by T.K. Whitaker from notes of taped interviews with Delargy, reprinted in the *Irish Times*.

Ignatius Donnelly, *Atlantis, the Antediluvian World* (New York 1882), pp. 17–19.

Paul Edwards, review of I. Van Sertima (ed.), *African Presence in Early Europe* (New Brunswick 1985) in *Research in African Literatures* (Texas 1987). In a personal note Dr Edwards kindly referred me to A.P. Smyth, 'The black foreigners of York and the white foreigners of Dublin' in *Saga Books of The Viking Society*, vol. 29 (1974–7), pp. 101–17.

R.F. Foster, *Paddy and Mr Punch* (London 1993).

Robert Graves, *The White Goddess* (London 1961), p. 224.

Douglas Hyde, *A Literary History of Ireland* (New York 1901), pp. 622–3.

James Joyce, 'Ireland, island of saints and sages' in Richard Ellman and Edward Ledwich, *Antiquities of Ireland* (Dublin 1790).

Geoffrey Keating, *History of Ireland* (London 1902).

Mary Lefkowitz (ed.), *Black Athena Revisited* (North Carolina 1996).

Edward Lhuyd, *Archaeologia Britannica, giving some account additional to what has hitherto been publish'd of the languages, histories and customs of the original inhabitants of Great Britain: from collections and observations in travels through Wales, Cornwall, Bas-Bretagne, Ireland and Scotland*, vol. 1 (Oxford 1707).

Eoin MacNeill, *Celtic Ireland* (Dublin 1921); *Phases of Irish History* (Dublin 1937).

Ellsworth Mason (eds), *The Critical Writings of James Joyce* (London 1959), p. 156.

G. Frank Mitchell, *Reading the Irish Landscape* (London and Dublin 1986).

M.A. O'Brien, 'Irish origin-legends' in Myles Dillon (ed.), *Early Irish Society* (Dublin 1954).

Padraig Ó Snodaigh, *Hidden Ulster, Protestants and the Irish Language* (Belfast 1995).

Paul-Yves Pezron, *L'Antiquité de la nation et la langue des Celtes Autremont appelez Gaulois* (1703).

Colin Renfrew, *Archaeology and Language* (London 1987); see also his 'Essay on culture, migration: Models in prehistory', *Antiquity*, 42 (1968).

Michael Ryan, *Ireland's First Inhabitants*, Bulletin of the Department of Foreign Affairs, no. 983 (Dec. 1981).

Kamal Salibi, *The Bible Came From Arabia: Radical Interpretations of Old Testament Geography* (London 1985).

F.R. Scott, *Selected Poems* (Toronto and Oxford 1966), p. 44.

Jeanne Sheehy, *The Rediscovery of Ireland's Past: The Celtic Revival 1830–1930* (London 1980).

Edmund Spenser, *View of the State of Ireland* (1596), W.L. Renwick ed. (Oxford 1970).

Charles Vallancey, *Collectanea de Rebus Hibernicis*, vol. 4, no. 14 (1786).

David Wilson, *The New Archaeology* (New York 1976), p. 261.

Peter Woodman, *The Mesolithic in Ireland* (British Archaeological Reports [BAR] 1978).

2: *Sean-nós Singing and Conamara's Boats* [pp. 33–47]

Charles Acton, 'Sean-nós and the Arab style', *Irish Times* (4 Nov. 1974); see also letter to *Irish Times* (July 1985) in which he claimed to have first given Ó Riada the idea of a North African connection. He also quoted Joan Rimmer's attribution of an ultimate Northern Indian origin to the music.

Seóirse Bodley, 'Technique and structure in sean-nós singing', *Ceol Tíre*, 1 (1973).

Hugh Brody, *Inishkillane: Change and Decline in the West of Ireland* (London 1974).

For background to Conamara in the late nineteenth century, see Dr Charles R. Browne, 'The ethnography of Garumna and Lettermullen, in the County Galway', *Proceedings of the Royal Irish Academy*, series III, vol. 5 (1898). See also *Graceville, The Connemaras in Minnesota*, documentary film by author with Seosamh Ó Cuaig (1996) available on VHS from Gael Media, Na Forbacha, Conamara.

Tomás Canainn and Gearóid Mac an Bhua, *Seán Ó Riada: A Shaol agus a Shaothar Gartan* (Dublin 1993). The best introduction to Ó Riada's life and work.

Rhys Carpenter, *Beyond the Pillars of Hercules* (Auckland 1973).

John de Courcy Ireland, *Ireland and the Sea* (Cork 1983); *Ireland and the Irish in Maritime History* (Dublin 1986); 'The corsairs of North Africa', *The Mariner's Mirror* (May 1974).

Frank Forde, 'Tragic end for a heroic venture', *Sunday Press* (18 Nov. 1984); *The Long Watch* (Dublin 1981). The author served with Irish Shipping, whose demise he laments.

Paul Gosling, compiler of *Archaeological Inventory of County Galway*, vol. 1, Commissioners of Public Works, Stationery Office (1993).

For sample analyses of the emigration phenomenon see: Seamus Grimes and Michael Connolly, 'The migration link between Cois Fharraige and Portland, Maine, 1880s to 1920s', *Irish Geography*, 22 (1989), 1–64. Also Kenneth Nilsen, 'Thinking of Monday: The Irish speakers of Portland, Maine', *Eire/Ireland*, 25 (1991), 619, which draws attention to 'Seán Palmer's voyage to America', collected by the Irish Folklore Commission in Kerry (1933) and reported by R. Dorson, *American Folklore* (1953), as having been heard by him in Ireland.

Michael D. Higgins, 'The tyranny of images', *The Crane Bag*, 9, 2 (1984).

Alan Lomax, Dept of Anthropology, Columbia University, NY, in letter to the author (23 Sept. 1985).

Michael McCaughan, *Ethnology and Irish Boatbuilding Traditions*, Fourth International Symposium on Boat and Ship Archaeology, Porto 1985 (BAR 1988).

Lawrence Millman, *Our Like Will Not Be There Again, Notes from the West of Ireland* (London 1977).

Paul Mohr, *Rain and Rocks: The Discovery of West Connacht Geology, 1800–1950* (Galway 2000).

Seán O'Baoill, 'Traditional singing in English', *Treoir* (1974).

Máirtín Ó Cadhain, quoted by Seán Mac Réamoinn on record sleeve of Seosamh Ó hÉanaí, *Seosamh Ó hÉanaí* (Gael Linn 1969).

Brian O'Rourke, *Blas Meala: Gaelic Folksongs with English Translations* (Dublin 1985).

Arthur Reynolds, 'Mainly boats and people', *The Irish Skipper* (Aug. 1980), 20.

Abdelhamid Sabra, 'The exact sciences' in John R. Hayes (ed.), *The Genius of Arabic Civilization* (Cambridge, Massachusetts 1978), p. 121.

Richard J. Scott, *The Galway Hookers, Working Sailboats of Galway Bay* (Dublin 1983).

Kevin Whelan, 'Introduction' in *Letters from the Irish Highlands* (Clifden 1995). An example of the excellent work the Gibbonses have done in revising the image of Conamara.

O. Wright, 'Science: Music' in Joseph Schacht and C.E. Boswirth (eds), *The Legacy of Islam* (Oxford 1979), p. 489.

3: *Gaels and Arabs: The Common Ground* [pp. 48–60]

Bertil Almgren (ed.), *The Vikings* (Stockholm 1975).

Aziz S. Atiya, *The Copts and Christian Civilization*, the 42nd annual Frederick William Reynolds lecture, University of Utah, 7 Feb. 1979 (Utah 1979).

Donald Attwater, *The Christian Churches of the East*, vols 1 and 2 (Milwaukee 1947, 1948).

Nora K. Chadwick, *Studies in Early British History* (Cambridge 1954), chapter 8.

Edward Clibborn, Curator of the Royal Irish Academy, related the O'Curry anecdote in a letter to Robert MacAdam (26 March 1859). In 1985, sculptor Colm Brennan told

me he had exactly the same experience playing a Seosamh Ó hÉanaí sean-nós recording for Salah Quarashi, a Saudi Arabian. The latter said it was 'fíor-cosúil' (truly like)
Bedouin singing.

Con Costello, *Ireland and the Holy Land*, op. cit.

Norman Daniel, *The Arabs and Mediaeval Europe* (London 1979).

Liam de Paor, 'Roots, the new nationalism', *Irish Times* (18 Aug. 1971).

Issam El-Said and Ayse Parman, *Geometric Concepts in Islamic Art* (London 1976).

Godfrey Goodwin, *Islamic Spain* (London 1990).

Washington Irving, *Tales of the Alhambra* (1832), Miguel Sanchez ed. (Granada 1994).

David James, 'Celtic and Islamic art', *Art About Ireland* (1979); also interview with the
author.

Chris Lynn, in conversation with the author. See *The Atlantean Trilogy* (1984), available on
VHS at Irish Film Institute, Eustace Street, Dublin 2.

M. Mansoor, *The Story of Irish Orientalism* (Dublin 1944).

The Palmer & Darling quotation comes from a poster for the 1866 event that is in my
possession. The Vallancey poem appears on the reverse side. Note that it was printed
at 'J. Darling's General Printing Office, 52 Henry St.' (Dublin).

Joseph Raftery, 'Ex Oriente', *Journal of the Royal Society of Antiquaries of Ireland*, 95 (1965).

David Talbot Rice, *Islamic Art* (London 1965).

Franz Rosenthal, 'Literature' in Schacht and Boswirth, *The Legacy of Islam*, op. cit., p. 321.

Eric Rowan (ed.), *Art in Wales* (Wales 1978).

Edward W. Said, *Orientalism* (London 1985).

Idries Shah, *The Way of the Sufi* (London 1975). In 1984 Anna Felton of Shankill passed
his reference to the Ballycotton Cross on to me and gave me the name of another
work by him, *The Sufis*.

Jeanne Sheehy, *The Rediscovery of Ireland's Past: The Celtic Revival 1830–1930* (London 1980).

Daragh Smyth, *A Guide to Irish Mythology* (Dublin 1988).

W.B. Yeats, *Deirdre* in *Collected Plays of W.B. Yeats* (London 1952).

Charlotte M. Yonge, *Christians and Moors of Spain* (London 1903).

4: Seafarers, Smugglers and Pirates [pp. 61–74]

Henry Barnaby, 'The sack of Baltimore', *Journal of the Cork Historical and Archaeological Society*,
1 (1895), 220.

Calendar of State Papers, Public Record Office, National Library of Ireland.

Anne Chambers, *Granuaile* (Dublin 1979).

John de Courcy Ireland, 'The corsairs of North Africa', op. cit. and personal correspondence.

Donald Harden, *The Phoenicians*, vol. 26 in the series *Ancient Peoples and Places*, Glyn Daniel
ed. (London 1963).

P.L. Henry, *Ulster is Mine: A Novel* (Galway 2002).

H.D. Inglis, *Ireland in 1834* (London 1835).

James F. Kenney, *Sources for the Early History of Ireland: Ecclesiastical* (Dublin 1993).

Peter Lamborn Wilson, *Pirate Utopias: Moorish Corsairs and European Renegadoes* (New York 1995).

David Mitchell, *Pirates* (New York 1976).

K.W. Nicholls, *Gaelic and Gaelicized Ireland in the Middle Ages* (Dublin 2003).
Jacques Ramin, *The Periplus of Hanno* (BAR 1976).

5: St Brendan, Sindbad and the Viking Connection [pp. 75–81]

Per Andreas Andersen, *Vikings of the West, The Expansion of Norway in the Early Middle Ages* (Oslo 1985).
R.D. Barnet, 'Early Shipping in the Near East', *Antiquity*, 32 (1958), 220–30.
Norman H. Baynes (ed.), *Three Byzantine Saints*, trans. Elizabeth Dawes (London 1948).
Ernst Bloch, *The Principle of Hope (Das Prinzip Hoffnung)*, vol. 2 (Cambridge, Massachusetts 1959), pp. 892–6.
Chambers, *Granuaile, op. cit.*
John de Courcy Ireland and David C. Sheehy (eds), *Atlantic Visions: A Definitive Collection of Essays on the Brendan Story*, papers from the 1985 conference, organized by the Society of St Brendan (Dublin 1989).
Máire and Liam de Paor, *Early Christian Ireland* (London 1978).
P.W. Joyce, *A Social History of Ancient Ireland* (London 1913).
Kenney, *Early History of Ireland, op. cit.*
Mark Kurlansky, *Cod: A Biography of the Fish that Changed the World* (London 1998).
John McNeill, *The Celtic Churches* (Chicago 1974), p. 182. Reference courtesy of John Goodwillie.
National Museum of Ireland, Excavations Catalogue 1962–73.
Tim Severin, *The Brendan Voyage* (London 1979).
Rev. Geo. Fyler Townsend MA (ed.), *The Arabian Nights Entertainment* (London 1886).
T.J. Westropp, 'Brazil and the legendary islands of the North Atlantic: their history and fable. A contribution to the "Atlantis" problem', *Proceedings of the Royal Irish Academy*, vol. 30, section C (1912).

6: Wales and Europe [pp. 82–97]

Barnet, 'Early Shipping in the Near East', *art. cit.*
E.G. Bowen, *Saints, Seaways and Settlements in the Celtic Lands* (Wales 1969); 'The St David of history, Dewi Sant, our founder saint', address given on 800th anniversary of the building of the cathedral (16 July 1981); *Britain and the Western Seaways* (London 1972). Also many personal communications: see *Atlantean Trilogy, op. cit.*
V. Gordon Childe, quoted in Daniel, *Megalith Builders of Western Europe, op. cit.*
O.G.S. Crawford and Glyn Daniel (eds), review of T.G. Powell, *Barclodiad Y Gawres* (Proc. Preh. Soc. 1956).
David T. Croke, 'Genetics and archaeology: synergy or culture-clash?', *Archaeology Ireland* (Winter 2001).
H.S. Green, A.H.V. Smith, Y.B.R. Young and R.K. Harrison, *The Caergwrle Bowl: Its Composition, Geological Source and Archaeological Significance*, Report of the Institute of Geological Science, no. 80.1 (1980), pp. 26–30.

Thor Heyerdahl demonstrated his theories on the *Kon Tiki* voyage in the Pacific and on his Red Sea adventure.

J. Geraint Jenkins, 'Bowl turners and spoon carvers', *Folk Life: Journal of the Society for Folk Life Studies*, vol. 1 (1963).

Tecwyn Vaughan Jones, 'Bando' (1982), two short commentaries given to the author by D. Roy Saer.

Gillies MacBain, *Common Ground* (Tipperary 2001). See also Anthony Murphy, 'Knowth: Archaeological and astronomical legacy', and Michael Purser, 'Some thoughts on neolithic astronomy', *The Pulse* (November 2000). (*The Pulse* is a periodical edited by Gillies MacBain and self-published under the imprint of the Cuttlefish Press.)

Mitchell, *Reading the Irish Landscape, op. cit.*

John Mitchell, *A Little History of Astro-Archaeology* (London 2001).

A.E. Mourant and Morgan Watkins, 'Blood groups, anthropology and language in Wales and the Western countries', *Heredity*, 6 (1952), pp. 13–36.

Stuart Piggott, 'An ancient Briton in North Africa', *Antiquity*, 42 (1968), 128–30.

Eric Rowan (ed.), *Art in Wales: An Illustrated History* (Wales 1978).

D. Roy Saer, Dept of Folklore, Welsh Folk Museum, Cardiff, supplied a list and map to the author (15 Dec. 1981) showing twenty-three Sunday schools, including Maenclochog, in which Cymanfa Pwync is sung.

Michael Viney, 'Earth light diminishes the beauty of the stars', *Irish Times* (25 Jan. 2003).

Heinrich Wagner spoke with me about the mutual unintelligibility of Welsh and Irish. See also James, *Atlantic Celts, op. cit.*

Morgan Watkins, *Genetic and Population Studies in Wales* (Wales 1987).

Gwyn A. Williams, 'Frontier of illusion: The Welsh and the Atlantic revolution', *History Today* (June 1980).

Nicholas Williams of University College Dublin kindly sent me a paper on the subject of atropaic plants in 1991. His book on this subject, *Díolaim Luibheanna*, was due from Sáirséal agus Dill the same year.

7: *Ireland and North Africa* [pp. 98–114]

Shabbir Akhtar, *Be Careful with Muhammad: The Salman Rushdie Affair* (London 1989).

F. Benoit, 'La Stele de Maaziz', *Bulletin de las Societé de Préhistorique de Maroc* (1932).

André Bertrand, *Tribus Berbéres du Haut Atlas* (Lausanne 1977).

George Coffey, *New Grange* (Dorset 1912).

Daniel, *Megalith Builders of Western Europe, op. cit.*

N.J. Dawood (trans.), *The Koran* (London 1979).

DeGraft-Johnson, *African Glory, The Story of Vanished Negro Civilisations* (New York 1954), p. 38.

Ahmed Galwash, *The Religion of Islam* (Cairo 1956).

Paul Johnson, *A History of Christianity* (London 1975). I am also indebted to Fred Johnson for sharing his insights based on his North African experiences with me.

Ibn Khaldun, *The Muqaddimah: An Introduction to History*, trans. Franz Rosenthal (London 1967).

Arthur Koestler, *The Act of Creation* (London 1971), p. 110.

Lauria Liman, 'Henri Lothe et les découvertes préhistoriques du Tassili' (24 March 1988). Unpublished thesis for the University of Stockholm, generously provided by Liman, an archaeology student, along with material and photographs from her researches in the Algerian Sahara. Of particular interest is a picture of a triple spiral, identical to that in the Newgrange inner chamber; a similar triple spiral has been found in the Canary Islands. She also gave me the following references, both of which evidenced prehistoric designs similar to those in Ireland: J. Bouyssonie, 'Statuette from Tin-Hinan', *Collections Préhistoriques Planches*, 1 (1956); R. Pyto and J.C. Musso, *Corpus des Peintures et Gravures Rupestres de Grande Kabylie* (Algiers 1969).

Robert MacAdam, 'Is the Irish language spoken in Africa?', *Journal of the Royal Society of Antiquaries of Ireland*, 7 (1859), 195.

George Mackay, 'Celtic tribes in Morocco', *Caledonian Medical Journal*, vii, 5 (Jan. 1908). Paper delivered at the Pan-Celtic congress in Edinburgh.

James W. Mavor, 'The Riddle of M'Zorah', contribution no. 2973 from the Woods Hole Oceanographic Institution, Graz, Austria (personal copy from the author).

Gavin Maxwell, *Lords of the Atlas: The Rise and Fall of the House of Glaoua, 1893–1956* (New York 1966).

Michael J. O'Kelly, *Newgrange: Archaeology, Art and Legend* (London 1982). Also personal letter to the author (1 March 1982) in which he declared himself unqualified to comment on my impressions.

Revue Marocaine d'Histoire et de Civilisation (Rabat 1980–81). These magazines are written in French, but each has a section of lessons in Tamazight.

George Souville, 'Engraved steles from western Morocco' in *Atlas Préhistorique di Maroc Atlantique* (Aix-en-Provence 1973). Also see the journal *Bollettino del Centro Camuno di Studi Preistorici* (1987) for essays on other stelae.

J.W.C. Wand, *A History of the Early Church to AD 500* (London 1937).

8: Deconstructing the Celtic Myth [pp. 115–132]

John Arden, *Silence Among the Weapons* (London 1982).

Robert Ball, 'Means used by the ancients for attaching handles to the stone and metal implements called Celts', *Proceedings of the Royal Irish Academy*, no. 43 (Jan. 1844).

Peter Beresford Ellis, *The Celtic Empire. The First Millennium of Celtic History 1000 BC–51 AD* (London 1990). This work seems to support my remarks about the reification of the term 'Celt', along with: Frank Delaney, *The Celts* (London 1986); and John Sharkey, *Celtic Mysteries, The Ancient Religion* (New York 1975).

Cormac (Mac Cuileannáin), Bishop-King of Munster, d. 908 AD, credited with *Sanas Cormaic* (*Cormac's Glossary*) a dictionary of unusual or obsolete Irish words, see Kenney, *Early History of Ireland, op. cit.* See also *Saltair Caiseal* by the same author. In fact, because Cormac's reign marked the transition from a Latin-speaking to an Irish-speaking Christianity, he might very well have been referring to a dialect of Irish as the 'iron language' (author's speculation).

Barry Cunliffe, *The Ancient Celts* (Oxford 1997); *Facing the Ocean, op. cit.*

Kevin Danaher (Caoimhín Ó Danachair), *A Celtic Origin of the Irish Folk Tradition?*, Arizona State University Anthropological Research Papers no. 27 (1982); 'Irish Folk Tradition and the Celtic Calendar' in O'Driscoll (ed.), *The Celtic Consciousness, op. cit.*

Myles Dillon, 'The Irish language' in *Early Irish Society (RTÉ Thomas Davis Lectures 1953)* (Dublin 1954).

Desmond Fennell, in personal communication, as well as his mid-1980s columns in the *Sunday Press.*

Robin Flower, *The Irish Tradition* (Dublin 1994).

David Greene, in conversation with Heinrich Wagner (1984); 'The Celtic languages' in Joseph Raftery (ed.), *The Celts (RTÉ Thomas Davis Lectures 1964)* (Cork 1964).

P.L. Henry, 'Anglo-Irish word-charts' in *Ulster Dialects* (Holyrood 1964), p. 147. Quoted in Evans, *Personality of Ireland, op. cit.*, chapter 3, note 16.

James, *Atlantic Celts, op. cit.*, p. 138.

Morris Jones, 'Pre-Aryan syntax in insular Celtic' in *The Welsh People* (London 1900).

D.H. Lawrence, *Sea and Sardinia* (London 1923). I am indebted to Barry MacDonnell for this reference.

Lhuyd, *Archaeologia Britannica, op. cit.*

Brian McEvoy, Martin Richards, Peter Forster and Daniel G. Bradley, 'The *Longue Durée* of genetic ancestry: Multiple genetic marker systems and Celtic origins on the Atlantic façade of Europe', *The American Journal of Human Genetics*, vol. 75, no. 4, (Oct. 2004).

J.P. Mallory, 'The origins of the Irish', *Journal of Irish Archaeology*, 2 (1984).

Sabatino Moscati (catalogue and exhibition coordinator), *The Celts* (Bompiani 1991), p. 53. I am grateful to Luke Dempsey OP for this gift. Note: a misprint in the catalogue (p. 51) places the migration of Irish to Scotland in the sixteenth century, a thousand years after the actual event.

Gerard Murphy, *Saga and Myth in Ancient Ireland* (Dublin 1961).

T.G.E. Powell, *The Celts* (London 1980).

Barry Raftery, *Barbarians to the West* (BAR 1989), chapter 8.

Joseph Raftery, interview with the author, *Atlantean Trilogy, op. cit.*

Renfrew, *Archaeology and Language, op. cit.*

E. Ben Rochd, *Structuralism* (Oujda, Morocco 1988), and many personal communications, including a letter (13 Aug. 1991) in which he said of Arabic: 'There is indeed a name of a tree/trees called Ad-Dar-Dar (*Ad* being the assimilated definite article, i.e. 'the') which stands for both the Ash and the Elm (according to the English/Arabic dictionary by Munir Ba'labaki').

Michael Ryan, in an interview with the author. See *Atlantean Trilogy, op. cit.*

John Strachan (ed.), *Stories from the Táin*, revised by Osborn Bergin (Dublin 1944).

J.J. Tierney, 'The Celtic ethnography of Posidonius', *Proceedings of the Royal Irish Academy*, vol. 60, section C, no. 5 (1960, 1985).

Theo Vennemann, 'Semitic>Celtic>English, the transivity of language contact' in Markku Filippula, Juhani Klemola and Heli Pitkaenen (eds), *Studies in Languages 37, The Celtic Roots of English* (Joensuu, Finland 2002). Also see Vennemann, 'English as a "Celtic" language: Atlantic influences from above and below' in Hildegard L.C. Tristram (ed.), *The Celtic Englishes 2* (Heidelberg 2002). I am indebted to Ms Tristram for many of these references.

Wagner, 'Near Eastern and African connections with the Celtic world', *art. cit.*; *Common Problems Concerning the Languages of the British Isles and the Iberian Peninsula* (Salamanca 1976).

Calvert Watkins, *Indo-European Origins of the Celtic Verb 1: The Sigmatic Aorist* (Dublin 1962).

9: *Pre-Celtic Place-Names* [pp. 133–143]

Ahmed Ali and Ibrahim Ali, *Pre-Celtic Languages: The African Substratum Theory* (Cardiff 1995).

David Bellamy, *The Wild Boglands* (Dublin 1986).

Winthrop Palmer Boswell, 'Irish wizards in the woods of Ethiopia' (unpublished thesis, San Francisco State College, revised 1972).

George Calder (ed. and trans.), *Auraicept na n-Éces* (*The Scholar's Primer*) (Edinburgh 1917).

Séamus Caulfield, *Landscape and Archaeology in Ireland* (BAR 1982–3); *Neolithic Fields – the Irish evidence* (BAR 1978), pp. 137–43; *The Neolithic Settlement of North Connaught* (BAR 1983), pp. 195–213.

Census 1851, *General Alphabetical Index to the Townlands and Towns, Parishes and Baronies of Ireland* (Baltimore, Maryland 1984).

Peter Coxon, *A Field Guide to the Quaternary in North Mayo*, IQUA field guide, no. 14 (1991); 'New biostratigraphic evidence of the post-glacial colonization of Ireland and for Mesolithic forest disturbance', *Journal of Biogeography*, 13 (1986), 487–509.

Seán de Fréine, *The Great Silence* (Dublin 1965).

Myles Dillon, 'The Irish language' in *Early Irish Society, op. cit.*

Desmond Fennell, in conversation with the author.

A.C. Forbes, 'Some legendary and historical references to Irish woods and their significance', *Proceedings of the Royal Irish Academy*, vol. 41, section B (1932); 'Tree planting in Ireland during four centuries', *Proceedings of the Royal Irish Academy*, vol. 41, section C, no. 6 (1933).

P.W. Joyce, *Irish Names of Places*, 3 vols (Dublin 1913).

Fergus Kelly, 'Trees in Early Ireland', Augustine Henry Memorial Lecture, Royal Dublin Society (11 March 1999).

Seán MacConnell, 'Uncovering the secrets of the Céide Fields', *Irish Times* (22 Sept. 1990).

James MacKillop, *Dictionary of Celtic Mythology* (Oxford 2000).

G. Frank Mitchell, 'The relative ages of archaeological objects recently found in bogs in Ireland', *Proceedings of the Royal Irish Academy*, vol. 50, section C (1945).

Karen Molloy and Michael O'Connell, 'Palaeological investigations towards the reconstruction of woodland and land-use history at Lough Sheeauns, Connemara, western Ireland', *Review of Palaeobotany and Palynology*, 67 (1991), pp. 75–113. For summary of above, see *Archaeology Ireland*, 2, 2 (Summer 1988).

Michael O'Connell, 'Origins of Irish lowland blanket bog' in G.J. Doyle (ed.), *Ecology and Conservation of Irish Peatlands* (Dublin 1990), pp. 49–71.

Donncha Ó hEallaithe, personal communication to author.

Tomás Ó Máille, *An Béal Beo* (Dublin 1937).

Tim Robinson, *Connemara, Part 1: Introduction and Gazetteer* (Galway 1990).

Heinrich Wagner, in a letter to the author (2 Dec. 1983), provided this reference to Brendan Adams.

T.J. Westropp, 'The forests of the counties of the lower Shannon Valley', *Proceedings of the Royal Irish Academy*, vol. 27, section C (1909).

10: *Ireland's Early Maritime History* [pp. 144–150]

A. Bede, *History of the English Church and People*, trans. Leo Shirley-Price (London 1983).

Julius Caesar, *Julius Caesar: The Conquest of Gaul*, trans. S.A. Handford (London 1951).

Cambrensis, *Topographica Hibernica, op. cit.*

Daniel, *Arabs and Medieval Europe, op. cit.*

Pádraig de Bhaldraithe, *Saothrú an Uisce, Feirmeoireacht éisc, slogéisc agus algaí* (Dublin 1990). In personal communication with the author, he told me he suspected the shipwrecked sailor might have been a remote ancestor of his own.

Miguel González Garcés, *La Coruna* (Leon 1974).

Hayes (ed.), *Genius of Arabic Civilisation, op. cit.*

Archibald R. Lewis, *The Northern Seas: Shipping and Commerce in Northern Europe* AD 300–1100 (New Jersey 1958).

Bernard Lewis, *Politics and War, the Legacy of Islam* (Oxford 1979).

The Merriman Summer School, Lahinch (1982), presented papers on Ireland and the Sea.

Charles Thomas, *Britain and Ireland in Early Christian Times* AD 400–800 (London 1971).

11: *Vikings and Trade in the Middle Ages* [pp. 151–161]

Almgren (ed.), *The Vikings, op. cit.*

American Numismatic Society, New York. Thanks to Dr Michael Bates, curator, for assisting researches and supplying images.

Andersen, *Vikings of the West, op. cit.*

Bolin, 'Mohammed, Charlemagne and Ruric', *op. cit.*

Hodges and Whitehouse, *Mohammed, Charlemagne and the Origins of Europe, op. cit.*

Bent Engelbreth Jorgensen, *The Viking Boats* (Roskilde 1994).

For interviews with Kenneth Jonsson and Jorgen Steen Jensen, see *Navigatio: Atlantean 2, op. cit.*

Quote from *Annales Bertiniani*, 1, 435, in Archibald Lewis, *The Northern Seas, op. cit.* See *Navigatio: Atlantean 2, Completing the Circle* (1997), documentary film by the author.

Sven-Olof Lindqvist, *Society and Trade in the Baltic During the Viking Age, Papers of the 7th Visby Symposium 1983* (Gotlands 1985).

Pirenne, *Medieval Cities* and *Mohammed and Charlemagne, op. cit.*

George Bernard Shaw, *The Genuine Islam*, vol. 1, no. 8 (1936); Arnold J. Toynbee, *Civilization on Trial* (Oxford 1948), p. 205. I am grateful to Dr E. Ben Rochd of Oujda University, Morocco, for these two references.

12: Moorish Spain and Ireland: A Golden Age *[pp. 162–174]*

Bede, *History, op. cit.*

Ludwig Bieler, *Ireland, Harbinger of the Middle Ages* (Oxford 1966).

Titus Burckhardt, *Moorish Culture in Spain* (London 1972).

Daniel, *Arabs and Medieval Europe, op. cit.*

de Paor, *Early Christian Ireland, op. cit.*

W.S. Howell (trans.), *Alcuin: The Rhetoric,* vol. 23 (Princeton 1941).

Dermot Moran, 'Johannes Scottus Eriugena', *Art About Ireland* (1979); *The Philosophy of John Scottus Eriugena* (Cambridge 1989). John J. O'Meara, *Eriugena* (Oxford 1969).

H.T. Norris, *The Berbers in Arabic Literature* (London 1982).

Stanley Lane Poole, *The Moors in Spain* (Beirut 1962).

Hilary Richardson, 'Christian Iconography in Early Irish and Armenian Art', extracts from *Atti del Quinto Simposio Internazionale di Arte Armena, 1988* (Venice 1992), p. 577.

Ryan, 'Derrynaflan Chalice', *art. cit.*

Philip Sherrard, *Byzantium* (London 1974).

Charles Singer, *Short History of Science* (Oxford 1941).

George T. Stokes, *Ireland and the Celtic Church* (London 1886); Stokes, 'Celtic, Syrian and Egyptian monks', *Journal of the Royal Society of Antiquaries of Ireland,* 22 (1891).

J.M. Wallace-Hadrill, *The Barbarian West: The Early Middle Ages AD 400–1000* (New York 1962).

Yonge, *Christians and Moors of Spain, op. cit.*

13: Myths and Storytelling *[pp. 175–188]*

S. Baring-Gould, *Curious Myths of the Middle Ages* (London 1875).

Henri d'Arbois de Jubainville, *Cours de Litterature Celtique,* 3, ser. x (1883); *Beltine* (1884), pp. 121–32.

Joachim de Villaneuve, *Phoenician Ireland,* trans. and illustrated with notes by Henry O'Brien (London 1833).

Donnelly, *Atlantis, op. cit.*

Niall Fallon, *The Armada in Ireland* (London 1978).

Flower, *The Irish Tradition, op. cit.*

J. Foster Forbes, 'The unchronicled past, this England – 4000 years ago', *The Listener* (Sept. 1937). See also E.F. Wills, 'Egypt in Bristol' in Rendel Harris (ed.), *The Migration of Culture* (London 1937); another title in this series is Marjorie J. Martyn, *Egypt in Gloucestershire* (London 1934).

Paul Gosling, *Archaeological Inventory of County Galway, Vol. 1: West Galway,* no. 124 (Dublin 1993).

Graves, *The White Goddess, op. cit.*

David Greene, 'Early Irish Literature' in Myles Dillon (ed.), *Early Irish Society (RTÉ Thomas Davis Lectures 1953)* (Dublin 1954).

Kenneth H. Jackson, *A Celtic Miscellany* (New York 1951), p. 68.

T.P. Kilfeather, *Ireland, Graveyard of the Spanish Armada* (Dublin 1979).

Bernard MacDonagh, *Spanish Armada*, Sligo School of Landscape Painting publication [n.d.], illustrated by MacDonagh, based on R. Crawford and Hugh Cunningham's translations of accounts of the disaster by Armada captains Duro and Cuellar. These are based on 'La Armada Invincible', Spanish archives: academy of history, collection Salazar, no. 7, folio 58.

James MacKillop, *Dictionary of Celtic Mythology* (Oxford 1998), p. 161.

James W. Mavor, *Voyage to Atlantis* (London 1977).

Pádraic O'Farrell, *Folk Tales of the Irish Coast* (Cork 1978).

P.A. Ó Síocháin, *A Journey into Lost Time* (Dublin 1984).

E.L. Ranelagh, *The Past We Share* (London 1979).

Lorna Siggins, 'Report on the work of the Sites and Monuments Records under the leadership of Michael Gibbons and Geraldine Stout', *Irish Times* (21 April 1992).

Daragh Smyth, *A Guide to Irish Mythology* (Dublin 1988).

Jurgen Spanuth, *Atlantis of the North* (Tubingen 1976).

Walter Starkie, *In Sara's Tent* (London 1953).

John Strachan (ed.), *Stories from the Táin*, op. cit.

R.A. Walshe, *A Residence in Constantinople* (1838).

14: North African Influences on Early Irish Christianity [pp. 189–208]

Atiya, *The Copts and Christian Civilization*, op. cit., pp. 186–7.

The Atlantean Trilogy, part 3, op. cit., Martha Roy interview.

J.R. Bourhis, J. Briard, H. Cabillic and Y. Onnée, *Tumulus et Coffres à Plouhinec (Finistère)*, extrait du bulletin de la societé archéologique du finistère, tome CVII (1979).

G.A. Bracken and P.A. Wayman, 'A Neolithic or Bronze Age alignment for Croagh Patrick', *Cathair na Mart, Journal of the Westport Historical Society* (Jan. 1993).

J.B. Bury, *The Life of St Patrick* (London 1905).

Francis John Byrne, *Irish Kings and High Kings* (London 1973). I am indebted to Rory Rapple for this reference.

Henri Cabillic showed the grave at Plouhinec to me.

Joseph Campbell, 'Peripheries of the Indo-European world' in O'Driscoll (ed.), *Celtic Consciousness*, op. cit., p. 7.

V. Gordon Childe, *The Prehistory of European Society* (London 1958), quoted in Daniel, *Megalith Builders of Western Europe*, op. cit., p. 128; for next Daniel quote, op. cit., p. 127.

de Paor, *Early Christian Ireland*, op. cit.

Jean Guitton, *Great Heresies and Church Councils*, trans. F.D. West from *Le Christ Écartelé*, 1963 (London 1965).

Raouf Habib, *The Contribution of Ancient Egypt in Coptic Art* (Cairo 1980); also *The Coptic Ikon; The Peacock and the Eagle in the Coptic Period; Coptic Manuscripts; The Development of the Ivory and Bone Industry; The History of Coptic Art and its Coptic Museum*. These five booklets, written by a Copt, were collected by the author in Cairo and in the Scetis monastery, 1982.

Patrick J. Hamell, *Patrology: An Introduction* (Maynooth 1963), borrowed from *an t-Athair* Pádraig Standúin and, *mea culpa*, never returned.

Peter Harbison, 'Iconography on the Dysert and Kilfenora crosses: A Romanesque renaissance', *The Other Clare*, 5 (1981); see also Arthur K. Porter, *An Egyptian Legend in Ireland*, reviewed in *Journal of the Royal Society of Antiquaries of Ireland*, 61 (1931), 72.

W.R. Inge, *The Church in the World* (London 1927).

Johnson, *History of Christianity, op. cit.*

Kenney, *Early History of Ireland, op. cit.*

Jean Lacarrière, *The God-Possessed*, trans. B. Arthaud from *Les Hommes Ivres de Dieu*, 1961 (London 1963).

I am obliged to H. Lyons, then Deputy Manager, Kildare County Council, for his courteous letter (14 Aug. 1991) giving me some background on the emblems of Naas. He confirmed that the original emblem, designed in 1898 by the county surveyor Edmund Glover, contained the snake and specifically referred to the town of Naas.

Wiltrud Mersmann, *Orientalische Einfluesse auf die insulare Kunst im Zeitalter des hl. Virgil: Sonderdruck aus* Virgil Von Salzburg (Salzburg 1985).

Fr Matta El Meskeen, *The Original Calendar of the Coptic Church* (Monastery of St Macarius, Scetis 1980).

J.D. Newport and D.D. White, *Latin Writings of St Patrick* (SPCK 1918).

Elaine Pagel, *The Gnostic Gospels* (London 1982).

C.A. Ralegh Redford, *Mediaeval Sources of Sculpture in Stone among Insular Celts* (BAR 1977).

Hilary Richardson, 'Art in Ireland in the eighth century', paper delivered at Salzburg (September 1984); also Richardson, 'Observations on Christian art in early Ireland, Georgia, Armenia', offprint from Ryan (ed.), *Ireland and Insular Art, op. cit.*

Information on the Brittany Pardon from a report by John and Elizabeth Rodenbeck, copied for me by Brian Ó Ceallagh, once Irish ambassador to Egypt.

Kurt Rudolph, *Gnosis* (Edinburgh 1983).

Sr Mary T. Ryan, personal communication (20 Jan. 1988).

Etienne Rynne, 'The Tau-cross at Killanaboy: Pagan or Christian?', *North Munster Studies* (1967).

Gerard Viaud, *Pratiques Populaires Communes aux Coptes et aux Celtes*, société d'archéologie, copte TXXIII (Cairo 1981).

Michael Viney, 'When the sun goes rolling down Croagh Patrick', *Irish Times* (14 July 2001).

Wand, *History of the Early Church, op. cit.*

15: *Irish and Eastern Illuminated Art* [pp. 209–223]

Carol Andrews, *The Rosetta Stone* (London 1987).

Bieler, *Ireland, Harbinger of the Middle Ages, op. cit.*, p. 11.

Titus Burckhardt, *Art of Islam: Language and Meaning*, trans. P. Hobson (London 1976). I am indebted to Mary J. Byrne for this reference.

James E. Doan, 'The Animal Style in Celtic and Thracian Art' in John T. Koch (ed.), *Proceedings of the Harvard Celtic Colloquium*, vol. III (Boston 1983); 'Mediterranean influences on insular manuscript illumination' in John T. Koch (ed.), *Proceedings of the Harvard Celtic Colloquium*, vol. II (Boston 1982).

W.B. Emery, *Archaic Egypt* (London 1961).

G.S.P. Freeman-Grenville, *The Beauty of Cairo: Historical Guide to the Chief Islamic and Coptic Monuments* (London 1981).

Henry, *Early Christian Irish Art*, op. cit.

Kenney, *Early History of Ireland*, op. cit., pp. 629–30.

Heinz Edgar Kiewe, *Origin of the 'Isle of Aran' Knitting Designs* (Oxford 1981); *The Sacred History of Knitting* (Oxford 1967); also many personal communications, and interview in *The Atlantean Trilogy*, op. cit.

Paul Lipke, *The Royal Ship of Cheops* (BAR 1985).

G. Frank Mitchell, 'Foreign influences and the beginnings of Christian art' in *Treasures of Early Irish Art*, op. cit.; 'Introduction' in *Treasures of Early Irish Art: 1500 BC to 1500 AD* (New York 1977).

Conor Cruise O'Brien, 'Last week in the Holy City', *Irish Times* (2 March 1982).

Hilary Richardson, 'Remarks on the Liturgical Fan, Flabellum or Rhipidion' in R.M. Spearman and J. Higgitt (eds), *The Age of Migrating Ideas* (Edinburgh 1993).

Michael Viney, 'Butterflies in a warm winter', *Irish Times* (10 Dec. 1994).

16: *The Sheela-na-Gig* [pp. 224–236]

Allegro, *Dead Sea Scrolls*, op. cit.; see also interview in *Atlantean Trilogy*, op. cit.

Jorgen Andersen, *The Witch on the Wall* (London 1977), p. 20; I am indebted to Edward Delaney, RHA, for bringing this book to my attention in 1979 and lending it to me.

Edward Clibborn, 'Discussion on the Lavey church and other Sheela-na-Gigs', *Proceedings of the Royal Irish Academy*, vol. 2 (1864).

Mary Condren, *The Serpent and the Goddess: Women, Religion and Power in Celtic Ireland* (San Francisco 1989).

Johann W. Von Goethe, *Faust: The First Part of the Tragedy*, trans. John R. Williams (Hertfordshire 1999).

Edith M. Guest, 'Irish Sheela na Gigs in 1935', *Journal of the Royal Society of Antiquaries of Ireland*, 66 (1937), 107–29; 'Some notes on the dating of Sheela na Gigs', *Journal of the Royal Society of Antiquaries of Ireland*, 67 (1937), 176–80.

James A. Jerman, 'The Sheela-na-Gig carvings of the British Isles: suggestions for a re-classification, and other notes', *Journal of the County Louth Archaeological and Historical Society*, 20, 1 (1981).

Eamonn Kelly, *Sheela-na-Gigs* (Dublin 1996).

Joanne McMahon and Jack Roberts, *The Divine Hag of the Christian Celts: An Illustrated Guide to the Sheela-na-Gigs of Britain and Ireland* (Cork 2000).

Brian Merriman, *The Midnight Court* (Cork 1982).

Rudolph, *Gnosis*, op. cit.

Etienne Rynne, 'Celtic stone idols in Ireland' in *The Iron Age in the Irish Sea Province* (CBA Research Report 1972); 'A pagan Celtic background for Sheela-na-Gigs' in Rynne (ed.), *Figures from the Past: Studies on Figurative Art in Christian Ireland* (Dublin 1987).

Britta Sandqvist, personal communication to the author (31 May 1993).

Anthony Weir, 'Exhibitionists and related carvings in the Irish midlands: Their origins and functions' in Harman Murtagh (ed.), *Irish Midland Studies* (Athlone 1980).

17: *La Tène Culture* [pp. 237–247]

Elizabeth Wayland Barber, *The Mummies of Urumchi* (London 1999).
de Latocnaye, *Frenchman's Walk Through Ireland, op. cit.*
D.W. Harding, *Prehistoric Europe* (New York 1978).
Paul Jacobsthal, *Early Celtic Art* (Oxford 1944); 'Imagery in early Celtic art', *Proceedings of the British Academy*, vol. 27 (1941), pp. 310–20.
Les Murray, 'Only a flat earth has margins: Footnotes on a deadly metaphor', Claudia Ortese Memorial Lecture, University of Florence (May 1993), reprinted in Gerald Dawe and Jonathan Williams (eds), *Krino: An Anthology of Modern Irish Writers, 1986–1996* (Dublin 1996).
William O'Connor Morris, *Hannibal, Soldier, Statesman, Patriot* (New York 1897).
Barry Raftery, review of Simon James and Valerie Rigby (eds), *Britain and Ireland in the Celtic Age* and Barry Cunliffe, *The Ancient Celts*, in *Times Literary Supplement* (12 June 1998); Raftery, *Barbarians to the West, op. cit.*
Hilary Richardson, in letter to the author (9 Nov. 1984).

Conclusion [pp. 248–250]

Luigi Luca Cavalli-Sforza et. al., 'The genetic legacy of paleolithic *Homo sapiens sapiens* in extant Europeans: A Y-chromosome perspective', *Science*, 290 (Nov. 2000), 1155–9.
Bryan Sykes, *The Seven Daughters of Eve* (London 2001).

Index

INDEX